UNEASY NEIGHBORS

OVERTURES TO BIBLICAL THEOLOGY

EDITORS

WALTER BRUEGGEMANN, McPheeters Professor of Old Testament
Columbia Theological Seminary, Decatur, Georgia

JOHN R. DONAHUE, S. J., Professor of New Testament,
Jesuit School of Theology at Berkeley, California

SHARYN DOWD, Professor of New Testament,
Lexington Theological Seminary, Lexington, Kentucky

CHRISTOPHER R. SEITZ, Professor of Old Testament
University of St. Andrews, St. Andrews, Scotland

UNEASY NEIGHBORS

CHURCH AND STATE
IN THE NEW TESTAMENT

Walter E. Pilgrim

FORTRESS PRESS

MINNEAPOLIS

To Jeanette, my best friend for forty-two years
To my colleagues in ministry in the Pacific Northwest

Uneasy Neighbors
Church and State in the New Testament

Copyright © 1999 Augsburg Fortress. All rights reserved. Except for brief quotations in critical articles or reviews, no part of this book may be reproduced in any manner without prior written permission from the publisher. Write: Permissions, Augsburg Fortress, Box 1209, Minneapolis, MN 55440.

Cover and book design by Joseph Bonyata.
Typesetting by Peregrine Graphics Services.
On the cover: Coin of Nero (Emperor A.D. 54–68). Sesterius, mint of Rome. Photograph copyright © BIBLICAL ILLUSTRATOR PHOTO/David Rogers. Used by permission.

Library of Congress Cataloging-in-Publication Data
Pilgrim, Walter E.
    Uneasy neighbors: church and state in the New Testament / Walter E. Pilgrim
    p. cm. — (Overtures to biblical theology)
    Includes bibliographical references and indexes.
    ISBN: 0-8006-3113-7
    1. Church and state—Biblical teaching.   2. Bible.   N.T.—Criticism, intepretation, etc.   I. Title.   II. Series.
    BS2417.C55P55 1999
    261.7'09'015—dc21   98-50385
                                                                 CIP

Manufactured in the U.S.A.   AF 1-3113
03   02   01   00   99   1   2   3   4   5   6   7   8   9   10

CONTENTS

EDITOR'S FOREWORD

THE FAITH OF THE BIBLE HAS BEEN MASSIVELY PRIVATIZED, REDUCED TO personal morality and family values in our society, thus leaving public matters outside the scope of biblical summons and critique. There is no doubt that the recovery of the public dimension of biblical faith is an important project when technological reductionism threatens to preempt all ethical questions. In the recovery of that public dimension, a very important issue is the relation of the believer and the believing community to the state.

The relationship of church and state is a very old issue. It has, however, been largely reduced in many discussions to simplistic formulations of "Romans 13–Revelation 13" ("13–13"), either submissive *confidence* in the state (as Paul seems to urge) or deep *resistance* to the state (as the Book of Revelation advocates). Walter Pilgrim has written a judicious and carefully nuanced book, which argues that the reductionist cliché of "13–13" is not adequate for the issue or the text. His scholarship powerfully contributes to the recovery of the public dimension of biblical faith.

The particular contribution that he makes is evident in two ways. First, the title of the book, *Uneasy Neighbors,* suggests that there is no single, easy posture for the church, either in rejection or in affirmation of the state. The church is a "neighbor" with the inevitable state, but, because of the deep and radical claims of the Gospel, that neighborliness is endlessly "uneasy." Every easy inclination, either subordination or resistance, is, therefore, destabilized. Second, Pilgrim's contribution escapes the familiar solution of "13-13" by arguing for three, and not two, possible New Testament attitudes toward the state. In addition to subordination and resistance, Pilgrim's argument includes critical distancing, which he finds evident powerfully in the Gospel narrative. Out of that conclusion, Pilgrim then revamps both of the "13–13" options to show that they may not be taken in the now conventional, flat way. Every New Testament writer, Pilgrim illuminates, was aware of the delicacy, difficulty, and complexity that allow no simple resolution of the issue.

In his discussion of Romans 13 and related texts, Pilgrim persuasively shows that even Paul's attitude toward Rome is not an unquestioning affirmation. In the end, Pilgrim brings the cross as the critical principle even to the Pauline stance, presented in a variety of texts including the later letter to the Hebrews. Thus Pilgrim concludes of the Pauline stance:

> The reality is that Christians will also suffer for doing right and at the very hands of those whom God intended to preserve peace and justice in this world.

The long, central chapter of the book is titled "Ethic of Critical Distancing: Jesus and the Gospels." This chapter most advances his argument and is a masterful job of careful textual work. Pilgrim shows that Jesus' attitude, as given in the Gospel narratives, is very different from that of Paul. Jesus' statements suggest no easy settlement with the state but propose "an alternative vision of authority." The outcome of the analysis shows it is important that Jesus is "unafraid" of Caesar and "uncowed" by Herod in Jesus' exercise of freedom in trust of another authority. The discussion takes up a rich variety of subjects including the Sermon on the Mount (informed by Walter Wink's important analysis), taxes to Caesar, the Magnificat, and the temple cleansing. Pilgrim ducks none of the hard subjects and, in the end, shows great theological sensitivity in seeing the cross standing sovereign over every claim of the state:

> [Jesus'] life from beginning to end is a history of conflict with those in power. It is the *pax Christi* versus the *pax Romana* . . . Jesus refuses to be deterred by those who oppose his mission, including his own ruler.

Pilgrim also shows that the resistance motif of the Book of Revelation leads to endurance and protest that may culminate in martyrdom. He charts three distinct positions but is able to show that the radical resistance of Revelation is inchoately present in the Gospel narratives themselves. His effort to resist flat categories is clear in his nice summary of options: critical-constructive, critical-transformative, and critically resistive. Every stance must be undertaken *critically* with full knowledge of the realities.

It occurs to me that Pilgrim pushes the discussion beyond the settled categories of the old European model toward greater complexity on the issue. In forming his splendid conclusion, Pilgrim is, of course, aware of the deep crises of the twentieth century that have shaped the on-going discussion . . . the unbearable state of Germany under National Socialism and the Confessing Church; the intense brutality of the Soviet Union; and the apartheid state in South Africa, which evoked the *Kairos* document. Before

Pilgrim is finished, he pushes matters toward the Vietnam War and the U.S. Catholic Bishops' pastoral letter, "Economic Justice for All."

Reflecting upon Pilgrim's conclusion, it occurred to me that for the reader in the U.S., given our nation's status as "the last superpower" and the emerging "global economy," the new issue is not church and state, but church and *corporate economy*. This is an issue left for another time and is not the agenda Pilgrim has taken up here. The move from state to corporate economy indicates how interpretive responsibility must always be in the real world. Catherine Gonzales suggests, in a reading of Revelation 18, how such an interpretive move might take Pilgrim's categories into a new question:

> What is at stake in this passage is the character of the economic system of the Roman Empire, which is not all that different from the system under which we live in terms of its values. It is not only the wealthy who are involved: the whole system of commerce is tied to bringing goods to the wealthy. Even the poorest sailor is tied into this system. The question then is how Christians can live faithfully in an economic system that does not have as its goal the values of the gospel in terms of loving the neighbor. How does the Christian live under a political system that supports such an economic structure? Granted, the role of the citizen is different today from what it was in the first-century Roman Empire, but the question remains for us just as it did for the Christians in John's day.[1]

Pilgrim thinks like a theologian, always bringing the critical principle of the Gospel to the claims of the text. He also thinks with the sensitivities of an exegete. The outcome is a huge contribution, closely text based, that refuses any easy or simplistic formulation. It is a delight to thank Professor Pilgrim for his careful and suggestive work.

Walter Brueggemann

---

1. Catherine Gonzalez, "Mission Accomplished; Mission Begun: Lent and the Book of Revelation," *Journal for Preachers* 32.2 (Lent, 1999) 11.

ABBREVIATIONS

AB	The Anchor Bible
BAGD	Walter Bauer, William F. Arndt, F. Wilbur Gingrich, and F. Danker. *A Greek-English Lexicon of the New Testament and Other Early Christian Literature*. 2d ed. rev. F. Danker. Chicago: University of Chicago Press, 1979.
CBQ	*Catholic Biblical Quarterly*
Chr & Cr	*Christianity and Crisis*
Chr Cent	*The Christian Century*
CurrThMiss	*Currents in Theology and Mission*
ETL	*Ephemerides Theologicae Lovaniensis*
HNT	Handbuch zum Neuen Testament
JAAR	*Journal of the American Academy of Religion*
JBL	*Journal of Biblical Literature*
LCL	Loeb Classical Library
NTS	*New Testament Studies*
NovT	*Novum Testamentum*
NRSV	New Revised Standard Version
REB	Revised English Bible
RSV	Revised Standard Version
TDNT	*Theological Dictionary of the New Testament.*
ZSTh	*Zeitschrift für Systematique Theologie*
ZThK	*Zeitschrift für Theologie und Kirche*

PREFACE

THIS STUDY BRINGS TO FRUITION A PROJECT I HAVE PURSUED OVER THE past decade. It became a serious and viable topic after I finished writing an adult Bible study on the book of Revelation.[1] In this study, it was apparent that the author of Revelation's attitude toward the imperial Roman state was not one of respect and subjection but rather one of resistance and defiance, if not hostility. This led me to examine more fully the other New Testament writings and their respective attitudes toward political structures and the possessors of power. The result is this book, which takes an intensive survey of the entire New Testament. I have tried to be sensitive to the diversity of the canonical writings regarding this important topic, as well as seeking to find the major themes that emerge. In the last chapter, I am bold enough to attempt a translation of the primary New Testament motifs to our contemporary North American setting. I believe it is necessary for biblical scholarship to help bridge the gap between the biblical world and our own time, difficult as this may be.

I owe a debt of gratitude to many people. I first proposed the subject matter with an outline to the late John Hollar, then editorial director at Fortress Press. Marshall Johnson, his successor, suggested its inclusion in the Overtures to Biblical Theology series, and he subsequently shepherded its development (including his thorough editing of the final manuscript). K. C. Hanson (the current biblical studies editor at Fortress Press) has, along with Debbie Brandt (production editor at Fortress Press), brought the book to completion. I am grateful to them for making the transition between editors no real obstacle to the book's publication.

For including this volume in the Overtures to Biblical Theology series, I am especially grateful to Walter Brueggemann, William M. McPheeters Professor of Old Testament at Columbia Theological Seminary; Sharon Dowd, Professor of New Testament at Lexington Theological Seminary; and John R. Donahue, Professor of New Testament at the Jesuit School of Theology, Graduate Theological Union, Berkeley. In particular, my thanks to Professor Brueggemann for his thoughtful foreword and to Professor Dowd who carefully reviewed the entire manuscript and made numerous helpful criticisms and improvements. I am pleased it will be a volume in this distinctive series.

My primary work on the manuscript occurred during a sabbatical term in Vienna, Austria, in 1995. This sabbatical was made possible through the efforts of the late Dr. Carl Mau, former General Secretary of the Lutheran World Federation. Through his connections with Lutheran leaders throughout the globe, he provided me with both a place to live and to study. I am also in debt to my colleagues in the Department of Religion at Pacific Lutheran University, who were vital to the publication of this book. They read, reviewed, and questioned most of its chapters. They will be glad it is finished. I also thank Pacific Lutheran University for the sabbatical leaves that encourage scholarly activity for busy teachers.

I also want to remember my ecumenical and Lutheran colleagues in ministry, whom I was privileged to serve in this region for some twenty years. As executive director of the Lutheran Institute of Theological Education from 1973–1993, I was involved in countless seminars, conferences, and forums to provide continuing theological education for this region. Our contacts and friendships continue. For those colleagues who received a gift certificate from Pacific Lutheran University for this long-promised book, it is time to pick yours up. I hope that this study will be a rich resource for leaders in the church as they grapple with the role of faith-communities amid a pluralistic, democratic, secular, and nationalistic culture. Perhaps this study will clarify some of the pressing issues for the church.

Of all those to thank, my companion for so many good years deserves the greatest commendation. Her patience is unending, her love steady. Thank you, Jeanette. And to my beloved daughters, Kathryn, Kristen, and Karyn, it is time to enjoy some of your father's labor.

---

1. Walter Pilgrim, *Revelation,* unit 20, in Search Weekly Bible Studies (Minneapolis: Augsburg Publishing House, 1988).

1.
INTRODUCTION

W HAT DOES THE NEW TESTAMENT SAY ABOUT THE ATTITUDE OF CHRIS-
tians and the church toward those who exercise political authority?
Fred Craddock observed, "For those who call Caesar 'Lord' the matter is
simply handled. For those who call Caesar 'Satan' the matter is just as simply handled."[1] The journey on which we are about to embark will demonstrate the complexity of the matter when we move beyond these two
extremes.

Few topics have caused more controversy in the history of the church
than that of the right relationship between the church and the state. From
the beginnings of Christianity as a Jewish offspring in the Greco-Roman
world, through the many centuries of alliance with Rome and its successors
from Constantine to Charles V, and from the Reformation and Enlighten-
ment into the modern era with all its twists and turns, the church has
struggled to know and define its link to the political realm. Questions
abound: Ought Christians support those who govern? Should they pay
taxes? What if those in power misuse their authority or become hostile to
the church? Is it permissible for Christians to resist those who rule and perhaps seek their overthrow? Should the church align itself with particular
governments? Can there be a "Christian" nation? What might that mean?
How can we deal with the constitutional separation of church and state in
our pluralistic democracy? And what should be the church's role in an
increasingly secular culture?

The twentieth century, as we know all too well, has proved to be especially troublesome with respect to these issues. During this century the
church has encountered totalitarian governments that sought to co-opt it
to their racist ideologies and goals. The church has experienced irreconcilable clashes with atheistic socialist regimes bent on destroying it. And the
church has faced powerful secular forces that sought to marginalize or
silence its public influence and substitute their own beliefs and agenda.
And all too often, the church has not known what to say or do.

1. Fred Craddock, *Luke* (Interpretation; Louisville: Westminster/John Knox Press, 1990).

What does the New Testament have to say concerning the political realm and the faith-communities' response to it? For Christians, the biblical norm is the Old and New Testament, which serve as the primary source for its faith and life. Of course, the Bible needs to be interpreted alongside the tradition of the church and its ongoing theological and ethical reflection in each new social and historical setting. Times do change, and altered contexts require different answers.[2] But the Bible and the New Testament in particular remain the central resource for the self-identity of the Christian community. So its witness is necessary not only for the content of the faith itself but also for the shape of the faith-response in both its personal and social dimensions, including the political.

This book focuses on the New Testament and the controversial question broached to Jesus, "Is it lawful to pay taxes to the emperor, or not" (Mark 12:14). As I will show, the subject of the relationship to the emperor is raised at many points throughout the New Testament, usually not as a major issue, yet one of vital importance for life in an alien and sometimes hostile society. With the book of Revelation, however, the matter of the state emerges as the key issue in the author's apocalyptic denunciation of Rome as a beastly oppressor of the church and humanity.

What is the New Testament attitude toward political structures— respect and subjection? Watchful caution, with moments of challenge? Uncompromising rejection of godless and corrupt states? I will show that no single attitude toward those in political authority dominates the New Testament, but that the New Testament exhibits a range of responses from subordination to resistance that reflects the early church's theological and ethical evaluation of the state in varying historical circumstances. I hope to demonstrate the rich diversity of these responses and especially to identify three distinct attitudes within the New Testament.

My own interest in this topic arose in part out of work on the book of Revelation. I was surprised—and for a time offended—by the apparent hostile attitude of the author toward imperial Rome. While this might be understandable in a context of perceived threat, it seemed excessive and vindictive. But I was gradually able to see that behind the apocalyptic visions of judgment on a tyrannical government lay profound prophetic insights. In fact, Revelation, perhaps more than any other New Testament writing, grasps the totality of the conflict between good and evil, order and chaos, God and the satanic, and in so doing reveals the potential for evil inherent in all earthly, human institutions. Even governments can and do

---

2. On the whole question of the use of the Bible in ethical decision-making in the church, see Bruce C. Birch and Larry L. Rasmussen, *Bible and Ethics in the Christian Life*, rev. ed. (Minneapolis: Augsburg, 1989).

incarnate demonic evil! My study of Luke-Acts also led me to different conclusions from many other contemporary interpreters on the Lukan perspective toward Rome.

I have been deeply puzzled and disturbed by the repeated failure of the church and individual Christians in the midst of twentieth-century crises. I do not say this to pass judgment or to claim a higher moral ground. But I wonder about the degree to which the failures may be due to a one-sided reading or misreading of the New Testament. In the case of German Evangelical Christians (my own heritage), it became far too easy to equate being a Christian with loyalty to one's nation or government. Victoria Barnett, the author of a provocative study of the church resistance movements in Germany, searches for the reasons why so few stood firm: "For those who weren't Nazis, the habits of complicity grew by degrees; its roots were in the tangled web of fear, nationalism, political naivete, *and traditional subservience to the state.*"[3] Why this subservience to the state? Among the complexity of answers may be biblical ones. Perhaps those Christians knew only the tradition of Romans 13 or a misinterpretation of Jesus' saying, "Give to the emperor the things that are the emperor's. . . ." The contrary witnesses in the New Testament, and especially the Apocalypse, may have been unknown, forgotten, or silenced. Therefore, one of my purposes is to enable Christians and the church to hear the full testimony of the New Testament, which includes both a critique of and resistance to those in political authority. Caesar is not Lord. Governments may or may not be servants of God.

To attempt a survey of any significant theme in the New Testament is a challenging, if not risky task. Most contemporary research focuses on smaller units or select topics within the various writings or perhaps produces commentaries on single books. Yet it is also necessary to see the larger picture or to paint on a broader canvas, as I have dared to do. In this way, one can bring into view the different ways in which the New Testament church dealt with the particular topic and at the same time lessen the temptation of choosing only one response to the issue.

On the subject of church and government, there are numerous studies on related texts. The bibliography on Romans 13 alone is immense; the same is true of Jesus' saying on payment of tax to the emperor or on the love ethic of the Sermon on the Mount (Plain). Individual commentaries in all their varying shapes and sizes and depths also touch on the texts and themes relevant to our purpose. Of special help are books on the ethics of

---

3. Victoria Barnett, *For the Soul of the People: Protestant Protest against Hitler* (New York: Oxford University Press, 1992), 180. Her work is a moving study of the Confessing Church, using oral histories of survivors at key points in the history.

the New Testament, which typically include sections on the relation of the Christian communities to the socioeconomic and political structures of society.

Nevertheless, despite the historic importance of the topic and its crucial relevance in recent church/state experience, there have been few attempts to survey the entire New Testament on the subject. I mention three.

One is the classic study by the respected Swiss New Testament scholar Oscar Cullmann. His book *The State in the New Testament* was published in 1956 and revised in 1963.[4] In his brilliant pioneering work, Cullmann recognizes the tension between the various New Testament positions regarding the state but finds an underlying unity in the "provisional" nature of all human institutions in light of the promised future already begun. But the study suffers from a narrow focus on the Zealot movement as the counterpart to Jesus' teaching on nonviolence and concerning political structures, tends to find too much unity among the distinct New Testament attitudes toward the state, and fails to grasp the full portrait of Jesus' prophetic critique of the political realm. Yet it is a seminal work of continuing importance.

Another survey, by the German scholar Wolfgang Schrage in 1971, has not been translated.[5] Like Cullmann, Schrage concentrates on key passages in the various New Testament documents. While noting their distinctiveness, he nevertheless argues for an underlying commonality among the New Testament writers, who view the state neither as a satanic nor a divine power and consequently neither commend disloyalty nor unconditional subjection. Without recognizing its uniqueness, he rightly grasps Jesus' nonrevolutionary yet critical stance. Among its weaknesses, it too strongly posits a unity among the diversity and omits significant material in its brief discussions (for example, the Pastorals, the three demonic images of the

---

4. Oscar Cullmann, *The State in the New Testament* (New York: Charles Scribner's Sons, 1956); rev. ed. (London: SCM Press, 1963). As I suggest in chap. 3, Cullmann's assumption that the Zealots were an organized Jewish resistance movement from 6 to 70 C.E. is now under serious doubt (pp. 38–39). Also, his interpretation of the "authorities" (*exousiai*) in Romans 13:1 as mythic powers never gained acceptance, despite his attempt in the revised edition to justify its possibility. But his insights as a whole are acute and helpful.

5. Wolfgang Schrage, *Die Christen und der Staat im Neuen Testament* (Gütersloh: Gerd Mohn, 1971). See also his *Ethics of the New Testament*, trans. D. E. Green (Philadelphia: Fortress Press, 1988). To my knowledge, Schrage and Cullmann published the only book-length studies on the relation of church and state in the New Testament since 1950. Schrage's bibliography, however, also lists nine articles or essays in German that review the subject from 1950 to 1970. Similarly, Lutz Pohle's book on Romans 13, *Die Christen und der Staat nach Römer 13* (Mainz: Matthias-Grünewald Verlag, 1984), includes thirteen other brief articles (all in German) that survey the topic.

state in Revelation); moreover, its Pauline ethic of obedience needs more careful qualification.

A third comprehensive look at the New Testament teaching on church and government is a 1972 essay by the English scholar Charles Kingsley Barrett.[6] Although brief, it relates the early church to Judaism and notes some differences between Jesus and Paul and especially the differences between Paul and the book of Revelation. Nevertheless, both its brevity and a strong desire to find a basic unity among the distinct New Testament writers lessen its value.[7]

A new look at an old subject is in order. While much can be learned from previous interpreters, all the differing voices in the New Testament must be heard, and the evidence in the Gospels and in the Apocalypse of John should be fully considered.

My methods and tools are those of historical-critical scholarship. Contemporary research has refined newer literary or narrative methodologies and models for illumining the social world of the biblical era.[8] While these currents have exciting potential for reading the Bible with fresh eyes, the approach in this book does not identify with any one method. I simply seek to employ the best of historical scholarship in order to understand the New Testament witness regarding the relationship between the church and the state.

My main purpose is to demonstrate three differing attitudes toward the state in the New Testament. Chapter 2 begins with the traditional ethic of subordination in the Pauline, post-Pauline, and Petrine literature. Special attention is given to Romans 13 and its proper interpretation within Paul's thought. In the next chapter, I turn to the Gospels and their representation of Jesus' ethic of critical distancing from the possessors of religious and political authority. Both Jesus' public ministry and the passion history (suffering and death) are included. An extended excursus on Luke-Acts continues the debate on Luke's attitude toward Rome and opts for Lukan opposition to the imperial government. In chapter 4 I look at the book of Revelation and its ethic of resistance toward a totalitarian and idolatrous

6. C. K. Barrett, "The New Testament Doctrine of the State," in his *New Testament Essays* (London: SPCK, 1972).

7. Other problems with Barrett's overview are that (a) he thinks Luke-Acts adopts a positive attitude toward the state as do Paul and the Pastorals (pp. 5–6, 17) and (b), while he grasps the sharp attack in Revelation on an oppressive state, he does not seem to find any continuing relevance for Revelation's position against those in political power.

8. For a helpful introduction to recent studies on the social world of the New Testament, see John E. Stambaugh and David L. Balch, *The New Testament in Its Social Environment* (Library of Early Christianity, 2; Philadelphia: Westminster Press, 1986). On literary approaches, see E. V. McKnight, *The Bible and the Reader: An Introduction to Literary Criticism* (Philadelphia: Fortress Press, 1985).

state. The concluding chapter, which attempts to relate the New Testament themes to the contemporary life of the church, seeks to hold together the three New Testament responses in such a way that they can be drawn upon in varying historical contexts by the church. A contextual paradigm is given, with twentieth-century illustrations of its potential usefulness.

I hope that this book will enable individual Christians and the church not only to affirm the divine mandate of the state under God but also to raise up the ethic of critical distancing and resistance as authentic New Testament options.

2.
ETHIC OF SUBORDINATION

Pauline, Post-Pauline, and Related Texts

THIS CHAPTER WILL EXPLORE THOSE NEW TESTAMENT TEXTS THAT
regard governments as earthly structures instituted by God and therefore advocate an ethic of Christian subordination toward those in authority. Our New Testament sources are the Pauline and deutero-Pauline epistles, along with 1 Peter and Hebrews (Rom. 13:1-7; 1 Thess. and 2 Thess.
2:1-10; 1 Tim. 2:1-2; Titus 3:1; 1 Pet. 2:13-17; Heb. 11–13). These New Testament
passages have shaped the dominant attitude of Christians toward the state
and those in political office down through the centuries. I begin with a cap-
sule summary of this position.

The government is understood to be a gift of God, divinely established
for the common good. Its God-given purpose is to encourage and maintain
what is beneficial for our life together and to discourage what is harmful
and disruptive. Or, put another way, the state is God's instrument in the
human community to preserve law and order and to promote justice and
peace. Its power consists in its responsibility to exercise its authority toward
these beneficial ends. Christians, in turn, owe to the government their loyalty and respect. Because government is a divine gift they support its
preservation of the good and opposition to evil, pray for those in authority, pay taxes, and try to live as model citizens of human communities. In so
doing they act in accordance with God's intent. Conversely, to resist the
state is to risk both punishment and divine disapproval.

The preceding paragraph is a paraphrase of Romans 13:1-7, the most
developed and familiar text on the relationship between church and government in the New Testament. Because the understanding of church-state
relations in this significant, yet difficult passage in Paul continues in certain
later New Testament traditions, I will need to examine them as well.

The Texts

Romans 13:1-7[1]

Romans, one of Paul's later letters, was written ca. 55 C.E., during the reign of Nero (54–68 C.E.).[2] Paul himself had never visited the church in Rome, though he anticipated a future visit and further missionary work in Spain (15:22-29). He obviously knew something about the church and its members, as well as the political winds that surrounded it. The long list of names in chap. 16, once thought to be a fragment from a lost Ephesians letter, may in fact reflect a Roman audience. Rome was the imperial center of the world.

Paul wrote both to introduce himself and his gospel and to prepare for his imminent visit to the mother church in Jerusalem (15:30-32). Chapters 12–15 conclude the letter with extended ethical instructions on the new life in Christ. Two themes seem pertinent to Paul's remarks concerning the Christian response to the political powers. One is the love command that surrounds the passage. Paul states that love, not vengeance or evil for evil, should govern Christian conduct (12:9-21). "Love your neighbor" fulfills the law (13:8-10). He also encourages the Christians in Rome to live in peace with everyone (12:18). May there be a link between the call to love the neighbor and willing subjection to those who rule? Many think so. The other theme is the nearness of the end (13:11-14). Does this eschatological (i.e., future) expectation, so prominent in Paul, lessen his concern over earthly structures in light of their imminent demise (cf. 1 Cor. 7;1 Thess. 4:13-18)? After all, if the world is about to end, why get so bothered with temporary human institutions? Again, many think this may influence Paul's thought. I will respond to these possibilities later.

13:1-2. "Let every person be subject to the governing authorities ... those authorities that exist have been instituted by God." This section is clearly meant to be ethical instruction ("be subject ..."), not theological or philosophical reflection on the nature of government. Every person is to be subject. Paul here employs a word that refers to subjection or subordination to persons worthy of respect (*hypotassesthai*). Elsewhere in the New Testa-

---

1. The scholarly literature on Romans 13:1-7 is immense. Both commentaries and numerous articles are available. Some commentaries: Ernst Käsemann, *Commentary on Romans*, trans. and ed. Geoffrey Bromiley (Grand Rapids, Mich.: Eerdmans, 1980; C. E. B. Cranfield, *A Critical and Exegetical Commentary on the Epistle to the Romans*, 2 vols. (Edinburgh: T. & T. Clark, 1975–79); James D. G. Dunn, *Romans 9-16* (WBC 38B; Dallas: Word Books, 1988); Joseph A. Fitzmyer, *Romans*, vol. 2 (Anchor Bible; New York: Doubleday, 1993). For a helpful article on the overall argument of the passage, see Robert H. Stein, "The Argument of Romans 13:1-7," *NovT* 30.4 (1989), 325–43.

2. Along with the majority of New Testament scholars, I regard the Pastorals (1–2 Timothy, Titus) and Ephesians as deutero-Pauline.

ment, the term can refer to the subjection of believers to God or Christ, or as a household metaphor expressing the relationship of children to parents, of slaves to masters, of wives to husbands, as well as of Christians to secular authorities (Rom. 13:1, Titus 3:1, 1 Pet. 2:13, *1 Clement* 61:1). With one exception (Acts 5:29), the New Testament avoids the normal Greek words for "obey" when expressing the church's relationship to the state. This may be due to the desire to emphasize the willing subordination of Christians to the powers that be, possibly even some sense of reciprocal obligation.[3] Why should persons be subject to those who govern? Because the authorities (*exousiai*) receive their authority from God. In fact, it is said that all existing authorities have been appointed by God. And who are these authorities? There is no doubt that Paul has political rulers, imperial representatives, and other officials in mind.[4]

3. So C. E. B. Cranfield, *Romans: A Shorter Commentary* (Grand Rapids, Mich.: Eerdmans, 1985), 320; also Dunn, *Romans 9-16*, 761. John H. Yoder argues vigorously that *hypotassesthai* should be translated as "subordination," not "subjection" or "submission" or "obedience," in order to avoid any thought of involuntary or blind submission. "Subordination means the acceptance of an order as it exists, but with the new meaning given to it by the fact that one's acceptance of it is willing and meaningfully motivated" (*The Politics of Jesus* [Grand Rapids, Mich.: Eerdmans], 175. While I agree, he does constrict the meaning of "subjection" too narrowly. Even the word "obedience" need not imply unwilling or abject submission (cf. Christ's obedience to God [Phil. 2:8] or the believer's obedience to Christ or the gospel; or the willing obedience of children to parents or slave to master [Col. 3:20-22; Eph. 6:1,5] and especially the mutual subjection of husbands and wives [Eph. 5:21]).

Yoder provides a sharp and provocative analysis of Romans 13 (193-214). Although it is cogent in many respects, I have two fundamental disagreements. First, Yoder sees the purpose of Romans 13 as singularly that of calling Roman Christians "away from any notion of revolution or insubordination," or "to a non-resistant attitude toward a tyrannical government" (204). As I will demonstrate below, this is but one of many hypothetical guesses about Paul's specific intent for writing Romans 13.

Second, Yoder rejects any interpretation of this passage that sees governments per se as divinely created or ordained or appointed institutions in the orders of creation (200-204). He argues instead that Paul simply recognizes that whatever powers exist, God somehow orders for his purposes, and thus Christians should respond in willing subordination. But the force of Paul's words goes far beyond that of merely affirming God's ordering of whatever exists. They assert without qualification that the ruling authorities exist according to divine purpose for ordering the common good. Six times he repeats that the authorities exist in relation to God or as servants of God (13:1-2, except from God, instituted by God, appointed by God; 13:4-6, God's servants thrice). There may be reason to question the concept of "orders of creation" in these verses, but they minimally understand governing rulers and structures as part of God's intended or providential way for preserving the public good. However, Yoder is right to observe that the term *hypotassesthai* means "willing and deliberate subordination," not uncritical obedience. "The Christian who accepts his subjection to government retains his moral independence and judgment" (207).

4. Oscar Cullmann, *The State in the New Testament* (New York: Scribner, 1956), 93ff., and a few others have argued that Paul may have had in mind angelic powers who stand behind

But can one say so easily that all political authorities, without exception, have been de facto established by God? Here is where one must begin to press Paul further (see below). Note that Paul does not say or claim in any way that political rulers are themselves divine. Clearly, they stand under God's authority.

Nevertheless, to resist the authorities is to go against God who appointed them and will result in judgment (from God or the rulers?). Were some Christians in Rome calling for resistance, possibly in sympathy with fellow Jewish nationalists? We know that Nero's early years were tolerable for Jews and Christians, but then he turned against the vulnerable Christians with bloody vengeance, using them as a scapegoat for rumors to the effect that he himself set fire to Rome.

> Consequently, to get rid of the report, Nero fastened the guilt and inflicted the most exquisite tortures on a class hated for their abominations, called Christians by the populace. (Tacitus, *Annals* 15.44; early second century)

This and other possible historical contexts for Paul's counsel of subjection will be explored later in this chapter.

13:3-5. "Do what is good . . . it [civil authority] is God's servant for your good . . . or to execute wrath on the wrongdoer." Christians who might be afraid of those possessing political power are assured that they have nothing to fear. Their good conduct will meet with welcome approval.

Conversely, if they do wrong, look out, for then they have reason to expect punishment and the sword. The "power of the sword," the government's right and responsibility to preserve justice and order, even by force if necessary, derives classically from this Pauline verse. It is assumed rulers have the duty to prevent and to punish all kinds of wrongdoing.

Does the "power of the sword" include capital punishment and war? This question is much debated. Paul's primary reference is the maintenance of the social order, what one might describe as the police function of the state. In the first century, this did include capital punishment, permit-

---

the earthly rulers. But Cullmann himself offered this explanation only as a hypothesis in his second, revised German edition (see *The State* [1963], 68ff.). See Walter Wink, *Naming the Powers* (Philadelphia: Fortress Press, 1984), 45–47, for a vigorous defense of its primary meaning here as historical, earthly rulers. Yet he does think it possible that supernatural powers may lie in the background. It is true that elsewhere in Paul the *exousiai* are hostile "principalities and powers." Not so here. Käsemann, *Commentary on Romans*, 353, correctly states that this means they do not always carry a metaphysical background and cites frequent Hellenistic examples as evidence.

ted and practiced by all governments. This passage does not really address the question of war, since it limits itself to internal "law and order" issues, not national military policy.[5] Once again it is repeated that the governing authorities act on God's behalf. Three times, in fact, they are termed "servant of God" in promoting the good and exercising judgment. Although the words used for "servant" most often carry a distinct Christian meaning (v. 4, *diakonos*; v. 6, *leitourgos*; cf. Rom. 1:1), here they simply have the generic meaning of "civil servant." But as servants of God, their authority is something derived, not inherent in their own office and appointment.

Another urgent question needs to be raised concerning Paul's counsel. What if the political authorities do not act on the side of justice or the public good? What if they persistently misuse or abuse the power of the sword? What then should be the Christian response? On this obvious and vital question, all one hears throughout this passage is a deafening silence! The weight remains one-sidedly on the assumption of good and just governments (see discussion below).

13:6-7. "Pay to all what is due them . . . taxes . . . respect . . . honor." Paul closes this section with some practical examples of subjection to those in authority.[6] One pays taxes to support their work as God's servants to foster what is right and prohibit evil. The strong emphasis on paying to everyone what one owes (*phoros* = tax; *telos* = revenue) may indicate this was a controversial issue in Rome, as well as in Palestine. Jewish nationalists fought against the imperial tax to their death (66–70 C.E.). Jesus left the question

5. Yoder argues vigorously against the tradition that says the government's "mandate to wield the sword and the Christian duty to obey the state combine to place upon the Christian a moral obligation to support and participate in the state's legal killing"(*Politics*, 194). Here Yoder reflects his pacifist stance. I agree "the sword" refers chiefly to the judicial and police mandate of the state. But Yoder tries to separate the Christian support of the state and its wielding of the sword from the death penalty, an impossibility in the first century (so Dunn, *Romans 9-16*, 764, and others). However, to what degree this decides the issue for today and how consistent this is with the love ethic of Jesus remains an open question. As for war, unfortunately the "power of the sword" has been used throughout history to legitimize war by those who govern, whether in the name of Christ or not. This de facto claim of nations to declare war has been tempered in the Christian tradition by concepts of "justifiable war" and by powerful impulses toward pacifism in the love-your-enemy ethic of Jesus (Matt. 5:43-48; cf. Rom. 12:14-21; 13:8-10). With some exceptions, pacifism did seem to be the norm for the pre-Constantinian church, although some recent studies question this assertion.

6. Yoder makes the intriguing suggestion that the participle translated, "busy with this very thing" (*proskarterountes*, v. 6), be treated as an adverbial phrase: "to the extent" the rulers busy themselves with good and evil; or "only to the extent" they do so (*Politics*, 207–208). This would make the obedience of Christians conditional upon the authorities' response. Although this translation is possible in Greek, it seems unlikely, given the thrust of the whole passage on the necessity of obedience to divinely appointed rulers.

open, as we will see (chap. 3). Paul here sides against Christian resistance, at least under the present circumstances of his writing to Christians in Rome.[7] In addition to the payment of taxes, Christians owe respect and honor toward those who govern. Absent, however, is any request to pray for the emperor, though this will appear in the later deutero-Pauline letters (see below, p. 15).

Before I take up some of the critical questions that arise from Romans 13:1-7, it will be helpful to examine the other New Testament writings that reflect a similar tradition of subjection and loyalty to the state.

First and Second Thessalonians

First Thessalonians

No direct word is found in this letter about the Christian response toward political rulers. Yet Paul does reflect indirectly on the matter within the context of the Christian attitude toward persecution (*thlipsis*). Paul wrote to the Thessalonians only a short time after he had been forced to leave abruptly when violent opposition broke out against his preaching (1:6; 2:1-2; cf. Acts 17:1-9). Both he and the neophyte Thessalonian Christians had experienced public animosity and suffering (Gentile and Jewish? 1:6; 2:1-2, 14-16; 3:1-3).[8]

What should be the Christian response in the face of such hostility? Paul in effect urges them to accept it as part of their Christian calling. He reminds them that he had forewarned them that persecution for the sake of Christ belongs to their new identity (3:3-4). By suffering, they become "imitators" of the Lord, of Paul, and of other Christians in Judea and elsewhere (1:6; 2:14-16). In fact, because of their willing submission to suffering, Paul holds them up as examples of "faith in the midst of persecution" for the younger churches of Macedonia and Achaia (1:6-8). Nowhere in the letter do we find any hint or suggestion of resistance to those who cause their suffering. Rather, they are reminded that Christians do not repay evil for evil but seek to do good toward everyone (5:15).

---

7. Dunn especially argues that Paul is offering a pragmatic policy of "political quietism" for Roman Christians in light of the suspicion toward Jews (and thus Jewish Christians) by Rome. In this sense it is a wise missionary strategy that tells Rome that Christians do not seek to subvert the social order (*Romans*, 759, 766–68).

8. Most interpreters view the persecution (*thlipsis*) as a reference to external conflict with local religious and political authorities. One recent commentator has argued, however, that the conflict refers to the internal anxieties and difficulties of believers as a consequence of their conversion (Abraham Malherbe, *Paul and the Thessalonians* [Philadelphia: Fortress Press, 1987], 48). But Paul's equation of their suffering with his own experience of conflict in Philippi and Thessalonica seems to rule out this possibility.

The general ethic of the letter is the encouragement to live quiet and peaceable lives and to seek to live in harmony with their non-Christian neighbors (4:9-12). While Christians love one another above all, they also exhibit concern for all people as an extension of their Christian love.

Second Thessalonians

There is one passage in 2 Thessalonians that some commentators interpret as a positive reference toward imperial Rome. This reference occurs within the apocalyptic-like passage 2:1-10. Here Paul (allegedly) mentions the expected coming of "the man of lawlessness," an Antichrist figure of the end-time (2:3-4). Paul's purpose for writing is to assure the confused believers in Thessalonica that neither the "day of the Lord" nor "the coming of our Lord Jesus Christ" are at hand, despite claims (and forged letters) to the contrary (2:1-2). He insists the end will not come until "the man of lawlessness" appears amid the final rebellion of evil. For the present moment, however, the Antichrist is prevented from appearing by a mysterious entity, "the restraining one" (2:6-7, *to katechon*).

Who is this restraining figure holding back the coming of the end-time Antichrist? The author assumes the original readers know, but this has not been true of subsequent readers. Interpreters have made several suggestions: angelic or supernatural powers, Paul's own preaching of the gospel to the Gentiles, or the Roman Empire.

This last suggestion arose very early and has remained a common explanation. According to this view, Paul regarded the Roman Empire as functioning in some way to preserve the civil order in the present and thereby to restrain the anti-Christ figure, whose coming will unleash the rebellion and chaos of the last days.[9] This end-time scenario is a familiar one in both Jewish and Christian apocalyptic. The author of 2 Thessalonians believed the forces of lawlessness were already at work, yet they would remain hidden until the end, at which time the coming of the Lord Jesus (the parousia) would destroy the man of lawlessness (2:7-8). If this is a valid interpretation of the restraining power, then Paul did recognize a positive role for the Roman imperium in the present interim. And this would agree with Romans 13 and Paul's view of the state as fulfilling a divinely given mandate in the preservation of peace and order.

At least two arguments raise serious doubts about this interpretation. One is the growing uncertainty over the authorship of 2 Thessalonians. Many think this letter was written later by an unknown follower of Paul. Among other problems, they find serious contradictions in the eschatology

9. See C. K. Barrett, "The New Testament Doctrine of the State," in his *New Testament Essays* (London: SPCK, 1972) 13.

of the two letters.[10] Second—and of greater importance—the identity of the restraining force is simply unknown. Since the first mention of the name occurs in the neuter case ("the restraining thing," v. 6) and the second uses the masculine ("the restraining person," v. 7) it has been plausibly suggested that the writer himself did not know for sure who or what it might be.[11] I find equally persuasive the argument that the author (Paul?) regards the preaching of the gospel to the Gentiles as the reason for the divine restraint with respect to the end (cf. Rom. 11:25). Whatever might have been in the author's mind, one cannot use this text with any certainty concerning the Pauline attitude toward the state.

The Pastoral Epistles (1–2 Timothy, Titus)

Although they are written in Paul's name, there is a near consensus among New Testament scholars that these epistles belong to a generation or two after Paul, around the turn of the first century. The unknown author saw himself as a loyal disciple of Paul and wrote what he considered to be an appropriate word from the apostle for the church leaders and congregations of his own generation.

The Pastorals show the church settling in for the long haul. The vivid expectation of Jesus' return has largely subsided. In this changed milieu, the writer responds to the need for the stabilization of the church and for institutional structures. We find a growing concern for tradition, for church order, for creeds, and for a scriptural canon. At the same time, there arises the need for a new look outward toward life in society and for the kind of conduct that will present the Christian community in a favorable light. All of this tends toward a more cautious and conservative ethic. "For the grace of God has appeared . . . training us to renounce impiety and worldly pas-

10. E.g., 1 Thessalonians needs to deal with the unexpected delay of the end-time and the death of believers (4:13-18); 2 Thessalonians finds believers overly excited by its supposed nearness ("it is here," 2:1-2). How could the two moods be so different in letters thought to be written only months apart? Some propose that the reverse order of writing makes better sense: 2 Thessalonians with its overenthusiasm for the end; then 1 Thessalonians with the problem of its delay. While all agree 1 Thessalonians is genuine, other arguments question the authenticity of 2 Thessalonians as well.

11. So Martin Dibelius, "Rom und die Christen im ersten Jahrhundert," *Botschaft und Geschichte* 2 (J. C. B. Mohr [Paul Siebeck], 1956), 187. Dibelius also thinks the mythological background argues against any historical reference. The early church father Tertullian (220 C.E.), seems to be the first Christian exegete to propose the identity of Rome. Since Tertullian wanted the empire to continue, he urged prayer to postpone the end and prevent the Antichrist's coming. Paul, however, longed for the coming of the end-time. Another church father, Irenaeus (c. 200), does not make the identification with Rome but instead sees the Antichrist as destroying the Roman Empire (cf. Revelation 17).

sions and to live lives that are self-controlled, upright, and godly" (Titus 2:11-12).[12]

One striking example is found in the so-called household codes. The household codes, which appear frequently in the New Testament letters, were intended to order domestic relationships between husband and wife, parents and children, masters and slaves. What is important for our purposes is to observe their increasingly hierarchical and patriarchal tendencies from the earlier to later letters. This is especially true of husband-wife relations, where the role of the wife becomes severely limited (cf. Col. 3—4:1//Eph. 5:21—6:9 with 1 Tim. 2:8-15//Titus 2:3-10//1 Pet. 2:18—3:17).

With respect to the Christian attitude toward the government, one might therefore expect the same cautious and pragmatic ethic. Two passages require our attention.

1 Timothy 2:1-2. Within the larger text, the author seeks to encourage the practice of prayer (2:1-15; note that women are admonished only to modesty and good works, not prayer, vv. 8-15). He begins by urging prayer for everyone. But those in particular singled out for prayer are "kings and all who are in high positions" (v. 2). This refers to civil authorities, including the emperor. While it is true that we did not find any appeal for public prayer on behalf of officials or the emperor in the Pauline letters, this prayer appeal nevertheless seems consistent with the spirit of Romans.

The practice of prayer on behalf of the emperor and empire was a regular part of Jewish religious life in New Testament times, until the disastrous events of 70 C.E. (the fall of Jerusalem and the Temple). Prayers were offered daily in the Temple, along with sacrifices for the welfare of the empire. Inscriptions from synagogues of Hellenistic Judaism outside of Palestine (the diaspora) reveal as well that these communities made strong affirmations of loyalty to the empire.[13] Therefore Christian prayer in like manner is not unexpected. As with Judaism, the appropriateness of such prayer will become problematic only when the state becomes increasingly hostile. Then the question will arise, Should a persecuted church continue

---

12. One scholar characterized the ethic of the Pastorals with the controversial phrase, "christliche Bürgerlichkeit"; this means something like "middle-class, bourgeois, ordinary or common": so did Martin Dibelius, *The Pastoral Epistles,* trans. Philip Buttolph and Adela Yarbro Collins (Hermeneia; Philadelphia: Fortress Press, 1972), 39–41. The translators use the term "good Christian citizenship." This description sparked considerable dispute, but in our judgment it is a fair generalization of the Pastoral ethic. However, another study, by Reggie M. Kidd, *Wealth and Beneficence in the Pastorals: A "Bourgeois" Form of Early Christianity?* (SBLDS 122; Atlanta: Scholars Press, 1990), questions the radical distance between the Pauline and Pastoral ethic and argues "there is more that unites the Pastorals and Paul than there is that divides them" (195).

13. See pp. 22–24 on the loyalty traditions in early Judaism.

to pray for kings and those in authority? As we will see, different answers are given by different New Testament authors.

In 2:2 the author explains why Christians should pray for those who hold political office. This will lead to quiet and peaceable lives. No doubt this concern for a peaceful life reflects the hope that Christians will be seen as model citizens rather than troublemakers. But it also seems linked to continued evangelistic efforts (2:3-7). By their exemplary conduct as loyal and praying citizens, Christians will promote the cause of the gospel. Nowhere do we get the feeling here or elsewhere in the Pastorals that there might be any inherent conflict between the Christian community and the government. Intercession for civil authorities and those who rule seems the natural and right thing to do.

Perhaps one caveat needs to be made. While the act of intercession does demonstrate honor and respect, it also makes clear that the emperor is not divine. "Intercession, however positive, is an absolute denial of worship. Anyone who stands in need of intercession—emperors, king, or governor—is human."[14]

Titus 3:1-2. This letter likewise preserves a positive affirmation of those in political power. The author begins a lengthy exhortation to good deeds with the admonition to be subject to rulers and authorities (3:1-8). The language contains a clear echo of Romans 13. Both the same verb for subordination (*hypotassein*) and the same nouns for those who rule ("rulers and authorities," *archai, exousiai*) appear. Only the use of the verb "to obey" is slightly different. Even though brief, we hear again the theme of Christian subjection to and respect for civil authorities.

As in 1 Timothy, the motivation appears to be both moral and evangelistic. "Remind them" indicates that this is thought to be typical ethical conduct for Christians (3:1). Such obedience and respect also proves to outsiders that Christians play a positive role in society.

Taken together, then, we find in the Pastorals a tradition of loyalty and respect for government that affirms the Pauline tradition of Romans 13.

1 Peter 2:13-17

Although this letter is identified with Petrine authorship (1:1, "Peter, an apostle . . ."), most interpreters attribute it to an unknown author writing in the post-martyrdom period between 65 and 90 C.E.[15] And, although it

---

14. Wolfgang Schrage, *The Ethics of the New Testament*, trans. D. E. Green (Philadelphia: Fortress Press, 1988), 268 (cited from Gerhard Kittel, "Das Urteil des Neuen Testament über den Staat," *ZSTh* 14 [1937] 665).

15. See John H. Elliott, *A Home for the Homeless* (Philadelphia: Fortress Press, 1981), 80–85; David L. Balch, *Let Wives Be Submissive: The Domestic Code in 1 Peter* (SBLMS 26; Chico, Calif.:

likely preserves Petrine tradition, there is a striking similarity throughout the letter with genuine Pauline themes.

First Peter was no doubt written from Rome ("Babylon," 5:13) to Christians in Asia Minor (1:1, described as "exiles of the Dispersion," with five provinces in Asia Minor named). Of significance for our purposes is an understanding of its particular sociohistorical context. The letter reflects a social milieu of growing conflict and tension between Christians and their non-Christian neighbors. This context of suffering and persecution, however, does not come from the imperial authorities, as later in Revelation. Here it seems more local, sporadic, and unofficial, the result of being perceived as "outsiders" and adherents of a new and exclusive religious sect.[16] There is heavy pressure to conform and surprise when converts to the new religion reject some of their former associations (4:4). Christians are distrusted and accused, possibly even facing sporadic trial and prosecution from the civil authorities. First Peter thus exhibits a Christian community trying hard to live as good and loyal citizens in the shadow of increasing conflict and alienation. The author hopes to avoid any confrontation. Yet there is the awareness that it cannot always be done (3:13-15, 17).

Christians are described as "aliens and exiles" in this kind of threatening world. They receive strong assurances that their "time of exile" will be short (1:17; 2:11). In the between-time, they are to conduct themselves as people already freed through the death of Christ, who now possess a living hope through the resurrection (1:3-6, 17-19).

As might be expected in view of their own potential suffering, the author expends considerable effort to hold up the sufferings of Jesus. Christ's passion becomes the model for them to remember and follow. "Christ also suffered for you, leaving you an example that you should follow in his steps" (2:21). The way of Jesus is the way of suffering. In addition, the teaching and conduct of Jesus toward one's enemies is recalled and affirmed. Jesus did not return evil for evil, nor abuse for abuse, but placed his trust solely in God (2:22-23; 3:9).

Scholar's Press, 1981), 137; and Paul J. Achtemeier, *1 Peter* (Hermeneia; Minneapolis: Fortress Press, 1996), 42, 49.

16. Elliott says there is only social pressure, religious discrimination, and local hostility such as is customarily directed against outside religious groups (*A Home*, 79–80). Balch is in essential agreement. "The socio-political tensions reflected in 1 Peter are best explained by the conversion of some persons in Greco-Roman culture to a despised religion and the predictable reaction of their domestic superiors to such conversions" (*Let Wives*, 137). Although local, it was nevertheless real and most likely involved some physical danger as well (against Elliott, *A Home*, 80); similarly Achtemeier, *1 Peter*: "The suffering therefore seems to be due more to social pressure with occasional intervention by officials than to any wide-ranging judicial attempt to locate and root out all Christian communities" (35).

What then should be the attitude of Christians toward those in political power? One can imagine that this was much debated, given the tenuous and dangerous circumstances they faced. Some Christians may have strongly advocated political resistance.[17] Perhaps others urged withdrawal and quietness. Still others (and this seems most probable) may have argued for more openness and accommodation with their pagan neighbors. Whatever the arguments, the response of the author comes down forcefully on the side of subjection to authorities. Like their Lord, they should be ready even to suffer, if need be (2:13-17). The letter indicates a willingness to try to get along, to remain loyal and obedient citizens, even though they may and do experience unjust hardship and suffering.

The passage on the government in 2:13-17 has close affinities to Romans 13. Some have even called it the first commentary on Paul's teaching. We will note both the striking similarities, as well as several significant differences, sometimes overlooked.

The verses preceding this text urge Christian exiles to conduct themselves honorably among the Gentiles (2:11-12). Even when mistreated they should let their good deeds speak well for them. No accusations against Christians should be based on their own actual misdeeds. In 2:13 believers are told "to be subject" to every human institution (the NRSV translates rather clumsily, "accept the authority of . . ."). The same verb occurs here as in Rom. 13:3 and Titus 3:1 (*hypotassein*). The phrase "every human institution" is unique to 1 Peter, and there is some disagreement over its exact meaning.[18] But the following phrase makes it certain that political officials are in mind. Christians are to be subject both to the emperor, as the highest authority (*basileus*, king) and to governors (*hēgēmon*) appointed by the emperor.

In 2:14 there is another paraphrase of Romans 13. Those who govern by authority of the emperor do so "to punish those who do wrong and to praise those who do good" (Rom. 13:3-4). In the subsequent verses, Christians are encouraged to do right and so silence the malicious slander of ignorant accusers. All of this sounds very Pauline.

---

17. Bo Reicke, *The Epistles of James, Peter, and Jude* (AB 37; Garden City, N.Y.: Doubleday, 1964), 73–74, 95–96, suggests that 1 Peter was written to quell Christian opposition to Nero's rule, a kind of Christian Zealotism. Against this view, C. Freemann Sleeper, "Political Responsibility According to 1 Peter," *NovT* 10 (1968) 270–86, argues that the evidence allows only a deep sense of alienation from society, not any kind of political revolt. I basically agree with Sleeper.

18. Schrage points out correctly that the Greek word translated "institution" (*ktisis*) never has that exact meaning elsewhere in ancient Greek literature (*Ethics*, 278). He suggests that we translate "human creature," so that the reference is to individuals who hold office, not the office itself. Nevertheless, these individuals are still understood to be the agents of the emperor or state.

Nevertheless, there are also some key points of difference from Romans 13. Despite the command to be subject, nowhere does it say that the authorities have been appointed by God. Christians are subject "for the Lord's sake" (2:13), that is, as their Christian duty. But they are not subject because rulers are divinely instituted, as in Paul. Nor are the authorities ever called "servants of God" (repeated three times in Rom. 13). In 1 Peter only Christians are "servants of God" (2:16) and so can act as free people.

In fact, the idea of freedom adds a new dimension to the discussion. Within the political context of this verse, it must mean that Christians are free with respect to the authorities. They should and do subordinate themselves to their rulers, but as free persons.[19] They give to God alone their highest allegiance and so are not bound to any lesser authority. They are "servants of God," not "servants of the state." Therefore they owe to the emperor only what they owe to everyone else: honor. The final verse sums up the status of Christians as servants of God with succinct clarity. Christians honor all people, love the family of believers, and honor the emperor. But they fear only God.[20]

In addition to the section on political powers in 2:13-17, two further relevant references occur in 1 Peter. As part of the closing exhortation, the author warns his readers to resist the devil (5:8-9). This resistance is linked to the same suffering their Christian sisters and brothers throughout the world are experiencing. So behind their mutual suffering at the hands of local and civil authorities stand evil powers. This means that institutions too can come under demonic influence.

There is also the illuminating closing greeting from their sister church "in Babylon" (5:13). Babylon, a pseudonym for Rome, was no compliment! Christians began to use it after Nero's brief but bloody persecution in Rome. It always carried negative connotations. We will see later how this is especially true in Revelation, where Babylon symbolizes the Roman Empire as the beastly enemy of God on earth (see chap. 4). A Christian reader of 1 Peter would certainly hear it as a red flag of caution and warning. And the

19. Schrage argues that Christian freedom "normally" manifests itself in respect and loyalty, submission and honor" (*Ethics*, 278). This might require qualification, and I will argue below that obedience and respect depend on other factors and especially on how the church assesses the role of a government: Does it stand essentially on the side of justice and the common good or not? (See chap. 5.) Of course, those in the Pauline and post-Pauline loyalty tradition would agree with Schrage.

20. Ethelbert Stauffer, *Christ and the Caesars* (London: SCM, 1955), 247, cites a dramatic example of how early Christians reserved the attitude of fear (i.e., ultimate respect) for the worship of God. When the Carthaginian Christian martyr Donata (N. Africa, second century) was asked to swear "by the divine spirit of the Lord our Caesar," she responded by saying she would "honor Caesar as Caesar but fear only God."

churches of Asia Minor soon did experience something of Babylon's fury and power.

Both 1 Peter and Romans 13, therefore, affirm the ethic of Christian respect for and subjection to political rulers.[21] Yet we find in 1 Peter an absence of the Pauline statement that all governments are appointed by God and a more realistic assessment of the authorities' potential for harm. Christians were beginning to face the hard truth of civil authorities who do not respect them, even the possibility of violent opposition. But the author's response was not to resist or to withdraw or to name the authorities as demonic enemies of God and the church.[22] Here we find unjust suffering and isolation and potential persecution met with acceptance and nonresistance and willingness to suffer, all modeled after the life of Jesus Christ, who also suffered unjustly. Here, too, suffering does not provoke apocalyptic visions of judgment on Babylon or the call to heroic and patient endurance or the readiness for martyrdom. We will see later how different this is from the response in the Apocalypse.

Hebrews

Several passages in Hebrews are of interest because they point to a Christian community that has obviously experienced some persecution, yet it responds without any apparent hostility or resistance. This letter was probably written to Hellenistic Jewish-Christians some decades after Paul.[23] Its author remains unknown. But he writes to offer a hopeful word of encouragement to "a community threatened by exhaustion, resignation, and indifference."[24]

21. Achtemeier notes six key differences between 1 Peter and Rom. 13:1-7 and thus concludes that they do not make the same point regarding the Christian's attitude toward the state (*1 Peter*, 180–82). I agree that the differences indicate no direct literary parallel between the two texts; I also agree that the main difference is the omission of any reference to the divine authority of civil authorities in 1 Peter. The two passages nonetheless make the same essential point, namely, that Christians are to be subordinate to those who rule. Rebellion or resistance is not a Christian option. Here the loyalty traditions in Judaism and early Christianity are reflected.

22. So Elliott, *A Home*, 86. He says that in 1 Peter the Roman government is "viewed neither as a servant of God [Rom. 13:1-7] nor as a henchman of Satan [Apocalypse] but simply as a human institution designed to administer justice [1 Pet. 2:13-14] and worthy of respect [2:17]."

23. Both the addressees and date are in dispute. Commentators argue between Jewish and Gentile Christian communities, and dates vary between 60 C.E. and 90 C.E. See Harold W. Attridge, *The Epistle to the Hebrews* (Hermeneia; Philadelphia: Fortress Press, 1989), 6–12. There is agreement the community was undergoing persecution from the civil authorities and experiencing a waning commitment to their new faith. But martyrdom was not yet involved (12:4).

24. Schrage, *Ethics*, 323.

One passage recalls a number of past difficulties they had faced as new converts (10:32-36). Among the sufferings named are public abuse and persecution, imprisonment, and loss of possessions. It is possible that the reference to the "earlier days" points to a period of persecution before or during the reign of Nero (v. 32).[25] But whatever the past problem may be, the present community is urged to possess the same kind of confident and courageous spirit they had formerly displayed. One hears no call to struggle against the persecutors or to pray for their downfall. To the contrary, Christians are exhorted to help one another and to even accept the plunder of their property cheerfully, knowing they possess a greater reward. The single, repeated admonition is to endure, lest they lose out on the promise (10:36-39).

The familiar passage Hebrews 11 recounts the heroic examples of faith. The author draws upon a host of biblical and extrabiblical figures for his "cloud of witnesses" to the meaning of genuine faith. Among them are Moses, who twice is said to be unafraid of the king's anger (11:23, 27), and the later Maccabean martyrs executed by the Seleucid ruler, Antiochus IV Epiphanies, as they fought and died for the freedom of Israel (11:35-38, ca.167 B.C.E.).

But Jesus is the supreme model of steadfast endurance: "looking to Jesus the pioneer and perfecter of our faith, who for the sake of the joy that was set before him endured the cross, disregarding its shame, and has taken his seat at the right hand of the throne of God" (12:2). In the subsequent verses Christians are challenged to possess the same kind of perseverance. The author notes that "they have not yet resisted to the point of shedding blood" (v. 4). To resist does not mean to defend oneself by force or by political action of some kind. Rather, it carries the sense of courageous acceptance of one's sufferings. This suffering is a distinct possibility as the community faces growing hostility. We learn that some are already in prison and must endure torture (13:3; cf. 10:34). To these and others, the example of Jesus' willingness to suffer is held up once more for emulation (13:12-13).

In the face of such troubling threats, the discouraged community is encouraged not to lose heart (12:3, 12-13). The author even dares to suggest that they might understand their present suffering as a sign of godly love and discipline (12:5-11). Out of parental love, God may even allow painful

25. Dibelius, "Rom und die Christen," 188, thinks it refers to Nero's persecution 64 C.E. But since martyrdom is specifically excluded (12:4), many argue for an occasion prior to Nero (Claudius, 49 C.E. See F. F. Bruce, *The Epistle to the Hebrews* (NICNT; Grand Rapids, Mich.: Eerdmans, 1964), xliii, 267-70. Others think of a Christian community in Rome that escaped Nero's persecution or Christian communities after Nero or outside of Rome. Any time in the first century may be that of the addressees (Attridge, *Hebrews*, 290). The terminal date for the writing of the book is 90 C.E. (*1 Clement*).

suffering to occur. Such suffering is not retributive or without purpose, for in the end it brings the "peaceful fruits of righteousness" (v. 11). And Christians look to one who experienced suffering and temptation as do they, so that he can sympathize with them (2:10; 4:14—5:10; 12:3).

Nowhere in the letter does one find any negative references against the authorities who caused the problems. Christians are told to live in peace with everyone (12:14). Voluntary acceptance of suffering in imitation of Jesus' own suffering best describes the attitude of Hebrews. In this sense it stands within the tradition of loyalty to the state we are examining.

Summary
The post-Pauline texts in the Pastorals, 1 Peter, and Hebrews continue the tradition of respect and honor and subordination to the state articulated most fully in Romans 13. One also finds a growing concern to demonstrate that Christians are peaceable and loyal and pious citizens, who in no way pose a threat to society or the emperor or good government. Perhaps the imperative "Honor the emperor" (1 Pet. 2:17) epitomizes in a stark way this New Testament tradition. As noted above, this tradition became the dominant one in Christian history.

Before I attempt to evaluate this tradition more fully, I observe its continuity with themes found in early Judaism and early Christianity outside the New Testament.

Loyalty Traditions in Judaism and Early Christianity

There is considerable evidence in both Judaism and Christianity at the turn of the first century for a long-standing tradition affirming the divine establishment of rulers and the corresponding ethic of respect and obedience.

Judaism
Despite the ambiguity about kingship in Israel, one royal tradition unequivocally claims divine authorization (2 Sam. 12:7-8, "I [the Lord] anointed you king . . ."). Both the authority to rule and a sense of divine accountability derive from God. But all those who govern on earth, not only the kings of Israel, do so by divine appointment. Since God is the ultimate ruler over all nations and the sovereign Lord of history, all earthly powers serve under God's providential will. This conviction especially comes to the fore during the time of the exile, when diaspora Jews saw their future tied to those of pagan society. Accordingly, the prophet Jeremiah counsels the exiles to seek peace with Babylon (Jer. 29:4-9). Even the imperial Babylonian oppressor, Nebuchadnezzar, can be called God's "servant"

and receive a prophetic endorsement and warning not to resist his temporary rule (Jer. 27:5).

In Ezra, the biblical narrative remembering the return from exile, we find what is probably the earliest reference to prayer and sacrifice for the king in the restored temple, during the reign of Darius, the Persian prince: "that they may offer pleasing sacrifice to the God of heaven, and pray for the life of the king and his sons" (Ezra 6:10). Similarly, the apocryphal Baruch, written sometime after 210 B.C.E., also mentions daily prayer and sacrifices for rulers and invokes their protection (Baruch 1:10-13). Likewise, the Letter of Aristeas, authored in Egypt around 250 (or 150) B.C.E., urges fellow Jews to obey those in power (*Aristeas* 45). And the apocryphal Wisdom of Solomon, written by a Hellenistic Jew ca. 150 B.C.E. (Alexandria?), affirms that it is God alone who raises up those who rule, as well as brings low those who act contrary to the divine law (Wisdom 6:3-4; cf. Proverbs 8:15-16).

The apocalyptic book of Daniel has a mixed attitude toward those who govern. On the one hand, the author seeks to encourage heroic resistance against political tyranny. Written during the Hasmonean struggle against the Seleucid tyrant Antiochus IV Epiphanes (167–164 B.C.E.), Daniel and his four companions steadfastly refuse to deny their God or their sacred tradition and risk death to defy the king's edict. On the other hand, the book recognizes that all rulers, including pagan ones, receive their power and authority from God. So they deserve honor and respect, as long as their rule does not conflict with the will of God (Dan. 1:2; 2:37-45; 5:18-23). Nevertheless, the sovereign God not only permits but also takes away the right to rule, especially when pride and arrogance and gross injustice prevail (5:20-28, 30).

The apocryphal 1 Maccabees likewise originated in the time of the Hasmonean revolt against Seleucid oppression (175–163 B.C.E.). While it chronicles the history of the heroic resistance, it also observes that daily sacrifices were offered in the Jerusalem temple on behalf of those who rule (1 Macc. 7:33). Apparently this practice was long-standing and reflects the conviction that all earthly authority somehow derives from God.

This loyalty tradition is found in first-century Judaism as well. With regard to temple sacrifice, we know that daily prayer and sacrifice on behalf of the empire/emperor continued until the great Jewish War of 66–70 C.E., in spite of the hated occupation by Roman puppets and numerous Jewish resistance movements. Josephus, the first-century Jewish historian who chronicles the history of the times (after abandoning the Jewish cause), makes several references to the common Jewish belief in the divine appointment of rulers (*War* 2.140; *Ant.* 12.406). In one writing, he explains the Jewish attitude toward political authorities by distinguishing between the honor due to emperors and their worship. Only the latter, Jews cannot do (*Apion* 2.75). He also notes the daily temple sacrifice for the empire. In addition to Josephus, other early rabbinic evidence echoes the same motif of respect for those who govern ("Pray for the well-being of government," *Aboth* 3.2; *Tos. Sukka* 4).

As one might expect, this loyalty tradition is especially evident in first century diaspora Judaism. Philo, the learned Jewish philosopher and apologist from Alexandria and contemporary of Jesus and Josephus (d. 50 C.E.), in several texts affirms obedience to those who rule. In one, Philo insists that the Jewish nation has been as favorably disposed toward Rome as any other nation: "In its prayers, its erection of votive offerings, its number of sacrifices, not only of those offered at general national feasts but in the perpetual and daily rites through which is declared their piety" (*Emb. Gaius* 10.80; also 10.317, 356–57).

In addition, synagogues of the diaspora provide a rich variety of evidence for the loyalty tradition. On shields, wreaths, pillars, and especially dedicatory inscriptions of synagogues, one finds the names of secular rulers and donors, including mention of the imperial house.[26] "The obvious aim of these acts of veneration and dedication is to express loyalty to rulers and to give thanks for political protection."[27] Diaspora Jews keenly desired to prove they were good citizens, even though they worshiped another God to whom they owed their ultimate allegiance.

The Pauline and post-Pauline New Testament tradition of loyalty and respect toward those who govern, therefore, has its roots in the Old Testament and contemporary Judaism. For both, God is the one who stands behind all earthly power. They are to rule with wisdom and justice for the peace and welfare of the nations. Prayer and sacrifice are therefore offered on their behalf, even when they may threaten the people of God. But there is a limit to one's obedience, as Daniel, 1 Maccabees, Josephus, and Philo make clear. Worship belongs only to God. Loyalty to earthly rulers ceases when the line between honor and worship is transgressed.

Early Christianity

The loyalty tradition found in contemporary Judaism and the New Testament continues in the earliest post-New Testament period as well.

First Clement, a letter written from the church in Rome to its sister church in Corinth ca. 96 C.E., seeks to encourage peace and concord with-

---

26. Philo, *Emb. Gaius*, 133; *Flacc.* 97.48; also see the article by Wolfgang Schrage on "synagogé," *TDNT*, 8: 826–827.

27. Schrage, ibid., 827.

in the Corinthian community. The whole tone of the letter is highly positive toward the Roman state. Although it recognizes the martyrs (under Nero), their misfortune seems to come less from the Roman state than from their own inner strife and jealousy. Even the Roman army, with the emperor at its head, serves as a model for church hierarchical order (37:1-3). Of greatest interest is the liturgical prayer which concludes the letter and which preserves the earliest Christian prayer for the state. It reads in part:

> Grant that we may be obedient to thy almighty and glorious name and to our rulers and governors upon earth. Thou, Master, hast given the power of sovereignty to them, through thy excellent and inexpressible might, so that we may know the glory and honor given them by thee and be subject to them, in no wise resisting thy will. To them, O Lord, give health, peace, concord, stability, so that they may administer without offense the governance which thou hast given them. For thou, heavenly Master, King of the ages, hast given the sons of men glory and honor and power over what is on earth; do thou, O Lord, direct their will according to what is good and pleasing before thee, so that with piety in peace and gentleness they may administer the power given them by thee, and may find thee propitious. (60:4—61:2).[28]

As with Paul, this prayer acknowledges that God bestows power on earthly leaders, asks divine grace for "good and pleasing" and peaceful rule, and teaches subjection to God and to those who govern (cf. 60:2; 57:2). Harmonious coexistence with the Roman state is the desired norm for the church. But there is a sense in which this prayer goes beyond anything in the New Testament, not only in its length, but in its repeated positive assessment of those who rule. Yet its endorsement of civil authority is not without qualification. The prayer does not equate the ruler's sovereignty with God's. To the contrary, "Only God has absolute power. All others hold their *exousia* [authority] under God's direction and subject to God's will. Only insofar as their actions conform to God's will can those in power continue to rule."[29] And this prayer does recognize, unlike Paul in Romans 13, that conflict could erupt between church and state.

28. Robert M. Grant, *The Apostolic Fathers*, vol. 2 (New York: Thomas Nelson, 1964), 91.

29. Barbara E. Bowe, "Prayer Rendered for Caesar? 1 Clement 59:3-61:3," in *The Lord's Prayer and Other Prayer Texts from the Greco-Roman Era*, ed. James H. Charlesworth (Valley Forge, Pa.: Trinity Press International, 1994), 94. While her article calls for a more moderate evaluation of Clement's attitude toward civil authorities against some recent studies (Klaus Wengst, *Pax Romana*, trans. John Bowden [Philadelphia: Fortress Press,1987],108; and J. S. Jeffers, *Conflict at Rome: Social Order and Hierarchy in Early Christianity* [Minneapolis: Fortress Press, 1991]), she agrees that "this prayer sets a potentially dangerous precedent by its endorsement of the imperial power," 94. She also recognizes, "There is little comment or critique of corrupt rulers and the need to 'resist' such evil powers," 92. See the look at Revelation for a striking contrast to 1 Clement.

The *Epistle of Polycarp* was written by Polycarp, bishop of Smyrna, to the church in Philippi in the early second century. Polycarp himself was eventually martyred ca. 156 or 167 C.E., by order of Rome's representative in Asia Minor. In his letter to the Philippians, he urges his readers to pray for emperors, authorities, and rulers (12:3). At the same time, he is keenly aware of opposition to the church, and he therefore encourages intercession "for those who persecute and hate you."

The *Martyrdom of Polycarp*, a letter from the church in Smyrna to the neighboring church in Philomelium (Phrygia), describes the martyrdom of the aged Polycarp in Smyrna. While the attitude of the Roman official is conciliatory but firm, Polycarp steadfastly resists all attempts to persuade him to recant, even when he is burned at the stake. In the midst of the dialog between Polycarp and the political leaders, Polycarp states that Christians have been taught to render suitable honor to powers and authorities appointed by God (*Mart.* 10:2). But the conflict here remains unresolved.

Ignatius, bishop of Antioch (Syria), wrote seven letters on his journey to Rome and martyrdom (d. 110 C.E.). Unlike Polycarp, Ignatius was eager for martyrdom. In fact he wrote one letter to Rome to forestall all attempts by influential Roman Christians to prevent his execution. Accordingly, nowhere in his letters do we find any discussion about the justice of his case nor any criticism of the Roman state. He simply accepts Rome's right to exercise its power against him, without further reflection.

This motif of support and prayer for those who rule becomes the dominant theme in the second-century apologists and beyond.[30] But a very few do take a different direction.

In the *Shepherd of Hermas*, written in Rome by an unknown author ca. 140 C.E., one finds a sense of deep conflict between church and state. Like other apocalyptic visions (Daniel, Revelation; see chap. 4), here too there is hostility toward the existing political structures and even predictions of their imminent collapse. In Vision 4, the church is threatened by a beast that foreshadows a great tribulation and a time of fearful martyrdom (4.1–2). Doubtless, imperial Rome is in view. Another apocalyptic expression of hostility toward Rome occurs in the Sibylline Oracles. Regarding the Jewish oracle of book 5, Collins comments, "the outburst against Rome in verses 162–78 is unparalleled in bitterness anywhere in the Sibylline Oracles."[31] In the Christian adaptation of book 8, there is a fierce hatred toward Rome, fueled by persecution. Rome is named directly, unlike in Revelation, and there are several references to the feared return of Nero (8:65-72).

---

30. See Knopf, *Die apostolischen Väter, Zwei Clemensbriefe* (HNT: Tübingen: Mohr-Siebeck, 1920), 139–48.

31. John J. Collins, "Sibylline Oracles," 391; in *The Old Testament Pseudepigrapha*, vol. 1, ed. James H. Charlesworth (Garden City, N.Y.: Doubleday, 1983–85).

Much of book 8 contains a powerful indictment of Rome for its greed and injustice (8:1-216). Similarly, the *Epistle of Barnabas* (early second century), considered Scripture by many early Christians, alludes to Rome as the final end-time beast, who subdues all the nations (4:4-5). Quite obviously, this sounds another theme contrary to that of the loyalty tradition of Paul and the literature surveyed above.

Early Christian writings in the post-New Testament period generally reflect the tradition of subjection to political powers and their divinely established rule, continuing the trajectory from the Pauline and post-Pauline traditions. There is perhaps greater awareness of potential conflict with the state, but the goal remains peaceful coexistence. But several writings envision another possible relationship caused by a hostile government, a relationship to be explored below.

Critique: Interpreting Romans 13 and Related New Testament Traditions

Most branches of Christendom, though not all, developed their basic understanding of the state from Pauline and post-Pauline traditions. As such, the government is regarded as divinely established, a gift for the common good of humanity. Some Christian theologies speak of the "orders of creation," which include the family, society, and government. One popular catechism offers this explanation within the context of the Fourth Commandment: "Honor your father and mother. Question: what does this mean? Answer: We are to fear and love God so that we do not despise or anger our parents and others *in authority*, but *respect, obey, love and esteem them*" (emphasis added).[32] This and similar expressions represent reasonable faithfulness to this New Testament strand of tradition.

But is there more to be said about the Christian attitude toward the state in the New Testament as a whole? Subsequent chapters will explore this question with some potentially surprising results. For the moment we need to ask whether there is more to be said about the Pauline and post-Pauline traditions themselves.

Most troubling about Romans 13 is not the understanding of the state as a divinely willed institution for the common good but rather its apparently unqualified acceptance of governments, no matter who or what, as somehow fulfilling their divinely intended purpose. We know from tragic experience this is simply not true! "For there is no authority except from God and those authorities that exist have been instituted by God. Therefore

32. *The Small Catechism*, by Martin Luther, in *Contemporary English* (Minneapolis: Augsburg; Philadelphia: Fortress Press, 1979), 5.

one who resists authority resists what God has appointed . . ."(Rom. 13:1-2). The logic seems faultless. But we ask, is it true that all governments or persons in authority have been appointed by God? Do Christians owe any and all governments their loyalty and obedience? Might one in fact resist the authorities, not be submissive, refuse to pay taxes, burn the flag, and still honor God?

Klaus Wengst raises the problem with Romans 13 this way: "Paul states the theological basis of Christian loyalty in that those in authority are virtually appointed by God to their function. But by doing that without caveat, qualification, and dialectic, he at least exposes himself to the *danger of providing theological legitimation for de facto power no matter how it may come into being, and how it may be used"* (emphasis added).[33] How true this danger has proved to be in Christian history and particularly in the twentieth-century tragedies of the Christian church under Nazism and apartheid.

How then shall we respond to the Romans 13 tradition? History itself teaches us to proceed with care. Perhaps the first task is to try to grasp more fully its historical setting in Romans. Unfortunately, despite a wealth of studies attempting to explain why Paul said what he did, little consensus has emerged. I here survey the most common explanations.

1. A few deny Paul wrote Rom. 13:1-7.[34] They regard the passage as a later insertion by a Christian representing the more conservative communities, similar to those of the Pastoral epistles. In favor of this suggestion is the fact that the text seems to interrupt the thought sequence of the context (cf. 12:21 and 13:8ff.). Further, only here does Paul speak of "authorities" in positive terms, as noted above. Against these arguments is the complete lack of any textual evidence for an insertion. Moreover, ethical teaching very often is loosely linked together in Paul. Like most interpreters, we think it best to view it as genuinely Pauline and in need of interpretation within Paul's entire thought.

2. By far the majority of commentators look for some historical reasons for Paul to speak so favorably of Rome and the governing authorities.

Many claim that Paul wrote Romans in a period of relative peace between the empire and the new Christian movement. The early years of Nero's rule were favorable until the charge of arson and outbreak of terror against Christians in 64 c.e. (Nero, 54–68 c.e.; Romans, 55–56 c.e.). So Paul

---

33. Wengst, *Pax Romana*, 83–84. Käsemann states the matter concisely: "The problem of political force does not come into view. This is the real problem of the passage" (*Romans*, 359).

34. James Kallas, "Romans xiii:1–7: An Interpolation," *New Testament Studies* (1964/65): 365–74, summarizes the main arguments against its authenticity.

may view Roman rule as providing a stable social order for the spread of
the gospel from Jerusalem to Spain (Rom. 15:23-24).

Others look toward the setting of the congregation in Rome. One suggests that Paul opposes Christian enthusiasts who want to negate all earthly authority.[35] Another posits the time in Rome shortly after the expulsion
of Jews and Christians for rioting by the emperor Claudius (49 C.E.). Consequently the emperor levied a heavy taxation on returning Jews and Christians. In this sensitive period, Paul advised obedience and the payment of
taxes.[36] Similarly, another hypothesizes on the general problem of taxation
during the time of increased Jewish conflict with Rome and the obvious
vulnerability of Christians as well.[37] Yet another suggests that Paul may be
writing to defend himself to the Christian community in Rome against
charges of disloyalty to the empire.[38] And still another argues that Paul
writes to urge Christians not to join Israel's cause against Rome.[39] Finally,
another finds that Paul is influenced both by the setting in Rome, as well as
by his deep fear of social disorder.[40]

Perhaps all of these and more have merit. Yet the lack of agreement and
their obvious hypothetical nature should make us wary. I agree that it is not
by chance that Paul includes these reflections on the government in his letter to Christians residing in the imperial city itself. This is a strong argument as well for the authenticity of the passage. But we cannot be sure
what immediate causes led him to write what he did. And since later New
Testament writings continue this positive attitude toward the state, even
though written thirty to fifty years later under differing historical circumstances, I find this argues persuasively that more than historical reasons are
present for Paul's ethic of obedience in Romans 13.

3. Other interpreters seek exegetical and theological reasons to explain
Paul's favorable view toward those in power.

As noted earlier, Romans 13 occurs within the wider context of Romans
12–15, where Paul sets forth the transformed life of the believer and love as
the shape of the new life. Romans 13 thus spells out the love ethic in the
public sphere, an ethic of subjection and respect for those who rule. In fact,

35. Käsemann, *Romans*, 357.

36. J. Friedrich, W. Pohlmann, and P. Stuhlmacher, "Zur historischen Situation und Intention vom Röm 13,1-7," *ZThK* 73 (1976): 131–66, esp. 157–59.

37. So Dun, *Romans 9-16*, 766.

38. Wengst, *Pax Romana*, 82–83.

39. Marcus Borg, "A New Context for Romans XIII," *NTS* 19 (1972/73), 205–218. Schrage,
Ethics, 235, finds nothing in the text or the epistle as a whole to suggest any anti-Roman or
antirevolutionary attitudes of Paul.

40. Ernst Bammel, "Romans 13," in *Jesus and the Politics of His Day*, eds. E. Bammel and C.
F. D. Moule (New York: Cambridge University Press, 1984), 365–83.

the verses immediately preceding this text urge love for the enemy and not to return evil for evil. Hence even hostile and unjust governments somehow need to be met with Christlike love. Although the command to love is absent from the passage on the government, Paul may intend these links. Nevertheless, this context still does not answer the problem of Paul's unqualified affirmation of those in political office: Does one obey out of love regardless of their conduct? Does love for the enemy require unquestioning allegiance and respect and payment of taxes to all authorities?

A second approach emphasizes the eschatological context of Paul's words (13:11-14). Paul may have regarded the government, like all earthly institutions, as a temporary human institution, necessary only for the moment. And during this brief interim, Christians could and should endure whatever may happen. It is true that Paul's view of the nearness of the end influenced his counsel on ethical matters,[41] and this may be at work here. However, the passage itself contains no eschatological motif. And since Paul was mistaken about the end-time, while for us history continues, we are left to struggle with Paul's apparent call to unqualified subjection to the state.

How then should Romans 13 and the related New Testament tradition of the ethic of obedience toward political authorities be interpreted?

1. Contrary to the majority of past interpreters, Romans 13 does not intend to provide a developed Christian doctrine of the state, good for all occasions. Paul's aims are more limited. He speaks first of all to the historical situation of Christians in Rome. We may not be sure why he counsels obedience as he does, but he addresses their setting in particular. If the context changes, different guidance might need to be given.

More important, his primary purpose is to offer ethical instruction on proper conduct toward rulers, not a political theory on the nature of the state. Paul grounds this ethical instruction in his conviction that governments have been divinely instituted to preserve order and peace and justice in the human community. Therefore Christians owe the government subjection and respect and support and payment of taxes. But this assumes that the state is fulfilling its divinely intended purpose.

2. Romans 13 and the other loyalty traditions cannot be used to give unqualified status to all earthly governments as somehow established by God nor to its corollary of unconditional obedience. Paul does say, "There

41. On Paul's eschatology as the dominant motif of his theology, see especially the writings of J. C. Beker: *Paul the Apostle: The Triumph of God in Life and Thought* (Philadelphia: Fortress Press, 1980; *Paul's Apocalyptic Gospel* (Philadelphia: Fortress Press, 1982; *The Triumph of God: The Essence of Paul's Thought*, trans. Loren Stuckenbruck (Minneapolis: Fortress Press, 1990).

is no authority except from God, and those authorities that exist have been instituted by God" (13:1). He also calls those who govern "servants of God" for the common good, both to uphold what is right and to counter wrongdoing. But as we have seen, Paul does not speak to the crucial issue regarding governments who oppose the good or do not resist evil. What if rulers betray their divine mandate for justice or fundamentally abuse or misuse their power? There is in Romans only a "deafening silence" on this question. The apparent assumption throughout Romans 13 is that rulers on the whole function as God intends. In that case, the question is left open about the Christian response to governments that may act contrary to the divine will. In fact, Christians are given the difficult but necessary task to decide when and where this may be happening. And they must also decide what the Christian response requires.

It follows that the Pauline and related New Testament ethic of subordination to the state cannot be turned into a fixed ethic of unconditional or unquestioning obedience. The critical question is whether the government seeks to uphold the public good. Does it use its power to prevent evil and encourage what is right? Is it an instrument for justice and peace or their enemy? The Christian response, it seems, depends on how one answers these questions.

3. Paul elsewhere gives evidence that Romans 13 is not the whole of his attitude toward those who hold political office. For Paul and the early church, there is only one sovereign Lord: "Jesus Christ is Lord" (1 Cor. 12:3; 8:5-6; Rom. 10:9; etc.). On coins and inscriptions, the ruling Caesar claimed to be *divi Augustus* (divine Augustus).[42] Paul preaches another as God and Lord. And only this Lord is worthy of unconditional or unquestioning trust and obedience. On this point, there is no room for compromise.

As noted earlier, Paul in Romans 13 uses the word *exousiai* ("authorities," 13:1, 3) to refer to the political rulers. Since *exousiai* in the deutero-Pauline literature refers to cosmic powers that oppose God and Christ (for example, Col. 2:15), some want to interpret the "authorities" here as angelic powers that stand behind nations and rulers. However, there is little doubt that in Romans 13 the authorities represent human beings in positions of earthly power.[43] Yet the term itself may convey a negative side of earthly or cosmic powers at work in the world.

In 1 Cor. 2:6-8, Paul refers to a divine wisdom hidden from "the rulers of this age." This wisdom is God's plan of saving the world through Christ. The rulers of this age proved their obvious ignorance of this plan by

---

42. See Laura Breglia, *Roman Imperial Coins* (New York: Praeger, 1968), 38–69, for representative imperial coins from Augustus to Nero.

43. See note 4, above.

crucifying Jesus and so inadvertently fulfilling it. This passage, brief as it is, shows that Paul was profoundly aware of the shadow side of human rulers and their great potential for evil. In this present age, they may be in control. But in the end, Paul states that those who rule are all doomed to perish. And he regards God as the one who both reverses the evil schemes of earthly rulers as well as the one who ultimately determines the course of human history.

Paul's own experience with Roman rule and the so-called *pax Romana* was decidedly mixed. Although a Roman citizen by birth, he often felt its harsh and cruel face. In 2 Cor. 11:23-33, Paul enumerates at some length his sufferings, beatings, tortures, stonings, imprisonments, banishment, and nocturnal escape over a wall. Both Jewish and Roman officials were responsible for these actions. Even though Acts may represent an idealized portrait of Paul's missionary labors, there is little doubt of the substantial accuracy of the reports about repeated conflict with synagogue and civic officials. Paul finally appealed to Caesar and Caesar (Nero) had him beheaded in Rome. Paul could scarcely have been naive about Roman justice.

At first glance, this makes it surprising that Paul could write so positively about obedience and respect toward political rulers as he does in Romans, one of his later letters. He had long felt the power of the imperial sword that trampled on people's rights and freedom and proclaimed peace where there was no peace. Yet, even in Paul's "prison epistles," written from Roman jails (Philippians, Philemon, Colossians, Ephesians),[44] there is no attack on Roman justice. Rather, Paul welcomes his imprisonment as an opportunity to spread the Christian message to the members of Caesar's household (Phil. 1:13; 4:22).

Nevertheless, Paul's obvious awareness of the misuse of political power should keep us from interpreting Romans 13 as any kind of blanket endorsement of power per se or of those who wield it. Unjust suffering and imprisonment and flagrant abuse of power are not God's intent for earthly rulers. They ought to uphold the right and good. Paul simply believed that God can turn evil into good. And he was willing to suffer, when necessary, for Christ's sake. He therefore made the best of whatever situation in which he may have found himself.

---

44. While Philippians and Philemon are authentically Pauline, Colossians and Ephesians are likely deutero-Pauline. Many other passages allude to times when Paul was a victim of Roman injustice or of civic authorities acting on Rome's behalf (1 Thess. 2:2; 2 Cor. 1:7-8; 4:8; 6:4-10; Gal. 5:11; 6:12; plus the prison epistles). Paul was obviously regarded as a disturber of the public order, and Paul himself knew this. See Wengst, *Pax Romana*, 72–76, for a detailed discussion of Paul's political conflicts.

In one passage Paul calls those who proclaim "peace and security" agents of darkness (1 Thess. 5:3). "Peace and security" represents the propaganda machine of imperial Rome. Rome claimed to have brought peace to the world. But it was peace by bloody conquest, security by the sword. It was the fictional peace of the *pax Romana*.[45] Paul exposes this kind of peace as pure illusion. In the end, for Paul, the only genuine peace and security comes through the *pax Christi*.

In brief, Paul reveals in diverse ways from his own negative experience that the authorities can be instruments of injustice as well as good. Hence Christians are scarcely called to side with governments blindly or unthinkingly. They may accept whatever comes, yet they trust and obey only God for their ultimate security.

4. For Paul and the early church, the Christians' true citizenship belongs in the kingdom of God (Phil. 3:20). In this life, believers are strangers and exiles, pilgrims on the move, as 1 Peter and Hebrews so movingly affirm. The government, as part of this present age, belongs to those structures that will one day pass away (1 Cor. 2:6). These human structures may serve in the interim as necessary for human community, but they remain part of the transient and fallen world, with no ultimate claim on believers.

There is one passage, however, where Paul might seem to oppose any Christian involvement with the structures of the state. In 1 Cor. 6:1-8, Paul argues vehemently against Christians going to civil courts to settle their disputes. He insists the church itself should have persons wise enough to act as arbitrators. In particular, he finds the whole matter of Christian suing Christian contrary to the mind of Christ ("why not rather be wronged?" 6:7). He also objects to the "unrighteous" judging Christians (6:1, 4, 6). This argument goes beyond that of mere competence to what appears to be a more fundamental objection to believers using civil courts.

Some Christian groups thus conclude that Paul here forbids any participation by Christians in civil or secular courts. Perhaps we should take this stance more seriously. It does stand as a strong witness to prior citizenship in God's kingdom, and it does reflect the core Christian ethic of willingness to suffer rather than seek redress. Nevertheless, it fails to preserve the tension between living in this world and living in the kingdom, a tension inherent to authentic Christian existence. For Paul and the early church, the kingdom is both here and not yet here. Christians already experience

---

45. Wengst cites numerous examples from the first century of Rome's proud claim to bring peace and security to the world and to subject nations. Some of the propaganda sounds very contemporary (e.g., "Peace through strength"). But naturally, it was peace only by willing or forced submission to Rome (*Pax Romana*, 19–21, 76–79).

the powers of the new age, yet they still live within the structures of the old. To collapse either side of the tension results in spiritual enthusiasm on the one hand or accommodation on the other. Pauline theology lives dynamically within the "both . . . and." With respect to government, it both honors the political structures for the common good as well as places them under divine authority. Even civil courts may thus serve the public welfare, possibly even for Christians. Paul's argument to the Corinthians is not directed against the courts per se but against the offensive spectacle of Christians against Christians.

Here, too, we can appeal to the theme of Christian freedom. As citizens of the coming age, Christians are essentially free with respect to the earthly powers (see pp. 78–80). They can live "as though" the forms and structures of this world are passing away (1 Cor. 7:25-35).[46] Yet out of love and responsibility for the neighbor and the world, Christians also live in submission to the powers that be and support good government and efforts toward greater justice and freedom and equality for all. The fundamental grappling with both Christian freedom and responsibility characteristic of the Reformation grows out of its attempt to interpret Pauline theology.[47]

5. Central to Paul's message is "Christ crucified" (1 Cor. 2:2; Gal. 3:1; etc.). Paul knows full well that the one he now proclaims as the crucified and risen Lord was executed by a Roman governor in Palestine. Crucifixion was the supreme penalty for political rebels against Rome, and Paul was keenly aware of the offensiveness of the message. A crucified Messiah was a scandal to Jews and nonsense to Gentiles (1 Cor. 1:23). Paul's own understanding of the cross must have grown out of his wrestling with the meaning of Christ's ignominious death, but even apart from its theological significance, the reference to a "crucified Lord" would constantly bring to mind the injustice of Roman power. Jesus Christ was crucified as an innocent victim of Roman power. His followers would live under the shadow of the same injustice. Neither Paul nor his hearers could be naive or sentimental about the empire that nailed their Lord to the cross.

6. Finally, consider Paul's understanding of Christian suffering. He himself imitates Christ as one who bears in his body the "sufferings of Christ" (2 Cor. 4:7-11; Gal. 6:17; Rom. 8:17; Phil. 3:10). This suffering is a direct result of his faithfulness to the gospel and the cause of Jesus Christ. And Paul calls

46. It is true that Paul's thought in 1 Corinthians 7 was strongly influenced by his belief that the end-time was near (7:26, 29, 31). But even apart from this, he saw believers living an "interim" existence until the consummation of God's plan for the world in Christ.

47. See, for example, the seminal essay by Martin Luther, "The Freedom of a Christian," in Timothy F. Lull, ed., *Martin Luther's Basic Theological Writings* (Minneapolis: Fortress Press, 1989), 585–629.

upon Christian believers to imitate him in their willingness to suffer with Christ (2 Cor. 1:7, Rom. 8:17).[48]

Paul's whole conception of Christian existence has been termed a theology of the cross.[49] By a theology of the cross is meant a theology that finds its center in God's self-revelation in the crucified Christ. Here, paradoxically, divine power becomes known in weakness, divine love in suffering, and divine wisdom in foolishness (1 Cor. 1:18-25). With respect to Christian existence, a theology of the cross places suffering love not only at the heart of God's character but at the core of faithful response. It understands the Christian life to be characterized by grateful obedience, neighborly service, and willingness to accept the cost of discipleship. A part of this cost is the suffering that faithful servanthood in a hostile world brings about.

What this means regarding the political authorities is that Paul does not necessarily expect peaceful coexistence as the only norm. He himself did not experience it, nor did Jesus, nor will the church of Jesus Christ. Where the church confesses only one Lord and lives by that confession with integrity, there will be an inevitable clash of loyalties. In Romans 13 Paul speaks only of the reward that the governing authorities give to those who do what is right and only of the fear of punishment when one does wrong. But there is far more than this ideal relationship that Paul describes. The reality is that Christians will also suffer for doing right and at the very hands of those whom God intended to preserve peace and justice in this world. Then what?

For the moment, Paul counsels acceptance of one's suffering for the sake of Christ. Here he is joined by the other New Testament writings advocating an ethic of obedience. But, as we will see in subsequent chapters, this loyalty tradition constitutes only one stream of New Testament thinking regarding the state. Other voices, perhaps dealing with governments that have become increasingly the enemy of the church, will counsel forms of resistance quite different from this tradition.

---

48. See J. C. Beker, *Suffering and Hope* (Philadelphia: Fortress Press, 1987), esp. 57–67, for a discussion of suffering in Paul. Beker distinguishes between redemptive suffering as a result of discipleship and tragic, meaningless suffering with its concomitant sense of abandonment. It is the former suffering for the sake of Christ that Christians are to imitate.

49. The term *theologia crucis* goes back to the Reformation and Luther's evocative way of doing theology. See Walther von Loewenich, *Luther's Theology of the Cross*, trans. Herbert Bouman (Minneapolis: Augsburg, 1976). On the contemporary discussion, see especially Jürgen Moltmann, *The Crucified God*, trans. R. A. Wilson and John Bowden (New York: Harper and Row, 1974); Douglas John Hall, *Lighten Our Darkness* (Philadelphia: Westminister, 1976); and Charles B. Cousar, *A Theology of the Cross* (Minneapolis: Fortress Press, 1990), esp. 135–75.

Summary

I began by observing that the Pauline and post-Pauline tradition of subordination to the state has represented for the majority of Christians the primary New Testament attitude. This tradition regards the government as God's gift to preserve and promote the public good—peace and order and justice and freedom and human dignity. In response Christians give to the state their respect, obedience, support, and prayers. In this view, the church and state can and should coexist as mutually supportive partners for the welfare of the human community as a whole. Each partner has its respective role and contribution to make but it seeks to work in harmony with the other.

How shall we respond to this tradition? This New Testament tradition of subordination needs to be taken seriously and responsibly by Christians as an expression of the divine intention for the state and the Christian response to it.[50] Can we take a further step and call this the normative New Testament tradition, as many have done? My answer to this question will depend in part on the remainder of this study. But for now I offer a tentative no, particularly in light of this tradition's troubled history of abuse and misuse. Most emphatically, we cannot absolutize or near-absolutize this position, as though all governments are ordained of God and Christians owe unqualified obedience. Within Romans 13 and within Paul's thought as a whole, we have shown good reason for thinking Paul himself did not intend such. Only Jesus Christ is Lord and deserves unconditional allegiance. The conservative ethic of the Pastorals, 1 Peter, and Hebrews depicts the church trying hard to live as loyal citizens in the midst of an increasingly hostile society. Perhaps Christian respect for those in authority as well as the good of the human family require this effort. But there is a limit beyond which the church cannot go and still be faithful.

---

50. The Barmen Declaration was written by members of the confessing church in Germany as a bold protest against the emergence of the Third Reich under Hitler. Nevertheless, in spite of its courageous opposition, it acknowledges that "the state has by divine appointment the task of providing for justice and peace" (Arthur C. Cochrane, *The Church's Confession under Hitler* [Pittsburgh: Pickwick Press, 1976], 241).

3.
ETHIC OF CRITICAL DISTANCING: JESUS AND THE GOSPELS

Method

EXAMINING THE GOSPEL TRADITIONS AND THEIR PRESENTATION OF Jesus' attitude toward those in positions of authority is a daunting task, to say the least.

Some problems immediately confront the interpreter. First, there are four Gospel portraits, not one. I will follow modern scholarship in distinguishing between the Synoptics (Mark, Matthew, Luke) and John. We will look first at the Synoptic Gospels and then the Gospel of John. However, for reasons noted later, I will include all four Gospels in the analysis of the passion narratives. Second, there is the problem of the historical Jesus. The Gospels' portraits of Jesus are inseparably intertwined with the faith of the early church. To decide what goes back to Jesus himself and what may represent the emerging faith in Jesus—the pre-Easter and post-Easter Jesus—is exceedingly complex and problematic; it is also necessary and rewarding.[1] Instead of attempting to uncover the teaching and activity of the historical Jesus, I invite the reader to hear the four canonical voices who remember, preserve, and pass on the story of Jesus in the early church.

---

1. Some recent studies include Marcus Borg, *Jesus: A New Vision* (San Francisco: Harper Collins, 1987); John Dominic Crossan, *The Historical Jesus: The Life of a Mediterranean Jewish Peasant* (San Francisco: Harper, 1991) and *Jesus: A Revolutionary Biography* (San Francisco: Harper Collins, 1994); John P. Meier, *A Marginal Jew: Rethinking the Historical Jesus* (New York: Doubleday, 1991) and *Mentor, Message and Miracle* (New York: Doubleday, 1994); E. P. Sanders, *Jesus and Judaism* (Philadelphia: Fortress Press, 1985) and *The Historical Figure of Jesus* (New York: Penguin, 1993); N. T. Wright, *Jesus and the Victory of God* (Minneapolis: Fortress Press, 1996). While providing new and fresh insights, the portraits differ widely, even fundamentally among themselves.

Third, I approach the Synoptic tradition with the help of contemporary scholarship. Apart from a few who argue for the priority of Matthew, most find Mark to be the earliest Gospel, along with Q, a source hypothesized from texts common only to Matthew and Luke. My approach to the Jesus tradition will begin with Q, followed by Mark and the parallel Synoptic texts and finally the material unique to Matthew and Luke.

Fourth, for reasons of clarity and emphasis, I divide this chapter into two major sections: Part one will survey the Synoptic and Johannine traditions from the public ministry of Jesus, and part two will examine the passion traditions, the narratives of Jesus' suffering and death.

Fifth, I will pay careful attention to the different voices of each Gospel. There are four distinct stories. The evangelists have taken up the traditions known to them and their respective faith communities and shaped the story of Jesus according to their own purposes. Redaction criticism and literary criticism have given special weight to the individuality of each evangelist. But, from early on, Christians had recognized the unique aspects of each Gospel's portrait of Jesus.

Sixth, Luke-Acts poses a special problem with respect to its attitude toward imperial Rome. This controversial topic will therefore be taken up in an excursus at the end of this chapter.

My thesis throughout this chapter is that the basic portrayal of Jesus in the Gospels with respect to those in power is quite different from the Pauline and other traditions explored in the previous chapter. Rather than an ethic of subordination toward earthly rulers as established by God, throughout the Gospels we find Jesus exercising a critical attitude toward those who rule. There exists at best an uneasy relationship, an evident tension between the kingdom of God inaugurated by Jesus and the kingdoms of this world. Jesus embodies this tension in word and deed throughout his ministry and above all in his journey to suffering and death. I will trace the key evidence in the Gospels that supports this understanding of Jesus.[2]

First, however, a brief overview of past scholarship on this disputed topic, particularly on the question of Jesus' attitude toward the Roman oppressor, is required. At one extreme, a few voices have argued vigorously that the historical Jesus was a Zealot, or at least a Zealot sympathizer.[3]

---

2. "Jesus" in this chapter refers to the Gospel's presentation of Jesus and not necessarily the historical Jesus.

3. So S. G. F. Brandon, *Jesus and the Zealots* (Manchester: Manchester University Press, 1967). This Zealot argument goes back to H. S. Reimarus in the eighteenth century. See the survey by E. Bammel, "The Revolutionary Jesus Theory from Reimarus to Brandon," in *Jesus and the Politics of His Day*, eds. E. Bammel and C. F. D. Moule (Cambridge: Cambridge University Press, 1984), 11–68.

They assume the Zealots were the chief advocates of freedom and resistance to Roman occupation in the first century. Zealots believed the land belonged only to Yahweh and the people of God. They opposed payment of the Roman tax, and, if need be, were ready to take up the sword against Rome. Subsequently, they were caught up in the devastating war of 66–70 C.E., ending in the destruction of Jerusalem and the Temple. Recent studies have raised serious questions about the Zealots, even denying their actual emergence as a distinct group until the war of 66–70.[4] Even if this proves correct, however, there was still continued, albeit sporadic, resistance to Rome and the tax throughout Jesus' lifetime.

To those unfamiliar with the controversy, the possibility of Jesus' siding with the Jewish resistance movements against Rome may seem absurd. None of the Gospels depicts this kind of Jesus. But those who advocate this view claim the politically dangerous Jesus has largely disappeared from the Gospels due to a concerted cover-up by his disciples and the early church. The motive for their transformation of Jesus was simple survival—the desire to get along with Rome and hide their founder's involvement in subversive revolt. Accordingly, the pacifist Jesus, who teaches, "Love your enemies," is the creation of the early church.

What possible evidence can one find in the Gospels for Jesus' participation in Zealot-like conduct? Several actions and teachings are adduced: Jesus' friendship with Zealots; a few sayings such as, "I came not to bring peace but a sword" (Matt. 10:34); the violent cleansing of the Temple; the possession of swords at his arrest; his trial and execution by the Roman governor for sedition.

Although this theory of the historical Jesus as a militant revolutionary or freedom-fighter, executed for sedition, has not been hard to refute, its arguments have been taken seriously.[5] Against the forced and often spurious interpretation of Gospel texts, interpreters point to key themes that illustrate another Jesus more consistent with the evangelists and the early church. Jesus' preaching of the kingdom may have political implications, but the kingdom of God is no political realm on earth. Jesus envisions instead the creation of a new community in history, where God's will is done on earth as in heaven. And Jesus' core ethic is the love command, radicalized to include even one's enemies.

4. R. A. Horsley and J. S. Hanson, *Bandits, Prophets, and Messiahs* (Minneapolis: Winston-Seabury, 1985); also R. A. Horsley, *Jesus and the Spiral of Violence* (San Francisco: Harper & Row, 1987), 77–89.

5. See Oscar Cullmann, *Jesus and the Revolutionaries*, trans. G. Putnam (New York: Harper and Row, 1970); Martin Hengel, *Was Jesus a Revolutionary?* trans. William Klassen (Philadelphia: Fortress Press, 1971); Martin Hengel, *Victory over Violence*, trans. D. E. Green (Philadelphia: Fortress Press, 1973).

There may be an element of overlooked truth in the suggestion that Jesus stood firmly on the side of political freedom over against the Roman occupation. He is depicted as sympathizing deeply with his people and their plight and as praying fervently for liberty and peace. We can also imagine Jesus protesting vigorously against the exercise of brute force by Rome or against excessive taxation or the marginalization of the poor and landless. But, for the Jesus of the Gospels, the kingdom comes not by violence or force or revolution but with compassion and peace and a love that embraces friend and foe alike. Similarly, the Gospels portray a Jesus who dies as a victim of injustice, not for crimes against the state.

At the other extreme are those interpreters who think Jesus has no political relevance at all. This has taken essentially two forms. One is the view that Jesus was an apocalyptic visionary whose eye was fixed on the future inbreaking of God's rule.[6] Since the world is soon to pass away, Jesus, it is said, has little or no interest in the structures of this world. This, the dominant understanding of the historical Jesus in modern New Testament study, has only recently been challenged.[7] There are some Gospel sayings, of course, that appear to support this view of Jesus as an eschatological prophet of the coming kingdom. Moreover, the early church from the very beginning had a hope for Christ's imminent return. One cannot therefore simply disregard this approach. But there is a growing suspicion that the early church may have been more apocalyptically minded than Jesus. New work on the social and historical backgrounds of the Gospels along with attempts to interpret them from the underside of history uncover a portrait of Jesus more profoundly involved in his culture than one suspected.[8] Jesus does not seem to preach and teach nor to model any escape from history.

The other nonpolitical view holds that Jesus' teaching and activity have to do with a spiritual gospel of salvation that has little or nothing to do with the real world of politics or history. Accordingly, Jesus' message consists above all in offering forgiveness and new life to persons broken by guilt or despair. One's relationship to God is the focal point, with the ethic of neighbor-love at best secondary. Moreover, it is believed the salvific death and resurrection of Jesus form the heart of what it means to believe in and follow Jesus.

6. See Albert Schweitzer, *The Quest of the Historical Jesus*, trans. W. Montgomery (London: A. C. Black, 1910), and Rudolf Bultmann, *Theology of the New Testament*, trans. Kendrick Grobel (New York: Scribner's, 1951–55).

7. See Borg, *Jesus*, especially the preface. His work mirrors that of the Jesus Seminar, a body of New Testament scholars seeking the historical Jesus. Despite publicity, they do not represent any real consensus in New Testament scholarship on the historical Jesus.

8. Especially Crossan, *The Historical Jesus*, and Borg, *Jesus*.

There is much truth in this traditional understanding of Jesus. According to the Gospels, the centrality of one's relationship with God stands at the core of Jesus' message and his own Spirit-anointed ministry. He offered God's forgiveness freely and indiscriminately to all, causing great offense. And the post-Easter church grasped the death and resurrection of Jesus as the saving events par excellence. But this is not the totality of Jesus' message. The Synoptic Gospels in particular present a Jesus who was deeply involved in the ordering of social life according to the will of God. He taught and lived an ethic of neighbor-love that broke down the religious and social barriers that divided people into holy or unholy, righteous or sinner. With prophetic passion he took the side of the poor and powerless against the rich and powerful. He called for a reform of his own people and nation that would bring peace and reconciliation, not war and destruction. His radical ethic of love for the enemy challenged the politics of hatred and violence. Jesus created new communities of followers imbued with a vision of mutual care and compassion and forgiveness in which the old hierarchies were replaced with egalitarian notions of servanthood and mutuality. In all of this and more, the Gospels depict a sense of mission that goes beyond a person's relationship with God and includes all the dynamics of life in the world.

In brief, neither a Zealot-like Jesus preaching freedom from the oppressor and the power of the sword to accomplish God's will nor an apocalyptic visionary nor a spiritually minded Jesus thinking only about God and the next world provides us with the proper background for understanding Jesus. The Gospels' portraits of Jesus' teaching and practice regarding those in civil and political power fits with a picture of Jesus that lies between these extremes. Above all, Jesus' relationship to the social and political and religious structures present in his world, as evident in the Gospels, must be taken seriously.

Jesus' Public Ministry

Mark is thought to be the earliest Gospel, used by both Matthew and Luke. But beyond their reliance on Mark for outline and content, Matthew and Luke also share a source known as Q. Its existence is posited from the large amount of material they hold in common, but which is not found in Mark. Q consists chiefly of sayings of Jesus, without any passion history. A vast amount of scholarly literature on Q has sought to establish its origin in early Christian communities, with their own theologies and historical settings.[9] In

---

9. See John S. Kloppenburg, *The Formation of Q* (Philadelphia: Fortress Press, 1987), or Richard Edwards, *A Theology of Q* (Philadelphia: Fortress Press, 1976).

general, we need not concern ourselves with this research, except as it may touch on questions of interpretation. There also is general agreement that Luke has preserved the earliest form and order of Q, although Matthew may often reflect earlier wording.

The Q Tradition

By beginning with the Q tradition of the Synoptic Gospels, I do not necessarily imply that it is earlier than Mark. Q and Mark are equally important and independent sources for the evangelists.

The Temptation of Jesus (Q Matt. 4:1-11/Luke 4:1-13; cf. Mark 1:12-13)
This Q text of Jesus' temptation, placed at the outset of Jesus' public ministry, provides us with basic insight into Matthew's and Luke's understanding of Jesus' ministry, including their attitude toward political powers. Mark has only a brief mention of the temptation (Mark 1:12-13), while Matthew and Luke share the expanded version found in Q. This is likely an attempt by the early church to fill in the Markan account with specific content concerning what seemed central to Jesus' mission. Both follow Mark by placing it immediately after the baptism. Their respective versions are closely similar, except for the reverse order of the last two temptations.

As the stories now stand in the Gospels, they represent reflections on the nature of Jesus' messianic vocation.[10] Called at his baptism to be the Son and anointed by the Spirit, Jesus withdraws into the wilderness to determine the kind of mission he will pursue. Accordingly, each of the Satanic temptations represents a false option for Jesus' fulfillment of his vocation.

The first tempts Jesus to fulfill his mission by the provision of daily bread, similar to the miracle of manna in the wilderness. Of course, Matthew and Luke do present a Jesus who multiplies loaves and cares for the hungry and teachers prayer for daily bread. Yet his task goes beyond earthly provisions: "One does not live by bread alone" (Matt. 4:4//Luke 4:4). The second temptation in Matthew (Luke's interest in the Temple may cause his reordering of the last two), to throw himself down from the pinnacle of the Temple, appeals to Jesus' ability to do mighty works. Again,

---

10. I follow a "messianic" interpretation of the temptations, which is true to the evangelist's intention in placing them at the beginning of Jesus' public ministry. Bultmann places the emphasis on "the paradigm of obedience" for new believers, which I consider to be a secondary theme (R. Bultmann, *The History of the Synoptic Tradition*, trans. John Marsh [Oxford: Basil Blackwell, 1963], 256). Kloppenburg offers four other possibilities, yet he is seeking only the Q editor's reason for preserving this "strange" story (*The Formation of Q*, 249–56). He does agree that the third temptation "amounts to a de facto rejection of Zealot ideology" (256).

Matthew and Luke depict Jesus' charismatic ministry as one filled with Spirit-empowered deeds. Yet they are evoked primarily to heal the sick and free the oppressed.

The third temptation, to rule over all the kingdoms of the world, represents the lure to earthly power and influence. Matthew and Luke (and the other Gospels) underscore this as one of the foundational temptations present throughout Jesus' ministry. His disciples and others repeatedly confuse their own nationalistic hopes and expectations with Jesus' own preaching of the inbreaking reign of God (for example, Acts 1:6-8). In truth, Jesus' own ministry is finally ended by a basic misunderstanding of his motives and actions in political and nationalistic terms. Yet as the Synoptics tell the story, the whole thrust of Jesus' preaching and activity has to do with the inauguration of God's rule of compassion and mercy and his rejection of any claim to earthly power and honor. In this Q temptation account, Jesus initiates his divine vocation by choosing a way ultimately in tension with all earthly powers—and uncompromisingly so.

Sermon on the Mount/Plain (Matthew 5–7//Luke 6:20-49)
A second group of significant Q texts is found in the familiar collection of sayings known as the "Sermon on the Mount" (Matthew) or "Sermon on the Plain" (Luke).[11] Q is the primary source for this extensive collection of Jesus' teaching. Much of the material is not relevant for our purposes. However, three sections are fundamental: the Beatitudes, sayings on non-retaliation, and love of enemies.

Both sermons have extensive points of similarity as well as striking differences. While Matthew has carefully constructed three long chapters of sayings on various themes, Luke has some of the same sayings elsewhere in his Gospel (for example, the Lord's Prayer, Luke 11:2-4). Which version of the sermon adheres most closely to Q is debated.[12] I will simply interpret the two collections as they now stand in their respective Gospels.

Beatitudes (Matt 5:1-12//Luke 6:20-26). The Beatitudes ("Blessed . . ."), which open both sermons, differ strikingly in number and content. It is clear the evangelists adopted the sayings of Jesus to their own literary and

11. For further study, see Joachim Jeremias, *The Sermon on the Mount*, trans. Norman Perrin (Philadelphia: Fortress Press, 1963); Robert Guelich, *The Sermon on the Mount* (Dallas: Word, 1982); Georg Strecker, *The Sermon on the Mount* (Nashville: Abingdon, 1988); Warren Carter, *What Are They Saying about Matthew's Sermon on the Mount?* (New York: Paulist Press, 1994); Hans Dieter Betz, *The Sermon on the Mount* (Hermeneia; Minneapolis: Fortress Press, 1995).

12. Most commentators think Luke's briefer and less spiritualized version is the earlier, although as we will see, Betz finds the two sermons to be independent traditions.

theological purposes. Nevertheless, there is profound agreement between them in the announcement of a radical reversal of values for those who belong to the kingdom.

In Matthew, nine Beatitudes flesh out the character of the followers of Jesus.[13] Taken together, they describe persons who renounce their own claims and seek to live the kingdom way of righteousness and compassion and single-minded devotion to God and neighbor.

Four of the Beatitudes touch on the question of Jesus' attitude toward those in authority.

(1) "Blessed are the meek . . ." (5:5, *praus*, gentle, humble, meek). This beatitude asserts that it is not the strong and mighty who are blessed but the lowly. "Meekness is the renunciation of power in human relations."[14] Jesus models meekness in Matthew when he enters Jerusalem as the "lowly king," forgoing any claim to political ambition or violent conquest (21:5).

(2) "Blessed are the merciful . . ." (5:7). The merciful act with compassion and forgiveness towards all persons, even enemies (5:43-48). They treat others as they know a merciful God has treated them.

(3) "Blessed are the peacemakers . . ." (5:9). This beatitude speaks with particular force against the holders of power and advocates of violence. To be a peacemaker is to practice *shalom*.[15] Peacemakers work for reconciliation between peoples and nations. Here and elsewhere the Gospels show Jesus taking a bold stance in opposition to the Jewish resistance movements that preached violence and hatred toward the oppressors and their collaborators.

(4) "Blessed are the persecuted . . ." (5:10-11//Luke 6:22-23). This beatitude, which is paralleled in Luke, recognizes the hostility that inevitably comes to those who practice the kingdom way. The persecuted are blessed because they know they are on God's side when they suffer for the cause of righteousness. Like Jesus, they too will experience rejection, betrayal, even death. Yet like him, they do not strike back (5:38-42). And they know God will reward them, along with a long and honorable company of God's messengers.

The Lukan version has only four Beatitudes, which are paralleled by four contrasting woes. Of special significance is the fact that the Lukan

---

13. Contrary to what some have thought, the Beatitudes are not entrance requirements for the kingdom (cf. Jeremias, *Sermon*, 1–12, who sketches three main interpretive approaches to the sermon). Rather, they describe those who respond to the kingdom invitation.

14. Robert H. Smith, *Matthew* (ACNT; Minneapolis: Augsburg, 1985), 83.

15. *Shalom* is the comprehensive Hebrew word for the rightness of relations in all circumstances of life.

Beatitudes and woes speak directly to persons in concrete need.[16] At some points, Matthew tends to spiritualize the Beatitudes (5:3, "poor in spirit" and "poor" in Luke 6:20; Matt. 5:6, "hunger and thirst for righteousness" and "hungry" in Luke 6:21), even though they still have concrete suffering in view. In Luke, however, the contrast is set forth in starkly literal terms: blessings on the poor, hungry, weeping, and persecuted (6:20-23); woes on the rich, full, laughing, and well-esteemed (6:24-26). With dramatic impact, the Lukan Jesus pronounces a great reversal of fortunes in the future. The suffering, despised, and hated disciples are promised that their needs will be met in the kingdom. At the same time, prophetic woes pronounce judgment on the rich and powerful, who have already received their reward in this life and who in the future are to experience the suffering of their victims.

Despite the differences in Matthew and Luke, the Beatitudes agree in upending the values that control and dominate this world and its structures. The community that seeks to follow Jesus lives by the ethics of the kingdom. Accordingly, it is not the rich and powerful and esteemed who will be blessed but those who look to God for their strength and whose lives are marked by righteousness, meekness, mercy, peacemaking, patient suffering, and longing for God's justice.

Nonretaliation (or nonviolent resistance; Matt 5:38-42//Luke 6:29-30) and Love of Enemies (Matt. 5:43-48//Luke 6:27-36). The Q tradition contains two of the most revolutionary sayings attributed to Jesus in the Gospels: the sayings on nonretaliation and love of enemies. Here we find the love ethic in its most radical and challenging form. Little wonder these teachings have become the subject of so much controversy and so many divergent interpretations, even within the Christian community. Interpretations vary from those who would limit their application to personal responses to wrongdoing or an inner spirit of nonretaliation to those who find here the source of Christian pacifism. If the Gospels present a Jesus who adopts an attitude of critical distancing from those who rule, how does that attitude relate to this teaching on radical love toward others, including one's enemies? And how does the teaching on nonretaliation toward evildoers relate to issues of war and peace and the need for governments to keep some semblance of order and justice in human societies?

Nonretaliation (or nonviolent resistance; Matt. 5:38-42//Luke 6:29-30). This saying exists in two forms. Matthew has an expanded version that is part of

---

16. See Walter Pilgrim, *Good News to the Poor* (Minneapolis: Augsburg, 1981), 74–77, 103–107, for a discussion of the Lukan Beatitudes and woes. I agree that Luke has the earlier form of the Beatitudes, although the origin of the woes is uncertain (Luke? Q?).

the six antitheses, in which the Matthean Jesus contrasts the old righteousness with the higher righteousness of the kingdom (5:21-48, "You heard . . .
but I say . . ."). The last two antitheses concern nonretaliation and love of
enemies. Matthew's sayings on nonretaliation begin with a thesis statement
("Do not resist an evildoer") followed by four examples of what this
means. Luke's version falls within the admonition to love one's enemies
(Luke 6:27-36) and consists of only three similar examples (6:29-30).[17] For
Matthew, the Law, the *lex talionis*, permitted certain kinds of limited retaliation: "an eye for an eye and a tooth for a tooth." In the Old Testament and
antiquity in general, the *lex talionis* was operative in beneficial ways to pose
restrictions on revenge and to find punishments suitable to fit the crime.[18]
Yet reciprocity was the norm, including "life for life" (Deut. 19:21; Exod.
21:23-25). The new righteousness of the kingdom espoused by the
Matthean Jesus, however, undercuts both the letter and spirit of revenge:
"Do not resist an evildoer" (5:39).

But what is meant by the command not to resist evildoers? This has recently become a matter of sharp dispute. The Greek verb, *antistēnai*, may be
translated "do not resist," as in most versions. Accordingly, the traditional
interpretation has understood the command as a counsel of submission, of
passive nonresistance to evil without any retaliation. This is a possible interpretation that has a long and noble history. Yet the notion of simple submission to evildoers has always posed ethical and practical questions and
seemed in tension at some points with Jesus' own activity in the Gospel.

Against this dominant view, two interpretations allow a more active
understanding of the prohibition. Walter Wink argues persuasively that
the Greek verb *antistēnai* should be translated, "do not resist violently."[19]
Thus the injunction, along with other related teaching and activity of Jesus
in the Gospels, offers a third way between mere submission and violence:
the way of active nonviolent resistance.[20] He interprets the four examples
of resisting evil in Matthew 5:39-42 in light of this (see pp. 47–49).

17. Walter Wink ("Neither Passivity nor Violence: Jesus' Third Way" [*Forum* 7, 1991], 6)
thinks that form critically the core saying is Matt. 5:39b-42, with v. 42 questionable. Betz (*The
Sermon*, 300), however, finds the two Q versions here and in the sermon as a whole to be independent traditions.

18. See Betz, *The Sermon*, 275–76, on the *lex talionis* in antiquity.

19. Walter Wink, *Engaging the Powers* (Minneapolis: Fortress Press, 1992), 185: "In short,
antistēnai means more in Matt. 5:39a than simply to "stand against" or "resist." It means to
resist violently, to revolt or rebel, to engage in an insurrection. . . ."

20. See also Wink's more detailed article, "Neither Passivity nor Violence," 5–28, where he
suggests a third way in Jesus' teaching that is neither submission nor assault but a way that
preserves human dignity while at the same time changes the power equation. He titles chapter 9 in his book, *Engaging the Powers*, "Jesus' Third Way: Nonviolent Engagement."

In a similar manner, Betz argues that *antistēnai* must be translated as "Do not retaliate," rather than as unqualified nonresistance to evil.[21] He finds the Jesus in the Sermon and elsewhere prohibiting retaliation and vengeance. Yet he insists the primary concern is not nonretaliation but "the combating of evil (*to ponēron*), that is, the establishment of justice."[22] Betz, too, interprets the four examples of nonretaliation as active resistance to evil.

I am attracted to these alternative understandings of *antistēnai* and Jesus' counsel as a whole. In many respects, they parallel the Pauline traditions echo of the Jesus tradition in Romans 12: "Do not repay anyone evil for evil . . ." (12:17, 19, 21). I now consider the four Matthean examples of nonretaliation or nonviolent resistance.

1. Turn the other cheek (Matt. 5:39//Luke 6:29). To strike someone on the right cheek with the back of the hand was an act of extreme insult and humiliation in the first century Jewish and Greco-Roman world.[23] Jesus' counsel to turn the other cheek could mean simply to yield submissively, without any retaliation, as many have thought. Or one could hear it more positively: By deliberately turning the other cheek without striking back the victim takes control of the situation and provocatively challenges the oppressor's actions.[24] While Luke preserves the essence of the saying, he presupposes a blow with the fist to injure someone and so misses the nuance of insult linked to the right cheek (6:29).

---

21. Betz, *The Sermon*, 280. Betz does not mention Wink's provocative work and especially Wink's similar conclusions on the saying on nonretaliation.

22. Betz, *The Sermon*, 283–84. "To conclude: The meaning of the controversial command *mē antistēnai* ("Do not retaliate") is not to recommend an attitude of resignation and defeatism concerning evil or a principled self-surrender to all kinds of villains. Rather, what is commanded is not nonviolence in general but desisting from retaliation in specific instances. The difference is that such desisting is in effect a positive method of fighting evil and helping justice prevail."

23. See Wink's colorful discussions of each example (*Engaging*, 175–84). Wink thinks "to hit on the right cheek" was a technical term of insult (369, #5). Pinchas Lapide, *The Sermon on the Mount: Utopia or Program for Action?* trans. Arlene Swidler (Maryknoll, N.Y.: Orbis, 1986), 121, agrees. The *Didache*, an early-second-century Christian writing, preserves a version of the saying that includes the right cheek as well as the second mile (*Didache* 1:4).

24. So Wink, *Engaging*, 176–77. "He [evildoer] has been stripped of his power to dehumanize the other." Betz, *The Sermon*, 290, provides an excellent summary of Jesus' counsel as a bold and positive directive. He writes that to turn the other cheek ". . . is a provocative invitation to receive a second strike. To do this is by no means a sign of weakness but . . . one of moral strength. The gesture exposes the act of the offender as what it is: morally repulsive and improper." "Thus the turning of the cheek is a mighty challenge demonstrating the *lex talionis* in reverse, by taking the initiative in accordance with the Golden Rule (7:12)."

2. Give your garments (Matt. 5:40//Luke 6:29). Matthew and Luke disagree on whether it is the outer (Luke) or inner (Matthew) garment that is being demanded. However, the Old Testament practice of giving an outer garment as a pledge supports Luke's version (Exod. 22:25-27, where the outer coat of the poor is to be returned at sunset). In Matthew, the needy victim is being sued in a court of law for his inner coat (*chiton*), no doubt the result of unpaid debt. Jesus' counsel is again striking: "Give your cloak (outer, *himation*) as well." By so doing, the victim gives away his most valuable garment. In Luke, a robber seizes the outer coat and gets the undershirt as well. In both, the victim gives away all his garments and stands naked before the court or his violator.

Rather than fight back or throw oneself on the mercy of the court, the command is to give up everything. Why? Wink proposes a novel interpretation. By stripping off all of his clothing, the victim "marches out of court naked" and thus shames the greed of the creditor, who stands with "the poor debtor's outer garment in the one hand and his undergarment in the other."[25] He also sees this action as a prophetic protest against the system that leads to poverty. While this interpretation probably reads too much into the text, it does capture the stance of protest embedded in the saying.

3. Go the second mile (Matt. 5:41; not in Luke). The practice of compelling the services of others by officials was common in the Roman world, and it was bitterly resented. The particular context for this saying was no doubt the Roman military occupation of Palestine, which allowed the legionnaires to force citizens to carry their gear or whatever (cf. Matt. 27:32, Simon of Cyrene). One mile placed limits on the potential for abuse, which was frequent. But Jesus advocates, "Go also the second mile." Such a saying would cause extreme offense to patriotic Jews or freedom-fighters.

Why such provocative counsel? Rather than revolt or murder or refusal, the command is to help the hated enemy. Why? Wink suggests that when the oppressed civilian takes the initiative, the soldier is caught off-guard and made uncertain about his role. One overcomes evil by doing an unexpected good.[26]

4. Give to everyone who asks (Matt. 5:42//Luke 6:30, 34-35). The fourth illustration concerning nonretaliation embraces the world of debt and economics. In Matthew, the saying simply says to give to anyone who wants to beg or borrow from you. Luke's version is more radical (consistent with his

---

25. Wink, *Engaging*, 177–79. Betz, *The Sermon*, 291, also notes the "absurdity" in the image of the victim standing naked but interprets it as an "exaggerated image," which shows that the person is following the Golden Rule.

26. Wink, *Engaging*, 143–79, who rightly includes this among the sayings of Jesus on nonviolence.

sayings on wealth and poverty): Do not ask for property forcibly taken; lend without expecting repayment or interest (6:34-35). A kind of egalitarian principle is at work (Acts 2:43-47).[27]

In effect, these Q sayings on nonretaliation mark a new path for disciples of Jesus. They reject the way of violence, of hatred, of getting even, of self-interest for a way that leads to justice and peace and reconciliation and sharing. The responses advocated in these verses involve more than passive nonresistance to evil. They have in view actions that resist the evildoer for the sake of greater justice.[28] With respect to those who rule by force, Jesus' injunction to go the second mile rules out violent retaliation or armed resistance. But it does not speak against prophetic protests of social injustices (for example, Jesus' cleansing of the Temple) or against exploitation by foreign powers or bold actions for freedom and justice in nonviolent ways. On the role of governments or questions of war, see the discussion below.

Love of Enemies (Matt. 5:43-48//Luke 6:27-36). Beyond nonretaliation, Jesus in Q teaches the way of love that includes even one's enemies. In Matthew, love of the enemy constitutes the sixth and climactic antithesis in the Sermon, the one that sums up the heart of Jesus' love ethic. According to the antithesis, the old way taught, "You shall love your neighbor and hate your enemy." In fact, Lev. 19:18 has only "love your neighbor," so that "hate your enemy" is an added interpretation. Neither the Old Testament nor Rabbinic literature taught hatred toward others. Yet it was commonsense morality. To love one's neighbor as a friend and to hate the enemy was taken for granted. Against this understanding, Jesus reinterprets the command to love your neighbor in terms of love for the enemy: "Love your enemies and pray for your persecutors" (5:44). This teaching is the most radical of all, because it reaches out to embrace the whole human family. No one is to be excluded as stranger or outcast or sinner or even as enemy.[29] If the neighbor includes the enemy, one must then also love the enemy.

The source for this revolutionary understanding of human relations is the character of God. The Q Jesus images a gracious God as the one who bestows love freely and unconditionally upon humankind.[30] This benevo-

---

27. Wink, *Engaging*, 183–84, sees the principle of the sabbatical year behind these words.

28. So Betz, *The Sermon*, 293: "The examples in vss. 39b–42 are imaginative in the sense that they envision situations of violence, pressure, and imposition in order to propose strategies of conduct that help to overcome injustice through justice." Betz sees the Golden Rule at work throughout this section.

29. Betz, *The Sermon*, 309, sees this as a "startling innovative interpretation" of the Torah and Lev. 19:18 by Jesus.

30. See Marcus Borg, *Meeting Jesus Again for the First Time* (San Francisco: HarperCollins, 1995), 46–61, for a fresh discussion of God's character as compassion in the teaching of Jesus.

lent God sends sun and rain on both the evil and the good, the righteous and the unrighteous (5:45). And Jesus invites his disciples to become children of their heavenly Father, that is to be perfect in love as God is (5:48, *teleios*, mature, complete). The call to perfection in love concludes the sixth antithesis and so stands as a summary statement of what the greater righteousness of the kingdom is all about. To imitate God's compassion for good and bad is to go beyond mere human reciprocity. Jesus holds up tax-collectors and Gentiles as caustic examples of how ordinary it is "to love those who love you!" (5:46-47). Everyone does that. But disciples are to practice the generosity of God who loves even the ungrateful and to pray for their persecutors.

Luke has a shortened and somewhat altered version (6:27-36). He combines the theme of nonretaliation and love of enemies. In fact, the command to love one's enemy frames the entire section (6:27, 37).

In the opening verses there are four imperatives on right conduct toward the enemy: Love your enemies, do good . . . those who hate you, bless . . . who curse you, pray . . . who abuse you (6:27-28). All of these imperatives counter evil with good. The Golden Rule concludes the section (cf. Matt. 7:12).

The remaining relevant passages in Luke parallel Matthew by urging the disciples to go beyond mere reciprocity in human relations (6:32-35). As in Matthew, the ground for this extraordinary generosity is the character of God. God is kind even to the ungrateful and wicked. As children of such a compassionate God, the disciples should imitate the divine goodness toward the enemy and the least deserving. Luke ends not with the call to be perfect but with the plea, "Be merciful, just as your Father is merciful" (6:36).

How should one interpret the counsel on nonretaliation and love of the enemy? Commentators often observe how we encounter in the teaching of the sermon a new kind of ethic, a new way to embrace everyone within the family of God. But how exactly is this ethic of love for enemies to be applied? Is this an ethic only for disciples or for everyone? Is it primarily an ethic that shapes personal relationships or does it also bear on society and public institutions, including governments? And if the latter, how so? These questions have vexed and provoked and challenged interpreters of Jesus' love your enemy ethic since the beginning.

The sermons seem to be directed above all to disciples of Jesus. Both Matthew and Luke have Jesus address the disciples, with the crowds listening in and responding with astonishment at his authoritative teaching (Matt 5:1; 7:28-29//Luke 6:17; 7:1). I take this to mean that for the evangelists, at least, Jesus teaches a discipleship ethic in which outsiders are invited to participate.

But is this discipleship ethic of nonretaliation and love of enemy only a norm and guide for personal relations, or is it a communal ethic? And if a communal ethic, how does it relate to the public realm? It is obviously to be practiced by individual disciples in their relationships to one another and with outsiders. Yet we hear this also as an ethic for the discipleship community. The community is to turn the other cheek, exercise nonretaliation towards its enemies, and pray for its persecutors. In this sense, the ethic of love for enemy belongs uniquely to the community of Jesus Christ, that is, the church. As such, it is not meant for secular states or governments or society as a whole.

But does the ethic of nonretaliation and love of enemy require a stance of pacifism on the part of the community that turns the other cheek, goes the extra mile, prays for its despisers, and desires to put into practice genuine love for the enemy? To this oft-disputed and nigh-irresolvable question, even among Christians, I answer both yes and no. Yes to pacifism, in that there can be no advocacy of war or crusades in the name of Christ, no desire to kill or use the sword to accomplish one's goals as an individual or community, no hatred or revenge as the motive for one's actions. Yes, also, in that the love ethic of the sermon stands for peace and reconciliation between neighbors and races and ethnic groups and nations.

But, at the same time, a possible no to pacifism. As noted above, there may be a third way between submission and retaliation, the way of nonviolent resistance. In this view, the Jesus of the sermons calls for nonretaliation, yet persistent and active nonviolent strategies to resist evil. Moreover, beyond this, the ethic of love for the neighbor may lead individual Christians or Christian communities to conclude reluctantly that the enemy or evildoer must be resisted or stopped, even with violence, to protect innocent victims or to preserve the greater public good. Christian "just war" concepts developed out of this concern for the common good of nations and people.[31] Yet great caution is required in rejecting pacifism, given the predominant history of the church, co-opted by the temptations of earthly power and holy wars and crusades and church-state alliances, as well as the contemporary memories of the horrors of "Christians" and "churches" blindly pursuing the siren call of nationalism or racism or ethnicism or national security, all too often in the name of Christ.

Finally, even though we find the call to nonretaliation and love of enemy intended primarily for the discipleship community, there is still a profound

---

31. The dual love-command summarizes Jesus' ethical teaching and acts as a critical principle for evaluating all other ethical judgments: The love ethic takes precedence over all other ethical criteria (Mark 12:28-34//Matt. 22:34-40//Luke 10:25-28). As stated, "just war" theories have been developed throughout Christian history in light of the "love your neighbor" ethic.

sense in which it does affect the social and political order. Not only do individual Christians live and work in the midst of their respective neighborhoods and nations and so have the opportunity to make their basic convictions and ethics known, but the Christian community itself exists within the same social and political structures. Here the faith community is called to serve as a model for an alternative kind of community, in which the spirit of love, forgiveness, nonretaliation, and care for the enemy is at work. This community is also called to serve as a conscience to the political structures when the spirit of revenge or national self-interest or the winds of war seem out of control (see chap. 5). By holding high the vision of another way to live together, a way of nonviolence and peace and reconciliation among nations and peoples, the community of Jesus Christ lets its "light shine."

The Beatitudes and the sayings on nonretaliation and love of enemies reverse the values of this world. In so doing, they create a community uncomfortably at odds with the earthly powers that rule and so arouse an inevitable conflict that persists throughout time. Moreover, the opposing communities battle with vastly different weapons. One fights with the power of the sword, the other with the power of love. Paradoxically, the victory is promised to those who choose the way of love.

"Those Who Live in Royal Palaces" (Matt 11:7-9//Luke 7:24-26)
Another passage that provides insight into Q's presentation of Jesus' critical attitude toward those in authority occurs within the context of praise for his predecessor, John the Baptist. John is in prison by order of Herod Antipas. When John hears reports of Jesus' activity, he sends his disciples to ask whether Jesus is the coming Messiah or not. Jesus responds by pointing to his ministry among the sick and oppressed (Matt 11:2-6//Luke 7:18-23). Subsequently, Jesus launches into a laudatory speech about his predecessor, calling him a prophet and more. In fact, until now, no one greater than John has been born! Since the coming of Jesus, however, "the least in the kingdom is greater than John" (Matt. 11:7-11//Luke 7:24-28).

In speaking of John, Jesus draws a sharp contrast between the rugged figure of the Baptist and that of royalty. Readers would no doubt remember the earlier description of John, clothed in camel's hair and a leather belt, eating locusts and wild honey (Matt. 3:4). So here Jesus refers to John's ascetic ways and to his stern and unyielding appearance as God's end-time prophet (Matt. 11:7, 18//Luke 7:24, 33). In stark opposition to the wilderness prophet are the figures of those who rule. In Matthew's version they are clothed in "soft robes" (REB, "finery"). Their rich attire is the badge of their wealth and status. They live in royal palaces. Luke heightens the contrast even more by adding "live in luxury" to his description of the affluent lifestyle enjoyed by the wealthy and powerful (Luke 7:25). In effect, the whole tone of the text is one of contempt for the lifestyle of kings and all those in positions of authority. God's messengers and God's people live differently. But in so doing, they suffer violence from those in power (Matt. 11:12).[32] Here there is also a possible echo of the mockery and contempt for Jesus as he is dressed in royal apparel and a crown of thorns, while the kings of the earth put him to death (Matt. 27:28//Luke 23:11).

"Not Peace . . . but a Sword" (Matt 10:34-39//Luke 12:49-53; 14:26-27)
In this series of Q sayings, Jesus speaks provocatively about his own mission and its results. Similar sayings appear in the *Gospel of Thomas* (*G. Thom.* 10, 16, 55, 101), a collection of Jesus' sayings originating in second-century gnostic circles.[33] The parallels seem dependent on Matthew and Luke.[34] The context for the sayings differ in each Gospel. Matthew places them within Jesus' missionary instruction to the Twelve (10:1—11:1), while Luke scatters them among other discipleship sayings of Jesus. What remains constant, however, is their reference to Jesus' mission and its divisive results for those who become disciples.

Matthew: "Not peace . . . but a sword" (10:34-39). According to Matthew, Jesus sends out the Twelve to preach the good news of the kingdom (10:7; 4:23; 9:35). Yet their message arouses hostility and dissension, and the coming of the kingdom inaugurated by Jesus marks a profound time of crisis for humanity. Persons must decide for or against the kingdom. Earlier in the missionary instructions, Jesus had spoken about future persecution from Jew and Gentile (10:16-25, "synagogues" and "governors, kings"). Now he describes his mission apocalyptically as that of bringing not peace "but a sword" (10:34). The following verses explain what this means. The sword is not a literal sword, as a few have argued, but a symbol for the deep division created between persons. Jesus comes to bring peace to those who receive his kingdom message (10:13, "peace" to the house that is "worthy," that is, accepts the messengers). But to those who refuse, it causes conflict

32. Matthew 11:12 is a difficult text to interpret. Some mss. read, "the kingdom of heaven has been coming violently," which would be a metaphor for the radical change needed to repent and enter the kingdom. I prefer the reading ". . . suffer violence." Forces of evil oppose the kingdom and "the violent take it by force," i.e., oppose it. In Matthew, King Herod has already massacred the innocents, Herod Antipas has imprisoned John and will soon behead him, and Jesus' encounter with "the violent who rule" lies ahead. The kingdom suffers violence!

33. See "The Gospel of Thomas," trans. Thomas Lambdin, in *The Nag Hammadi Library in English*, 3d rev. ed., ed. James M. Robinson (San Francisco: Harper and Row, 1988), 117–30.

34. So Joseph Fitzmyer, *The Gospel According to Luke X–XXIV* (Anchor Bible 28; Garden City: Doubleday, 1981), 994–95, 1061.

even within families. "One's foes will be members of one's own household" (10:36). Thus Jesus' coming effects a time of crisis that reaches into the most intimate fabric of human life.

Luke: "Not peace . . . but division" (12:49-53; 14:26-27). The Lukan version begins with three parallel sayings of Jesus about his disruptive, earth-shattering ministry (12:49-51). The first, "I came to bring fire to the earth," probably from Luke's own source, describes Jesus' coming as a time of purification or judgment for the world (3:9). The second, "I have a baptism with which to be baptized," reflects a saying of Jesus in Mark 10:38.[35] For Luke's readers the baptism that presses upon Jesus is his death. The third saying is a close parallel to Matthew's Q saying on the crisis caused by Jesus: "Not peace . . . but division." No sword is mentioned. Luke's Gospel especially underscores Jesus' mission as that of bringing peace on earth (2:14; 19:38; Acts 10:36). Beyond the *pax Christi*, nonetheless, lies the opposite effect of irreconcilable conflict, embracing even families (12:53). While Luke's wording is somewhat different, its meaning is the same. The inbreaking kingdom creates a division between people, not in a political or national or racial sense, but in terms of conflicting loyalties.

Luke also preserves a parallel to Matthew's saying on the cost of discipleship (14:26-27). But Luke's saying radicalizes the division even more. Jesus says one must "hate" one's own family and even one's own life to be a disciple (cf. Matt 10:37, "love me more than . . ."). Hate is the opposite of love. What "hate" involves, however, is not personal animosity toward those closest to oneself or personal self-hatred but making the kingdom the highest priority of all.

To conclude, the saying, "not peace . . . but a sword," has nothing to do with violent resistance or opposition to those in power. It reflects instead the reality of conflict inherent in the call to give prime allegiance to God and the kingdom proclaimed by Jesus. Yet there is a potential conflict in the political realm when loyalties and kingdoms clash. Persecutions, martyrdoms, and divided families may and do arise. In this sense, the sword cuts deep. And followers of Jesus' way may find themselves with no option but to accept the consequences, no matter what.

Mark and the Synoptic Tradition

Along with Q, Matthew and Luke tell their respective stories of Jesus based in large measure on the Gospel of Mark. I now turn to texts common to all

---

35. There is uncertainty how to translate the corresponding phrase, ". . . and what stress I am under until it is completed!" Helmut Koester argues for a positive sense to the Greek verb *sunexō*: "and how I am totally governed by this [his approaching death]!"; see "*sunexō*," *TDNT* 7, 884–85.

three Gospels (the triple tradition) that bear on our topic of Jesus' attitude toward those in power. In each case I begin with Mark as the earliest Gospel and then observe the similarities and differences in Matthew and Luke.

Mark's Gospel presents Jesus as a suffering Messiah, a motif that probably reflects Mark's historical setting.[36] After his baptism by John, Jesus begins his ministry by announcing the nearness of the promised reign of God and by manifesting its presence in his words and deeds (1:14-15). Within the first half of the Gospel, Jesus engages in conflict with the Jewish teachers of the law ("scribes and Pharisees," 1:16—8:26). While this struggle between Jesus and the teachers of the law is chiefly religious, Mark depicts the conflict as deep-seated, as in fact a cause of Jesus' eventual death (3:6). In the second half, however, it is the Jewish priestly and civil leaders in Jerusalem who become his primary opponents and plot his death at the hands of the Roman procurator (8:27—16:8). While Matthew and Luke have their own version of the story, there is general agreement between them on this outline of conflict and the nature of the opposition as described in Mark.

Conflict over Jesus' Authority
(Mark 2:1—3:6//Matt. 9:2-17; 12:1-14//Luke 5:17—6:11)

Mark presents five so-called controversy stories early in Jesus' public ministry, which show Jesus in bitter debate with the "scribes and Pharisees." The controversies arise over Jesus' authoritative claims to forgive sin (Mark 2:7, blasphemy), his fellowship with tax-collectors and sinners, his failure to emphasize fasting, and his alleged violations of the Sabbath.[37] In each case, Jesus defends himself as one who possesses his authority as God's representative (son of Man, 2:10, 28; "I have come . . . ," 2:17; bridegroom, 2:19). Over against the sacred tradition, Jesus presumes to interpret the law in a new and superior way. As a result, the Pharisees and Herodians (Herodians only in Mark) decide to seek Jesus' death—at the very outset of Jesus' ministry (3:6).

Both Matthew and Luke preserve the identical traditions, although Matthew places the Sabbath controversies later (Matt. 12:1-14). Matthew concludes the disputes with the same decision to destroy Jesus (12:14), while Luke states they were "filled with fury" and discussing what to do with Jesus (6:11).

36. Ancient tradition dates Mark's Gospel ca. 70 C.E. in Rome. While some today argue for a Syrian or Galilean origin, this date seems probable; it reflects a time of open conflict between the Jewish nation and Rome, ending in the tragedy of Jerusalem's conquest and destruction. Mark's call to suffering discipleship is most appropriate in this setting (Mark 8:27—10:45).

37. See Arland Hultgren, *Jesus and His Adversaries* (Minneapolis: Augsburg, 1979), for an excellent discussion of the controversy stories in Mark.

All three accounts of the controversies display Jesus on the attack and courageously challenging the traditional teachers of the law. In so doing, he risks blasphemy, a charge potentially worthy of death.

The Healing of the Gerasene Demoniac
(Mark 5:1-12//Matt. 8:28—9:1//Luke 8:23-39)

A text of special interest is this vivid story of Jesus' healing a deranged demoniac. Recent studies have suggested that behind the exorcism story may lie a strong anti-Roman sentiment.[38] The setting itself is Gentile territory (Mark 5:1, east side of the Sea of Galilee). The whole land was taboo for Jews (Gentiles, swine, cemetery), so that Jesus enters, as it were, forbidden territory. And by allowing the demons to enter the swine and drown in the sea, the author continues the anti-Roman theme.[39] But it is the use of "legion" for the demons that is most revealing (Mark 5:9, 15//Luke 8:30; Matthew omits this word in his abbreviated version of two demoniacs). Here is a Latin word in the mouth of demons! The allusion to the Roman occupation is unmistakable. The hostility toward the Roman occupiers is made clear when the demons express their wish to remain in the country. This is precisely what the Romans also want.[40] In effect, the story names the Roman oppressors the demonic power at work, and, by his exorcism, Jesus symbolically overthrows the oppressive legions and drives them into the sea, thus purifying the land of unclean forces.

As the exorcism story now stands in the Synoptics, it has lost much of its political impact. Nevertheless, the story does reveal the background of conflict between foreign oppressors and Jews, between the pollution of foreign demons and the struggle for holiness. Jesus here is on the side of those who would expel the demonic legions and liberate the land from its oppressors. But he does so by the power of God, not by the power of the sword.

Arrest and Death of John the Baptist
(Mark 6:14-29//Matt. 14:1-12//Luke 3:19-20; 9:7-9)

According to the Synoptics, Jesus begins his public ministry after the arrest of John the Baptist by Herod (Mark 1:14; the Gospel of John has a brief period of parallel ministries, 3:22-24). Herod Antipas, a son of Herod the Great, was the tetrarch of Galilee during the lifetime of Jesus (6–44 C.E.). Like his father, he remained a loyal vassal of Rome.

---

38. Gerd Theissen, *The Miracle-Stories of the Early Christian Tradition*, trans. Francis McDonagh (Philadelphia: Fortress Press, 1983), 255–57. Also Herman Waetjen, *A Reordering of Power* (Minneapolis: Fortress Press, 1989), 113–22.

39. Donald H. Juel, *Mark* (ACNT; Minneapolis: Augsburg, 1990), 80, notes that the standards of the Roman legions in Palestine bore the offensive image of the wild boar!

40. Theissen, *The Miracle-Stories*, 255.

Mark pays special attention to the popular tale of John's subsequent beheading by Herod. The Synoptics agree that John was murdered because of his fearless condemnation of Herod's adulterous marriage to Herodias, the wife of his half-brother Philip (Mark 6:17-19). Josephus also preserves an account of John's arrest and execution, but he attributes his death to Herod's fear of a popular uprising.[41] Both motives may be correct (cf. Matt. 14:5). Whatever the reason, the Synoptics describe John as a powerful prophetic figure, held in high regard by the people and by Herod himself. We learn that Herod issues the command for his beheading only under heavy duress (Mark 6:20; cf. Matt 14:4, 9). And, most important, Jesus himself was attracted to John's preaching and after his baptism by John saw his own mission as the culmination of John's eschatological activity.

No doubt Mark dwells on the arrest and death of John because it foreshadows Jesus' own fate. Although in Mark and Matthew Herod Antipas never becomes directly involved in Jesus' death, Herod is suspicious and fearful and thinks that Jesus may be the Baptist returned to life (Mark 6:14-16//Matt. 14:1-2//cf. Luke 9:9). Luke's account differs considerably by claiming that Herod himself has hostile intentions against Jesus and by preserving the story of Jesus' encounter with Antipas during his trial in Jerusalem (9:7-9; 13:31; 23:6-12). Luke also preserves the provocative comment by Jesus regarding his own provincial ruler (see below, pp. 87–88).

The fate of John and Jesus intermingle with frightening clarity. Like John, Jesus will be arrested and condemned unjustly. Like John, his will be another prophetic voice silenced forever. In the story of John, one hears the destiny that awaits Jesus at the hands of the political powers, both Jewish and Roman, who will later converge to execute the one greater than John. As the evangelists tell the story, the death of John stands as a sobering warning to Jesus and his followers about the uncertain road that lies ahead for prophets and messengers of God.[42] Yet they show Jesus intent on pursuing his mission with unflinching courage and conviction, even in the face of the political forces raised against him.

Passion Predictions (Mark 8:31; 9:31; 10:33-34//
Matt. 16:21; 17:22-23; 20:17-19//Luke 9:22; 9:44; 18:31-33)

Each of the Synoptics preserve three dramatic predictions by Jesus of his coming death and resurrection. These "passion predictions" occur within the narrative structure of Jesus' journey to Jerusalem (cf. Mark 8:31—11:1).

---

41. Josephus, *Ant.* 18.116-119.

42. "The fate of his mentor John the Baptizer must have been a vivid reminder to him of what happened to unauthorized leaders who attract a significant following in the tense atmosphere of first-century Palestine" (Marcus Borg, *Meeting Jesus Again*, 31).

In Mark, the first prediction names those responsible for his suffering and rejection as "the elders, chief priests, and scribes" (8:31). The second simply makes a general statement about his betrayal into human hands and subsequent death and resurrection (9:31). However, the third prediction offers a brief synopsis of the entire passion history (10:33-34). Both the Jewish leaders in Jerusalem ("chief priests, scribes") and the Gentiles are said to conspire to kill Jesus, although the initiative belongs with the priestly conspirators.

Matthew's version agrees with Mark, except that the ignorance and blindness of the disciples is lessened. Luke differs chiefly in the third prediction, which mentions only Jesus' maltreatment and murder by the Gentiles, a significant fact in considering Luke's attitude toward imperial Rome (18:32).

According to the passion predictions, Jesus not only has full knowledge of his approaching death and vindication but shares it openly with his disciples. However, they utterly fail to understand (Mark 9:32; 10:32//Luke 9:45; 18:34). Jesus himself accepts it as part of his divinely determined destiny (Mark 8:31, *dei*, "it is necessary," a divine must). But this conviction of its necessity as somehow willed by God results in the sharp, almost brutal confrontation between Jesus and Peter, in which Jesus rebukes Peter as Satan for thinking human thoughts rather than the things of God (*epitiman*, censure or reprove violently; Mark 8:32 par.).

The portrait of Jesus in the predictions[43] is a witness to one unafraid to die, who knows the political and religious forces aligned against him, yet who resolutely pressed forward to the end. Mark draws the unforgettable picture of Jesus courageously walking ahead of his disciples as they journey to Jerusalem, while the disciples follow in fear and amazement (Mark 10:32). Luke begins his lengthy "travel journey" to Jerusalem with Jesus determinedly "setting his face" toward his goal (Luke 9:51—19:28, a journey of ten chapters!). The evangelists do not present a meek and cowardly Jesus facing his political oppressors. His strength and heroism, however, stand in sharp contrast to that of his closest followers. They all flee when the going gets tough (Mark 14:50//Matt. 26:56).

Teaching on Authentic Greatness
(Mark 10:35-45//Matt. 20:20-28//Luke 22:24-27)

This text is one of the key passages in the Synoptic Gospels for illuminating their understanding of Jesus' critical stance toward those in positions of authority and the alternative vision of community that is set forth.

---

43. My concern here, as in this chapter as a whole, is not with questions of historicity but with the evangelist's story. Obviously the passion predictions raise many historical problems.

The Synoptics preserve an earlier controversy over greatness in which the disciples' desire for preeminence in the kingdom is vividly contrasted with the kingdom way of service (Mark 9:33-37//Matt. 18:1-5//Luke 9:46-48). At the heart of this controversy story is the saying of Jesus, "Whoever wants to be first must be last of all and servant of all" (Mark 9:35). To illustrate the authentic kingdom way of service, Jesus places a child in their midst and in Mark and Luke speaks of the necessity to welcome a child "in my name" (Mark 9:37//Luke 9:48).[44] Such welcome most likely means an attitude of openness toward or kindness to the least of the persons in the community.[45] And to welcome the least "in my name," means one is welcoming not only Jesus, but also the one who sent him.[46]

It is obvious that controversy over proper leadership within the Christian community was very much alive. In the tradition now before us, we find greatness in the kingdom of God deliberately set over against the exercise of authority in the political realm. This text consists of two interrelated passages: the request of James and John and the teaching on true greatness.

The request of James and John (Mark 10:35-40//Matt. 20:20-23; Luke omits) reveals their basic misunderstanding of the kingdom and their place within it. They covet positions of honor ("at your right hand . . . at your left," Mark 10:39; cf. Jesus' crucifixion, 15:27). As members of the select group of disciples, they desire a special place of prominence and recognition and authority. Jesus' response exposes their inability to grasp the new reality of life in the kingdom: "Are you able to drink the cup that I drink, or be baptized with the baptism that I am baptized with?" (Mark 10:38). Both images point to Jesus' imminent suffering and their necessity to share in it (cf. Isa. 51:17; Luke 12:50; 22:42; John 18:11). Despite their present lack of understanding, however, Jesus promises that they will participate in the new kingdom community by sharing in his sufferings. We learn from Acts that James did suffer martyrdom under Herod Agrippa I in 41 C.E. (Acts 12:2). Of John's fate, we are not sure. As for honored places in the kingdom, Jesus insists that is up to God (cf. Matt. 20:23).

In Matthew's version, it is the mother of James and John who piously initiates the request for chief places of honor (20:20). Yet Matthew betrays an awareness of the Markan tradition when he has Jesus address the two disciples in his reply, not their mother (v. 22, ". . . are you able?").

44. In Matthew, the child's own attitude becomes the model to imitate (18:3-4), while in Mark and Luke it is the attitude of others toward the child.

45. See Ernest Best, *Following Jesus: Discipleship in the Gospel of Mark* (JSNTSupp 4; Sheffield: JSOT Press, 1981), 78–79.

46. This accords with the Jewish legal principle (*sheliach*) that one's representative is to be regarded as the one who sent him (Best, *Discipleship*, 79).

In the related text, on authentic greatness (Mark 10:41-45//Matt. 20:24-28//Luke 22:24-27), introduced in Mark/Matthew by the indignation of the disciples over the request of James and John, the difference between the kingdom of God and the kingdoms of this world is drawn ever more sharply. The Markan Jesus here interprets with striking images the contrast between the two realms. The Gentiles represent the ordering of social and political institutions in this world. For them, the key words are "dominance over" or "authority over" others. The Greek verbs can be literally translated "lordship over" (*katakyrieuousin*; *kyrios*, lord, v. 42) or "authority over" (*kataexousiazousin*; *exousiazo*, authority, v. 42). (The Greek *kyrios*, "lord," is translated in Latin as *dominus*.) Accordingly, in the kingdoms of this world, their "rulers" (*hoi arxein*) and their "great ones" (*hoi megaloi*) exercise authority by domination, control, and power. This is the world as one knows it, the world as it is. This is the world arranged hierarchically so that there are patron and client, the strong and the weak, masters and slaves, privileged and exploited, benevolent and beneficiaries.

But there can be another way. "It is not so among you" (10:43). There is an alternate vision of authority and leadership and social relations that belongs to the realm of God. Here the key words are not "dominance and authority" but "service and self-giving." In this counter-community "the great one" (*megas*) is the "servant" (*diakonos*) and "the first" (*prōtos*) is the "slave" (*doulos*) of all. Life in this community clearly involves a revolutionary reversal of values and roles. It creates a community of shared authority in which control is abandoned for the sake of others. Here self-seeking and ambition and abuse of power become unacceptable. And especially do we find that leadership roles are reversed, for in this community the leaders wait on table (*diakonoi*, literally, those who wait on table) and adopt the role of slaves (*douloi*, 10:43-44).

The model for this unparalleled kind of community formation and its mutual sharing of leadership is Jesus himself. His life, consisting of both his words and deeds, exemplifies what authentic discipleship is all about. "For the son of Man came not to be served but to serve and to give his life a ransom for many" (10:45). This dominical saying summarizes for Mark the essence of Jesus' mission. Its central characteristic is a servant life dedicated to the good of the other. And as the ransom, Jesus makes possible the transvaluation of authority and leadership and egocentricity that can create the community he envisions.[47] "In the shadow of the cross, we get a

47. While Mark 10:45 represents for Mark a summary pronouncement regarding Jesus' life and salvific death, I am aware that the authenticity of the ransom saying is hotly debated. Because the Lukan version omits the ransom saying, many suggest that Luke preserves the more original form of the saying ("But I am among you as one who serves," Luke 22:27). While this may be so, I do not here intend to get involved in the debate on the historical Jesus.

brief glimpse of a new community in which relations are not governed by power and status but by service and hospitality for those without status—a community in which those who have been ransomed live for others."[48] Matthew's version is nearly identical with Mark's. But Mark provides a stronger critique of those who rule when he states (sarcastically?), "those who seem to rule [*hoi dokountes*, 10:42, RSV], lord it over others." The NRSV unfortunately obscures this pointed remark ("those whom they recognize as their rulers"). Matthew otherwise preserves the same contrasting parallels between the structures of this world and the structures of the kingdom: rulers = lordship, great ones = authority over, in contrast to great = servant, first = slave (20:25-27).

The Lukan version, however, differs considerably from Mark.[49] Luke places the story within the setting of the last supper and Jesus' farewell address to his disciples (22:14-38). In this context of a post-meal conversation, Jesus promises his disciples a place of honor in the coming kingdom, one even of preeminence (22:28-30, "judging the twelve tribes," a reconstituted Israel, that is, the church). Nevertheless, the dispute on greatness shows that in the ongoing community of followers there is to be a new definition of greatness and leadership at work. And this new understanding illumines the profound gulf that exists between all earthly political structures and the kingdom community begun by Jesus.

In this changed setting, the saying on greatness is occasioned by Jesus' revelation that one would betray him, not by the request of James and John for special favor. Yet the contrast between earthly rulers and leaders in Jesus' community is sketched with substantially the same effect, although employing somewhat different terms. "The kings of the Gentiles lord it over them; and those in authority over them are called benefactors" (22:25). The same two root verbs in Greek appear as in Mark 10:42: "lord over" (*kyrieuein*) and "exercise authority over" (*exousiazein*); only Mark uses the compound form. New is the term "benefactor" (*euergetēs*). This term was pervasive in the Hellenistic world, in which benefactor-client relationships formed the core of social relations.[50] Benefactors could be gods, princes,

48. Juel, *Mark*, 149.

49. Whether Luke's version comes from Mark or from Luke's own source is disputed. I think it originates in Mark (22:25-26//Mark 10:42-44), yet find Luke also drawing on his own source (22:27//Mark 10:45)). See Fitzmyer, *Luke*, vol. 2, 1412-1413.

50. See Frederick Danker, *Benefactor: Epigraphic study of a Graeco-Roman and New Testament Semantic Field* (St. Louis: Clayton, 1988), 317–66, for a survey of the term and the concept in the Hellenistic world. Although Danker has made a significant contribution in demonstrating its importance for the New Testament, I finally disagree with his conclusion that the author of Luke-Acts wants to present Jesus as the true "Hellenistic benefactor of Humanity" (see *Luke* [Proclamation Commentaries; Philadelphia: Fortress Press , 1976], 5). See the excursus on Luke-Acts, below.

and imperial rulers in the Roman world. Caesar Augustus was praised for his benefactions and Nero called savior and benefactor (*soter, euergetēs*). Rulers especially coveted the title as holders of power. But Luke is not about to praise those who are called benefactors, or as a better translation says, "those who acclaim themselves benefactors."[51] Pagan kings tyrannize their subjects. They possess power and use it for their own self-aggrandizement. Hence there is probably a note of sarcasm in Luke's use of the term—"self-proclaimed" benefactors.

Like Mark, the Lukan Jesus calls for another way to exhibit genuine greatness: "But not so with you" (22:26). Verse 26 presents contrasts: greatest/youngest (*neoteros*, newest, least important), leader/servant (*diakonon*; cf. Mark 10:43), great/servant (*diakonos*), and first/slave (*doulos*). Once more, greatness and leadership are defined by humility and service. The concluding verse drives this point home. To the rhetorical question of who is greater, the one who reclines or waits on table, Jesus responds by saying the one who reclines at table. This is so again in the real world, where distinctions of rank and honor prevail between the served and those who serve. But the text closes with the saying of Jesus, "But I am among you as one who serves" (22:27). The Greek *diakonon*, as mentioned above, literally means "to wait on table." With this saying the Lukan Jesus sums up his whole life and ministry. The similarity to the Markan saying is obvious (Mark 10:45), although the difference is also significant.[52] But there is profound agreement on servanthood as the overriding characteristic of those who follow Jesus. And those who belong to the community of disciples and those who want to exercise greatness are shown that authentic leadership must be in the service of others.

Some commentators have argued that Luke in fact has eliminated the sense of hostility regarding political rulers admittedly present in Mark. They point out that while Mark uses the expanded verbal compound to express their tyrannical manner of rule, Luke employs only the simple verb

51. See the NIV and the JB. The verbal form (*kalountai*) can be translated as either middle or passive (middle, "to acclaim oneself").

52. It is possible Luke draws this saying from "L." Yet that does not adequately explain his omission of the ransom saying, which would fit well within the context of the passion. As noted above, many think the Lukan version is the earliest and the "ransom saying" in Mark a later interpretation of Jesus' death. Others, however, think they represent two independent traditions (Vincent Taylor, *The Gospel according to St. Mark*, 2d ed. [New York: St. Martin's Press, 1966], 445-446). The matter is complicated by Luke's omission elsewhere of any sayings that directly link Jesus' death to atonement ideas. Luke's soteriology centers in the humiliated and exalted Lord who becomes the source of salvation for humanity, not on the cross per se. See Walter Pilgrim, "The Death of Christ in Lukan Soteriology" (diss., Princeton Theological Seminary, 1971).

(Luke 22:35: *kyrieuein/exousiazein*; cf. Mark 10:42: *katakyrieuein/kataexousiazein*). From this they conclude that Luke's judgment is less harsh than that of Mark's. They also question whether Luke uses the term "benefactor" with sarcasm and suggest that he merely wants to describe without making any kind of judgment about what exists in the secular Hellenistic world.

It may be that the omission of the compound verbs softens the judgment, although this is arguable.[53] But whatever slight softening there may be, Luke has not eliminated the negative judgment against earthly rulers. Luke intends to contrast the two kingdoms, not confuse them. The political way to rule exemplified by Rome and its sycophants is portrayed as the direct opposite of the kingdom way embodied in Jesus. Luke is not merely accepting or neutral about the rule of Hellenistic benefactors. The Lukan Jesus stands against their way and rejects their manner of exercising authority in the world. Luke is not saying that the Gentile rulers are truly benefactors of humanity. They may be called that by others or by themselves, but that is scarcely the reality. Behind their so-called benefactions lie the brute facts of conquest, tyranny, taxation, census, persecutions, and the like.

It is therefore not the case that Luke intends to describe Jesus as "the true Benefactor" of humanity for his Hellenistic readers.[54] It is instructive that Luke never applies the term "benefactor" directly to Jesus. Apparently, the risk was too great simply to call Jesus the benefactor of humankind, given the context of oppressive benefactors in the Greco-Roman world. So Luke

---

53. In *A Greek-English Lexicon of the New Testament and Other Early Christian Literature*, (BAGD; Chicago: Univ. of Chicago Press, 1979), the simple and compound forms are translated in the same manner. However, Luke T. Johnson, *The Gospel of Luke* (Collegeville, Minn.: Liturgical Press, 1991), 344, agrees that the Lukan use of compounds lessens the judgment; he also finds a slightly less negative overtone in Luke 22:26: "Luke recognizes the dominance without insisting on suppression." I think this fine-tunes the evidence overmuch. But Johnson agrees that Luke wants to contrast the two kingdoms, not minimize their differences. He also finds Luke opposing the term "benefactor." Like Jesus, "they [disciples] are neither to dominate nor to regard themselves as benefactors" (349).

54. See Danker's various writings on Luke and the Hellenistic world (*Benefactor; Luke*; and *Jesus and the New Age*, rev. ed. [Philadelphia: Fortress Press, 1988]). To make this point, Danker realizes he must present Jesus as "the *true* benefactor of humanity" (emphasis added) and as a political original. I think that for Luke it is not a matter of a true benefactor but of a different kind. This text shows Jesus to be something quite other than a Hellenistic benefactor or savior. The closest Luke comes to using "benefactor" for Jesus is Acts 10:38, where doing good (benefactions) is combined with Jesus' healing activity, scarcely a passage that can be used as a central motif of Luke (why not healing?). Moreover, I disagree that Luke intends this dispute on greatness "should lay to rest forever the ghost of subversiveness" (Danker, *New Age*, 348). This comment rests on the notion that Luke's two volumes are a pro-Roman apologia, a view I take to be mistaken and seek to correct (see the excursus, below).

uses other titles in order to keep distinct the unbridgeable gap between the way of Jesus and that of Hellenistic kingships and their imitators.

This passage on authentic greatness is no modest or offhand critique of social or political structures or of those who exercise authority in this world. Rather, it stands as a fundamental exposé of human structures gone awry. Some have argued that Jesus' teaching is concerned primarily with the discipleship community and that he only uses the Gentiles as an easy foil. But not so! This passage involves a devastating demythologizing of all "worldly structures" ordered by dominance, control, and brute power. It recognizes the abuse of authority, the oppression of the weak, and the disenfranchising of the majority of the human race that such authoritarian and hierarchical structures have caused. This may be the way it is, but not the way it ought to be. Nor does this passage offer some visionary utopia for the next world or some distant future. It defines the core of Jesus' ethic of community. This is an appeal for a basic reordering of community and leadership here and now, whenever the followers of Jesus come together.

There is here a critical distancing from those who rule and dominate in this world. The Synoptic Jesus calls for a radically new way of experiencing community and exercising authority. He appeals for subversive communities that resist the status quo and that model another kind of possibility. He seeks an end to all political, social, and religious structures that are fundamentally oppressive and where leadership is governed by dominance and self-serving. The new community models itself in the image of the one who came "not to be served but to serve." This is certainly not the way it is nor the way it will be until the final rule of God comes near. The challenge remains within the community of disciples continually to hear anew and reshape their life together more fully with that of Jesus' vision. But the faith community is also called to keep this vision alive for others and, in so doing, to shake the foundations and structures of this old world as well.

On Paying Taxes to Caesar
(Mark 12:13-17//Matt. 22:15-22//Luke 20:20-26)

Of all the texts in the Synoptic tradition, this controversy story is the most closely related to the question of Jesus' attitude toward the political structures in society. Despite its familiarity, however, this passage is notoriously difficult to interpret.

The Synoptics agree in placing the debate in the Temple, during Jesus' final week of teaching. They also agree that the setting is hostile, since the Jewish leaders are determined to arrest him (Mark 11:27; 12:12). Accordingly, in Mark the leaders send persons to trap him. Mark identifies the persons as Pharisees and Herodians (12:13). We know the Pharisees as the movement zealous to uphold the Torah as the guide for life. Although the Gospels depict Jesus in ongoing debate over their interpretation of the Law, they were in fact nearest to him in their desire to do the will of God. Politically, they were conservative, neither collaborating with the Roman regime, as did the Sadducees, nor opposing them violently, as did the Jewish resistance movements, including the Zealots and Sicarii. Their interest centered on religious matters, although they doubtless shared the longing for the liberation of Israel. Traditionally, they submitted to the Roman tax, with a few notable exceptions.[55] The Herodians are probably supporters of the Herodian family represented by Antipas in Galilee (Mark 3:6; 8:15). As Herodian nationalists, they would support the tax and Roman rule. This unusual alliance of Herodians and Pharisees, along with their Galilean location, may suggest that the story originated in Galilee.[56] But the real enemies for Mark are the religious leaders in Jerusalem.

The plotters approach Jesus with flattery, as one who teaches the way of God with truth and without respect of status (12:14). Then comes the trap question: "Is it lawful to pay taxes to Caesar or not?" (RSV). The issue was of burning importance to Jews and to Jewish Christians living under Rome's rule. Jesus' own contemporaries were deeply divided. The particular tax was the poll tax (not customs or property tax), levied since 6 C.E. directly on all inhabitants of Judea, Samaria, Idumea, and indirectly in Galilee. Obviously it was highly unpopular, both because it was the hated symbol of subjection to imperial Rome and because the coin used to make payment was a silver denarius, stamped with the name and image of Caesar. When it was introduced in 6 C.E., organized rebellions broke out, some led by Judas of Galilee. Josephus mentions continued Jewish resistance to the tax with outbreaks of violence, culminating in the revolt of 66–70. Although Josephus may incorrectly blame the Zealots, as "the fourth philosophy" of the Jews, for the continued active resistance, hostility was in the

---

55. For example, Judas the Galilean and Saddok the Pharisee mounted a strong resistance to the Roman imposition of the tax in Galilee in 6 C.E.. While most scholars have regarded Judas and Saddok as founders of the "fourth philosophy" (Zealots, following Josephus) and as advocates of violent resistance to the tax and Rome, Horsley (*Spiral*, 77–89, esp. 88–89) argues strongly against this common view. He concludes only that Judas and Saddok organized popular tax-resistance upon imposition of direct imperial rule and taxation in 6 C.E. While they were willing to die for their beliefs, Horsley does not think they were advocates of violent resistance or founders of the Zealot movement.

56. Klaus Wengst, *Pax Romana*, 58, argues for its Judean origin on the grounds that only in Judea, under direct Roman rule, was a poll tax levied by Rome. In Galilee, Herod Antipas collected the tax. But this overlooks the fact that all of Palestine had to pay the Roman *fiscus*, whether collected by the Roman procurator in Judea or Herod in Galilee. And every Jew knew that Herod was a loyal puppet of the Roman oppressor. Only on sabbatical years was the poll tax not levied.

air. Other Jewish groups took different positions, from withdrawal (Essenes at Qumran) to grudging acceptance (Pharisees) to open cooperation (Sadducees, Herodians). Whatever position Jesus took would put him in jeopardy. To say yes to the tax would brand him a traitor and affect his popularity with the people. To say no to the tax would bring political risk as a rebel and revolutionary (cf. Luke 23:2). Later Christians living under Rome had a huge stake in this question as well.

According to Mark, Jesus responds by exposing their hypocrisy and asking for a denarius (12:15). To his query about whose image and name it bears, they answer, Caesar's (*kaisaros*). Then follows Jesus' famous pronouncement, "Give to Caesar what belongs to Caesar, and to God what belongs to God" (RSV). The saying is clever, provocative, and open to more than one interpretation. For the moment, Jesus escapes the trap set for him. We read that the people and interrogators stand utterly amazed. But what does it mean? Matthew makes no real change from Mark, except to heighten the charge of hypocrisy against the Pharisees (22:15-22, v. 18, "you hypocrites"). Luke, however, differs by linking the account to the attempt by unnamed spies sent from the scribes and Pharisees to find accusations against Jesus to bring to the Roman governor (20:20-26, v. 20). This increases the political tension and points ahead to the charge of forbidding the payment of taxes brought later by the Temple authorities to Pilate (23:2).

How should one interpret Jesus' pronouncement? At one time there was a kind of consensus, but this is no longer the case. The following are the main types of interpretation today.

1. Two kingdoms: God and Caesar.[57] The traditional interpretation understood that Jesus recognized two legitimate realms, that of God and that of Caesar. Each has its rightful place and honor and respect and obedience are due to both. Accordingly, taxes are owed to Caesar, while to God belongs the inner loyalty of one's heart and life. When pressed, most interpreters would agree the greater loyalty belongs to God. Nevertheless, in this view the loyalty and respect owed to Caesar are not inherently in conflict with the things of God. A divinely intended partnership exists between the earthly political realm and the kingdom of God.

So understood, this text would seem to cohere with the Pauline counsel on Christian subordination toward those in authority and the whole subsequent tradition of obedience to the state (see chap. 2, above). This interpretation has also been instrumental in the development of the classical two-kingdom ethic of Lutheranism, with its political kingdom on the left

---

57. Fitzmyer, *Luke* vol. 2, 1292–93, attempts a helpful classification of three views. I follow his first but then offer different classifications.

and the spiritual kingdom on the right. Other formulations of Christian ethical theories on church and state are likewise anchored in this dual partnership approach.

The traditional view still has its articulate advocates and demands a serious hearing.[58] It attempts to do justice both to the reality of life in the world, with the need for structures to uphold the common good, and also the proclamation of the inbreaking rule of God in the ministry of Jesus. Yet questions arise. This view tends strongly to equate the two kingdoms. But, what exactly is Caesar's realm and what is God's? What belongs to each? Are they equal or is one subordinate to the other? Does this interpretation result, in part, from a search in the text for a peaceful coexistence between the realm of Caesar and that of God? And how consistent is this dual kingdom ethic with Jesus' own radical insistence on the priority of God above all else and with Jesus' critical stance toward those in power, as the Gospels demonstrate? Faced with these tough questions, and perhaps, too, as a result of the blatant misuse of this text and the Pauline and other texts on subordination throughout history, other interpretations have emerged.

2. *One kingdom: To God alone.*[59] A second interpretation is quite the opposite of the first. What Jesus intends is radical obedience to God alone. "Render to Caesar what belongs to Caesar, and to God what belongs to God." But what belongs to Caesar? In truth, nothing! Everything is God's. And since everything is God's, there can be no dualism of independent realms and obedience. From this perspective, Jesus refuses to allow Caesar any legitimate sphere of authority. Only one kingdom deserves human loyalty.[60] "No one can serve two masters: for a slave will

58. Cullmann, *The State*, 20, 34–37; Ethelbert Stauffer, *New Testament Theology* (New York: Macmillan, 1956), 197–98; E. Earle Ellis, *The Gospel of Luke* (NCB; Grand Rapids: Eerdmans, 1986), 233.

59. Fitzmyer, *Luke*, vol. 2, 1292, refers to this view as the "ironic interpretation," in the sense that payment to Caesar is only "a flash of wit" not to be taken seriously. Indifference or even hostility to Caesar clearly marks this view. Fitzmyer, however, fails to see the link with an imminent eschatology found in the adherents of this view (see below). A classification of the various interpretations should keep the language of the two realms explicitly in mind.

60. See Horsley, *Spiral*, 306–17, who finds that beneath Jesus' seemingly ambiguous response "Jesus was asserting the absolute and exclusive sovereignty of God" (309). Thus Caesar has no legitimate claims at all. He admits that Jesus' statement was sufficiently clever and noncommittal so as not to be charged with treason. But the saying "suggests that the people would almost certainly have understood that, since Caesar has no legitimate claims anyhow, nothing need be rendered. All belongs to God, the true Lord" (316). Richard J. Cassidy, *Jesus, Politics, and Society* (Maryknoll, N.Y.: Orbis, 1978), 57–63, likewise argues strongly against any dualism of two spheres, one temporal and the other spiritual. He posits one realm that belongs to God alone. In a lengthy argument he opposes the idea of an autonomous, separate

either hate the one and love the other, or be devoted to the one and despise the other" (Matt. 6:24).

One variant of this position combines it with Jesus' expectation of the imminent end. As such it has found some significant advocates.[61] Since Jesus thinks the world was fast coming to a close, he exhibits, at best, passing interest in the realm of Caesar and focuses everything on the coming reign of God. While Jesus permits the payment of tax, it possesses no importance. "Men should perform the first [that is, pay taxes] . . . but they should concentrate above all on their relationship to the God whose coming is now so imminent."[62] A few have even concluded that, on religious grounds, Jesus may have advocated a refusal to pay any tax.[63] As evidence they cite the charge against Jesus at his trial in Luke 23:2: ". . . forbid us to pay tribute."

How shall one evaluate this approach? Its appeal is that it takes with utmost seriousness the priority of God's kingdom in Jesus' teaching and recognizes also the tension in the Gospels between the claims of the inbreaking rule of God and all lesser, temporary claims. But its negative conclusions regarding Caesar and the political realm seem exaggerated. In particular, the proponent's dependence on Jesus' belief in the nearness of the end has become questionable. Even if Jesus did proclaim its nearness, he still called his followers to act responsibly toward the present world and its structures.[64] Moreover, the conclusion that Jesus advocated the nonpayment of tax seems most unlikely. If he did, this would place him in the Jewish resistance camp and bring swift retaliation from Pilate or Rome. That Jesus was a subversive and political revolutionary is not convincing. Nor do the evangelists or the early church interpret this saying of Jesus as a call to refuse the imperial tax.

---

realm "outside of God's creation" (163, n. 28). Hence, one gives to Caesar only when Caesar follows the way of God. But, since all belongs to God, one gives to God, even if contrary to Caesar. Cassidy correctly objects to the idea of two autonomous spheres, one independent of God, a problem that has plagued some two-kingdom theories, sometimes with tragic consequences. Nevertheless, there can be an understanding of two separate realms, even though both are under or within God's realm.

61. Martin Dibelius, *Jesus*, trans. Charles Hedrick and Frederick Grant (Philadelphia: Westminster, 1949), 114–15; Günther Bornkamm, *Jesus of Nazareth*, trans. Irene and Fraser McLuskey (New York: Harper, 1960), 120-24; Dennis Nineham, *The Gospel of St. Mark* (London: Penguin Books, 1963), 316.

62. Nineham, *Mark*, 316.

63. See Horsley, *Spiral*, 316, although with little direct link to Jesus' imminent expectation. Included in this view also are those who think Jesus was a Zealot sympathizer.

64. The link between ethics and eschatology has been carefully rethought in modern scholarship. Contrary to earlier views, concern for the coming world need not lead to indifference toward the present. Quite the opposite can be the case (see chap. 4, below).

Another variant on the one-kingdom approach suggests that Jesus' words are aimed at the Jewish religious leaders, who have already sold out to Rome.[65] This is why Jesus asks for the coin, a silver denarius that bore Caesar's image and inscription.[66] For faithful Jews, this was a clear violation of the prohibition against images (Deut. 7:5). As one commentator dryly remarks, "This money was not theologically neutral."[67] By asking for the coin, Jesus exposes the leaders as religiously and ethically compromised. They obviously did business with Caesar's coin. By saying, "Give to the emperor . . . ," he in effect indicates paying the tax, since they have already bought into the system. And in this way Jesus also avoids a no to the tax and any political retaliation. Yet by saying, "Give to God . . . ," Jesus challenges the whole presupposition that Caesar has a place apart from God. In fact, it is argued that in principle Jesus rejects the use of all coins and currency with Caesar's image and urges his opponents to do the same. Here the model of Jesus and his disciples, living without earthly vocations in sole reliance upon God, becomes the norm.

This a refreshing effort to shed light on this text. Its strength lies in its recognition of the dilemma posed by the use of the denarius and in its exposé of the compromised religious establishment. Yet there are at least two objections. First, it is doubtful whether this or any Gospel text shows that Jesus "in principle" rejected the use of currency. Although Jesus and his disciples lived an itinerant lifestyle, they accepted the support of followers with livelihoods and wealth (e.g., Luke 8:1-3). While sharply critical of wealth and its dangers, Jesus does not reject it per se in the Gospels. Second, Jesus does not direct his words primarily to the religious leaders. The saying is addressed both to those who resist the tax as a hated symbol of slavery and to those who accept it and the web of collaboration with Rome this entails. The dilemma posed by the interrogators is how Jesus can avoid taking sides so as not to fall into the trap of Jewish nationalism and fanaticism, on the one hand, or the embarrassing compromise of the religious leaders and their alliance with the oppressor, on the other.

3. Two kingdoms: God first, then Caesar. A third interpretation acknowledges the two kingdoms but insists on the priority of the kingdom of God.

---

65. Wengst, *Pax Romana*, 58–61.

66. The coin of Tiberius, emperor during Jesus' lifetime.

Obverse: Caesar's likeness, wearing a laurel wreath. Inscription: "Tiberius Caesar, son of deified Augustus, Augustus."

Reverse: Mother Linia, depicted as goddess of Peace. Inscription: "High Priest."

The denarius was "a visible symbol of Roman power and authority" (Wengst, *Pax Romana*, 59).

67. David L. Tiede, *Luke* (ACNT; Minneapolis: Augsburg, 1988), 344.

By saying, "Give to Caesar," Jesus does legitimate the political realm and rejects those who advocate nonpayment of tax or any form of open rebellion or violent resistance. This would be a decidedly (so-called) anti-Zealot stance in first-century Palestine.[68] Nevertheless, the two kingdoms are not equal. "Give to God" establishes the proper priority by affirming the singular importance of the rule of God. God's claim on humanity and the human response to that take precedence over all other claims, including that of Caesar or even that of the desire for political freedom. The priority of God also shatters all pretensions to divine rights of secular structures or authorities.[69]

A host of modern interpreters adopt this view with individual variations.[70] Their basic grasp of the relationship between the two realms is essentially correct, but their all-too-easy acceptance of the political realm is a vulnerable point.[71] I want to be even more cautious about Caesar's realm and more sensitive to Jesus' overall critique and stance toward political structures and systems, as found in the Gospels.

4. Two kingdoms: No peaceful coexistence. The same qualification needs to be made here as with Romans 13. This passage does not reflect any full-blown doctrine of the state. Rather, within the pronouncement-story preserved by the early church, we learn something of Jesus' attitude toward Caesar and God, which provides boundaries on the proper understanding of their relationship. The story deals with a conflict between opposing views in Jesus' time and with a problem in the ongoing life of the early church. How should they regard those in political power? What about

68. Fitzmyer, *Luke,* vol. 2, 1292–93, calls this "the anti-Zealot" interpretation. But he recognizes the historical problem of identifying the Zealots as a religious movement, and he himself goes beyond the setting of Zealotism in his reflections.

69. "In the light of what God requires, the demands of the state can have only limited authority and relative importance. Jesus' words take a mediating position between the extremes of rebellion and revolution on the one hand and the apotheosis and glorification of Caesar and the empire on the other, *but they leave no room for aspirations to divinity* (emphasis added)." See Wolfgang Schrage, *The Ethics of the New Testament,* trans. David E. Green (Philadelphia: Fortress Press, 1988), 114.

70. Schrage, *Ethics,* 107–115; Bornkamm, *Jesus of Nazareth,* 123; Fitzmyer, *Luke* vol. 2, 1289–1298; Rudolf Schnackenburg, *The Moral Teaching of the New Testament,* trans. J. Holland-Smith and W. J. O'Hara (New York: Seabury, 1982), 110–20.

71. For example: "The kingdom which Jesus preaches does not call in question Caesar's rightful kingship; but that is not the all-important aspect of human life. A human being belongs to God. . . . God has not only a right of possession over human beings, but also a claim to a basic recognition of his lordship" (Fitzmyer, *Luke,* vol. 2, 1293). While Fitzmyer strongly affirms the absolute priority of God's kingship, this statement appears to leave Caesar's realm untouched. The meaning of "rightful kingship" requires careful unpacking.

Rome and its imperial claims and its demand for taxes and obedience? What of the coins with Caesar's image and the divine titles inscribed on them? What did Jesus say? This story is of singular importance because it is the only authoritative "word from the Lord" on the subject in the tradition. Yet both its brevity and ambiguity place limits on its usefulness, then and now.

"Give to God": The priority of the kingdom. Despite the parallelism between the things of Caesar and of God, they are not equal. "Give to God what is God's"—the prior loyalty. God alone is Lord. All Israel and Jesus and the evangelists know this. It is a matter of the First Commandment (Mark 12:28-30). Here the freedom-fighters and Zealots were right: Tribute to Caesar can never be on a par with faithfulness to God. There are no divine rights of rulers nor anything approaching parity between the two realms. The natural pretensions so apparent throughout history of those who rule to make sovereign claims now meet their limits. "Give to God" establishes the absolute lordship of the living God, and no other.

If this is so, the possibility is opened for civil disobedience in the name of God and for the sake of Christ. Even the refusal to pay taxes may be possible. Whenever those in authority encroach on the ultimate loyalty owed to God, Christ's followers are inevitably thrown into the cauldron of conflict and potential resistance. "We must obey God rather than any human authority" (Acts 5:29).

"Give to Caesar": The political realm. While the priority of God's kingdom is unequivocal in this saying and in the teaching of Jesus as a whole, earthly political structures also have their place. "Give to Caesar" opens up the possibility of acknowledging the necessity and significance of the political realm for daily existence. The Jesus of the Gospels does not take the stance of those who in principle refuse to pay taxes to Caesar in the name of God nor does he advocate armed resistance to those in power. Even pagan political and civil authorities may have their role within the human community. One can give to Caesar what is Caesar's and seek to determine what is appropriate for Caesar. Payment of taxes includes also the attitude of respect and support for what affirms the structures of our common life together as people and nations. Even coins have their place as representatives of economic and commercial systems developed by human communities.[72] In itself, involvement in these structures does not necessarily mean disloyalty to God. Yet it is significant to observe that in this story Jesus does not call Caesar a servant of God nor claim that earthly rulers are instituted by God and so worthy of obedience from his followers (cf. Rom. 13:1-7).

---

72. Against Wengst's interpretation of this text (*Pax Romana*, 58–61).

No peaceful coexistence. At the same time, Jesus' words cannot be used as a blanket endorsement of Caesar or anything like a doctrine of two separate but equal realms. The priority of God's rule remains. The Jesus of the Gospels adopts a critical stance against those who govern, attacking their dominance over others, their violent use of force, their luxury, their injustice, and their self-aggrandizement. He refuses to be pressured into submission to authorities by fear or cowardice. He opts for the way of peace and reconciliation between people and nations and weeps over Jerusalem's self-destructive reliance on freedom by the power of the sword. Moreover, this text recognizes the temptation to idolatry that Caesar poses for humankind. The symbol of the coin, the Roman denarius with its blasphemous image of Caesar, graphically portrays the constant danger of idolatry and compromise. Disciples of Christ always live on the thin edge of compromise as they use and misuse the coins and systems of Caesar, whether in the political, economic, or military realm. For disciples, the decisive issue is finally not political or ethical but theological: "Which God do we serve?"

The relationship between the kingdom of God and the political structures embodied in this saying is not one of peaceful coexistence. It recognizes a profound tension between the two realms. The priority of faithfulness to God causes a conflict that is both inevitable and continuous. It would be utopian to think otherwise. Jesus' own life and death become the supreme witness to the risk and potential for suffering inherent in following the kingdom way, and the history of the church fills out the story. Obedience to God and Christ above all else does not sit well with the Caesars of this world, past or present. Jesus promises no easy way for those who give "to God the things that are God's" (Matt. 22:21; Luke 20:25).

Wars, Persecution, and the Desolating Sacrilege
(Mark 13:7-23//Matt. 24:6-28; 10:16-25//Luke 21:9-19)

Each of the Synoptics preserves a parallel collection of apocalyptic sayings about the end-time (the so-called "Markan apocalypse" and pars.). I shall concentrate not on the general nature of this difficult material but on the references to wars and persecution and the desolating sacrilege.

The collection begins with Jesus' prediction of the destruction of the Temple: "Not one stone will be left here upon another . . ." (Mark 13:1 pars.). While the conquerors are unnamed, the readers know all too well what the devastation by the Roman legions under Vespasian and Titus have done (66–70 C.E.). Especially Luke provides a graphic description of Jerusalem's siege and frightful demolition (19:43-44; 21:20; cf. Matt 23:37-38).

In the Markan apocalypse, among the signs preceding the end are both natural disasters (earthquakes and famines) and war between nations. "For nation will rise against nation, and kingdom against kingdom" (Mark 13:8). Within this context of end-time chaos and conflict, believers are warned that they too will suffer (13:9-13; no escape via the rapture!). Trials will occur before both Jewish and Roman religious and civil authorities: synagogues, governors, and kings (13:9). Beatings, trials, and imprisonment will take place; families will betray one another to death (13:12-13). And how should the faithful respond? Since they are forewarned, they are not to be afraid. When brought before the civil authorities, they make their testimony boldly and courageously (13:9). They trust the Spirit to give them the right words to speak (13:11). Above all, their chief mark is endurance, the toughness to hang on until the end, even in the face of martyrdom (13:13; on endurance as the primary Christian ethic in Revelation, see chap. 4, below). Not only here but elsewhere Mark has prepared his hearers for the possibility of future hostilities (Mark 10:30, the abrupt insertion of "with persecution" into his description of the new community; cp. Matt. 19:29). Most importantly, for Mark and the Synoptics, the core of Christian discipleship is readiness "to take up one's cross and follow me" (8:34; Matt. 16:24; Luke 9:23).

While Luke's sayings on war and persecution are nearly identical to Mark's (Luke 21:12-17), Matthew places them much earlier, within the setting of Jesus' missionary instruction to the Twelve (Matt. 10:16-23). Thus in the "Matthean apocalypse" Matthew edits a more general statement about persecution "by all nations" and omits any reference to the Spirit (Matt. 24:9).

The climactic sign preceding the end in the Markan apocalypse is the setting up of the "desolating sacrilege" with its fearful consequences for believers and the whole creation (13:14-23; cf. Matt. 24:15-28//Luke 21:20-24). Who or what is the "desolating sacrilege" (to bdelugma tes erēmōseōs; TEV, "the Awful Horror"!)? In the book of Daniel, it refers to the desecration of the Temple by Antiochus IV Epiphanes in 167 b.c.e., which led to the Maccabean revolt (Dan. 9:17, 27; 11:31; 12:11). Jewish memory remained alive and well regarding this infamous act of blasphemy by a hated conqueror. The same kind of sacrilegious action in the Temple may lie behind the fear expressed in Mark 13:14, only now applied to Christians and their expectation of the end. While the cryptic aside by the evangelist, "Let the reader understand" (13:14), indicates that his readers would doubtless understand the reference, we are not as certain. Two possibilities seem most likely. Either it refers to the threatened desecration of the Temple by Emperor Gaius Caligula, who ordered his statue to be erected in the Holy of Holies (37–49 c.e.), or, more probably, to the actual defilement by the Roman general Titus, the conqueror of Jerusalem, who entered the Holy of

Holies before the Temple's destruction by his legions in 70 C.E.[73] Whatever the exact reference, the "desolating sacrilege" represents the supreme embodiment of defiant evil by earthly powers. As with Antiochus IV in the time of Daniel, so with Rome in the present time: the "desolating sacrilege" is the symbol of the government as a blasphemous beast or anti-Christ, defying God and humanity (cf. Rev. 13:2; 2 Thess. 2:3-4). Therefore, Christian readers are warned to watch and be alert, for this will initiate a time of suffering and persecution unequalled since the beginning of creation (13:19). But they are also promised that God will mercifully cut short the time, for the sake of the elect (13:20).

While Matthew follows Mark's version in the warning about the desolating sacrilege, Luke rewrites this section in order to avoid any suggestion that the destruction of the Temple is related to the end-time (Luke 21:20-24). Instead, Luke makes them two separate events. On the one hand, he refers to the destruction of Jerusalem, omitting any direct reference to the desolating sacrilege, except to say the city's "desolation has come near" (21:20). On the other hand, he postpones the end-time into the unknown future.

What these apocalyptic sayings attribute to Jesus is a keen awareness of a world full of war and bloodshed. To feel the boot of the conquering army was a part of Israel's long and tragic history. Jesus, too, experienced the sights and sounds of marching legions and brutal occupation. The Synoptics hint that he foresaw the disastrous fate of his own people and nation and beloved city crushed by the superpower Rome.[74] In the Danielic symbol of the "desolating sacrilege," the state is portrayed as the supreme representation of blasphemous evil and corrupt power on earth. For Mark and the Synoptics, the government can become a beast, a persecutor of God's people and source of pervasive suffering. It can stand in ultimate defiance of God and humanity, so that only God can prevail

---

73. We learn from Josephus that Emperor Gaius Caligula, irritated by the fact that the Jews refused to reverence him as god, commanded the erection of his statue in the Temple. The Syrian legate, Petronius, delayed carrying out the order, fearing revolt and was saved by the assassination of the mad emperor in 41 C.E. (*Ant.* 18.257–309; *War* 2. 184–203). The early date, along with the fact that the threat was never carried out, creates doubt that this is the event referred to in Mark. The victorious general Titus did march into the Holy of Holies after the Temple area was captured, a frightful moment for the pious. Moreover, the Greek grammar allows one to translate the phrase "the desolating sacrilege set up . . ." as a reference to a person, since the participle is masculine (*hestekota*, "the one set up or standing"). See G. Beasley Murray, *Jesus and the Last Days* (Peabody, Mass.: Hendrickson, 1992), 408–16, whose thorough discussion of this term concludes that the reference to Titus's violation is the preferable interpretation.

74. See Borg, *Jesus*, 156–65.

against it. Yet even in this context of superhuman conflict and end-time chaos, God's people are called to stand firm. Like Jesus, his followers will be caught up in the struggle of allegiances and betrayals. Like him, they will face persecution from Jew and Gentile alike. But their response is not to be one of silence, fear, or compromise. When brought before the political and religious authorities, they make their bold witness, trust in the Spirit, and endure to the end. In so doing, they follow in the footsteps of their Lord.

Special Matthew

In addition to their use of Mark and Q, the evangelists Matthew and Luke draw upon sources of their own in writing their Gospels. We will first look at special Matthean texts (M) relevant to Jesus' attitude toward those possessing political and religious power and then the Lukan material (L).

Matthew presents Jesus as the promised Messiah/Son/Immanuel, as well as the teacher of the new righteousness of the kingdom (1:21-23; 5:20; 28:18-20). Within the Gospel itself, Matthew constructs five collections of Jesus' sayings on various themes for use in the church. Conflict is also central throughout the Gospel, with the conflict between Jesus and the religious authorities especially intense and bitter, culminating in his death (chap. 23, "scribes and Pharisees"; chaps. 24–27, high priests and Sanhedrin).[75] This obviously reflects the Jewish Christian milieu of Matthew's readers.

Matthean Infancy Stories:
The Child Born to Be King (Matthew 1–2)

While the infancy narratives do not deal with Jesus' own teaching and ministry, they do provide us with the evangelist's understanding of events and their significance. And we may presume the evangelist's understanding coheres with that of the community for whom he writes.[76] In this sense, the canonical infancy stories represent the faith of the early community and their grasp of what Jesus was all about.

While Matthew, chapter 1, tells the reader who Jesus is (1:21-23; genealogy, 1:2-17), chapter 2 narrates the founding events within the historical setting of Bethlehem and Nazareth and the rule of Herod the Great. The

---

75. See Jack D. Kingsbury, *Matthew: Structure, Christology, Kingdom* (Philadelphia: Fortress Press, 1975), and also his *Matthew as Story* (Philadelphia: Fortress Press, 1986).

76. One might compare the infancy Gospels written in the second century that were not included in the canon because of their fanciful and at times distorted portrayals of the child Jesus. See especially the *Infancy Gospel of Thomas* in Edgar Hennecke and Wilhelm Schneemelcher, *New Testament Apocrypha*, vol. 1, trans. A. J. Higgins, ed. R. McL. Wilson (Philadelphia: Westminster Press, 1963), 388–400.

theme of political conflict holds together this cycle of birth stories. As Matthew tells it, it is a monumental clash between two kings: Herod, tyrant king of Judea, and Jesus, the child born to be king of the Jews.

We are so familiar with reading the infancy stories in a nonpolitical way that we have inevitably missed their underlying social impact.[77] These are more than pious miracle-stories of dreams and moving stars. They are powerful stories of two worlds in collision. There is the world of the petty tyrant and dictator, Herod the Great, and his son Archelaus, puppet rulers of Palestine by favor of imperial Rome. This is the historical reality of occupied people, subject to mass terror, innocent victims, harsh taxation, and long-suffering exploitation. It is the reality of a priestly hierarchy clinging to power and privilege, cowing favor with bribes and collaboration with the oppressor. Into this kind of world comes the story of the child destined to be king. And this child-king, descendant of the royal line of David, comes to fulfill ancient promises of peace and liberation and to bring God's presence near. The holders of power rightly perceive this child-king to be a threat and plot to do away with him. His family must flee into exile, live like refugees, and await the death of the tyrant before they return home. Many innocent victims suffer and die.

For the evangelist, this is more than a human story. History and politics form the background for divine action within human history. Nevertheless, the story remains anchored in the concrete social realities of this world, with its interplay of innocence and cruelty, weakness and power, good and evil. It is a clash between two ways of living in the world, two claims to sovereignty. And this conflict continues to the end of Matthew's story, when the child-king come to bring peace is crucified by the imperial superpower and its local representative.

The visit of the Magi (2:1-12): Matthew 2:1 introduces the political setting. The birth in Bethlehem, the city of David, links Jesus to the royal line of David ("son of David," 1:1; 9:27; 21:9). Herod the Great, Rome's vassal, builder of the Temple and of cities, is ruler of Palestine (37–4 B.C.E.). Readers will soon learn his true character. Astrologers (*magoi*) from the East, alerted to the birth of a Jewish king by an uncommon constellation of stars, come to pay homage and seek the help of Herod and the high-priestly

---

77. See Richard A. Horsley, *The Liberation of Christmas* (New York: Crossroad, 1989), who attempts to rethink the birth stories in light of their sociopolitical background. He may exaggerate at points, but his work does breathe fresh life into the specifics of the historical setting in Jesus' time. Raymond Brown's magisterial commentary, *The Birth of the Messiah: A Commentary on the Infancy Narratives in Matthew and Luke,* 2d ed (ABRL; New York: Doubleday, 1977), is indispensable, especially for understanding the Old Testament influences on the stories. Yet at times Brown fails to do justice to the sociopolitical realities present in the story.

leaders. The conflict begins immediately between Herod and the child. Herod conspires to do away with the threat, while the priestly leaders will wait until the end of the story. The Magi find the child and worship, but divine intervention by means of a dream thwarts Herod's murderous plan. The clash has begun between those who rule by scheming and sword and the rule of this newborn king.

Matthew 2:13-23, the escape to Egypt, massacre of the children, and the return to Nazareth (2:13-23) centers on Herod's attempt to destroy the child-king and and on the divine acts of preservation. Behind this account are echoes of past escape and rescue stories in Israel's history (Moses, Joseph, exodus). Here God's power to save overcomes the human capacity to destroy.

Warned by a dream, the holy family flees under cover of darkness from their own ruler (Matt. 2:13-15). They live as refugees in Egypt, like Israel of old, and remain political exiles-in-waiting until the tyrant dies.

In Matthew's narrative of the massacre of the innocents (2:16-18), political tyranny and police brutality reveal their true colors. Enraged by the failure of his scheme, fearful of any rival to power, Herod sends his soldiers into action. All male infants in Bethlehem, two years or younger, are slaughtered en masse. Josephus relates that this same Herod succumbed to suspicion about plots from his own beloved wife and two sons and ordered them executed (*Ant.* 15.218-231; 16.392-394). The power of the sword becomes red with innocent blood. The child-king escapes for the moment but will later die as King of the Jews (27:29, 37). Much earlier, the prophet Jeremiah evoked the pathos of the matriarch Rachel weeping over her exiled children, "because they were no more" (Jer. 31:15). Now the scene is repeated in Ramah, near Bethlehem, "Rachel weeping for her children." Here is the same old story of innocent victims and grieving mothers, of power used and abused. Near Yad Vashem, the Holocaust memorial in Jerusalem, stands a statue of weeping Rachel.

Again, God intervenes to tell Joseph that the tyrant Herod is dead and their time of exile is over (2:19-23). It is time for homecoming. But the son of Herod, Archelaus, now sits on his father's throne in Judea and Samaria. He proves to be more cruel and rapacious than his father and is finally removed by orders of the emperor himself (4 B.C.E.–6 C.E.). Joseph hears the rumors about Archelaus and is afraid. One final time a dream guides him to Nazareth in Galilee, where Jesus of Nazareth grows up. Herod Antipas, another son of Herod the Great, becomes his ruler. They are safe for a time, but Herod Antipas will one day behead John the Baptizer and regard Jesus with suspicious eyes (14:1-2).

At the very outset of Matthew's Gospel, therefore, we encounter the conflict between those who hold power politically and the coming of Jesus. There are two kings, two ways to rule in the world. One governs by terror and armed might; the other will take the path of peace and gentleness and reconciliation. Jesus will die as innocent victim, like the infants in Bethlehem. Thus already here in the infancy narratives we experience the same tension with the political realm that will lead to Jesus' death and to the ongoing persecution of his followers. There can finally be no accommodation with rulers like Herod. "All authority in heaven and earth has been given to me" (28:18). With these words Matthew ends his Gospel by a call to undivided loyalty to the sovereign loyalty of Jesus and his way of exercising divine righteousness and mercy and healing for humankind.

Jesus and the Temple Tax: "Free ... but" (Matt. 17:24-27)
This tradition, preserved only in Matthew, sheds important light on the attitude of the Matthean Jesus toward religious and political authorities. Matthew also preserves the debate on paying taxes to Caesar, as noted above. But here the controversy has to do with payment of the Temple tax, which was levied annually on all male Jews twenty and over, whether living in Israel or the Diaspora (excluded were women and slaves and possibly priests and rabbis). The tax consisted of a half-shekel (Greek: *didrachma*) that went for the upkeep of the Temple: building maintenance, support of priests and Levites, offerings and supplies, vestments and vessels, and care of the poor (Exod. 30:11-16). It was paid faithfully by most Jews, as a sign of their religious and national loyalty.[78]

The Jewish people living in Palestine faced a repressive system of double taxation.[79] One was levied by Rome on goods and services, along with the hated poll tax. Judas the Galilean led a major anti-tax revolt in 6 c.e., and there was continued tax-resistance until the massive popular uprising in 66–70 c.e.. The other tax supported religious functions. These included tithes of all produce plus the annual Temple tax. Obviously this double taxation became a heavy, sometimes impossible burden for the majority, either landed or landless peasants or the numerous family craftspeople in the villages and cities.

78. Josephus, *Ant.* 18.312; *War* 7.216–218.
79. Richard A. Horsley and John S. Hanson, *Bandits*, 55–56; Borg, *Jesus*, 84–86. Borg estimates that up to 40 percent of a peasant's income could go to pay these taxes. A few argue that this estimate is far too high and even think the Jewish taxes were not much higher than other conquered lands in the Roman empire. Whatever the exact figure, when poverty is ever-present, taxation becomes a heavy burden for the masses.

As the story now stands, it presupposes a pre-70 period, when the Temple was still standing. Followers of Jesus were asking about the payment of the tax. Do we still have to pay the annual half-shekel tax? The answer of the Matthean Jesus, however, does not provide a simple response.

We are told that the setting of the story is Capernaum, Jesus' base for his ministry in Galilee (17:24; 4:12-13). Since Capernaum is also the home of Peter and the site of Jesus' healing of Peter's mother-in-law, Peter's role in the story is appropriate (8:14-15). Once a year in the spring, on the 15th of Adar (the 12th month), tax collection tables were erected in Jewish communities outside Jerusalem to collect the tax. Accordingly, tax collectors in Capernaum approach Peter and ask whether "the teacher" pays the half-shekel Temple tax. Peter responds yes, and no further dialogue occurs. But when Peter returns, Jesus initiates the conversation about taxes. He asks Simon (Peter), whether the kings of the earth collect tolls or tributes from their own children or from others. When Peter responds, "From others," Jesus replies provocatively, "Then the children are free" (17:26).

What is meant? The argument is theological in nature. The true king of the universe is God. Therefore, as daughters and sons of God, all persons are de facto free, subject to no human authority. In particular, Jesus and those who confess Jesus as the Son of God are free (16:16; 17:5). This means, in effect, that the disciples of Jesus are free from the rule of earthly kings and even free from any obligation to pay the Temple tax. "Jesus is free and so is the new community of his sisters and brothers."[80]

These are subversive words. They make the claim that disciples of Jesus owe tax or obedience to no one but God. And neither human rulers nor religious authorities can usurp that freedom. No other text in the Gospels declares the sovereign freedom of the people of God over against all human authority with such force and clarity. If this were all that was said, the Jesus movement would indeed be a threat to all religious and political institutions. And, in the declaration in this text of the inherent freedom of the people of God in relation to God, all those who rule have rightly perceived the limits of their own authority.

But this is not all.[81] Freedom is the first word, but not the only word. Peter had earlier insisted that Jesus does pay the tax. Now Jesus explains in what sense he does submit (17:27). While he and his disciples are under no obligation to pay, Jesus does so in order not to give offense (*skandilizein*, "to cause offense"). And the miracle of the coin in the fish's mouth allows him

80. Robert H. Smith, *Matthew*, 214.

81. Did the original text end at v. 26 and Matthew or the early church add v. 27 for the sake of showing their loyalty to Israel and Judaism? A few have thought so. But the whole passage depends on the yes of Peter to the payment of the Temple tax, which is then explained in v. 27.

to pay, since the coin, a stater, is the exact equivalent of the half-shekel coin (*didrachma*). At other times in the Gospel, Jesus is not afraid to scandalize others (9:1-13; 12:1-14; 15:12-14). But on this occasion he deliberately chooses to curb his freedom in order not to cause offense. Matthew links this voluntary submission to the tax with the greater obedience of Jesus to the destiny of suffering divinely willed for him (17:22-24).

Freedom is the fundamental word: Jesus is free with respect to the Temple tax and free with respect to subordination toward earthly rulers. Yet, at the same time, Jesus demonstrates free submission to the powers that be and their limited claim on humanity and the people of God. This passage recognizes that Christians live between the two worlds of freedom and submission. They are free indeed, yet also bound by the need to submit for the good of the human community for the sake of love.[82] At times this freedom is precarious, threatened, or denied. In this passage, Jesus insists "the children are free." There are times to claim that freedom. But there are also times for subordination and submission and for not giving offense. Christian wisdom is to know the difference.[83]

Special Luke

Luke follows the Markan outline and employs Q, but he also draws from his own source (L) and makes his own considerable literary and theological contribution.

Luke presents the story of Jesus as the promised savior of the nations (24: 44-48). Central to Luke's portrait is Jesus' friendship with outcasts and sinners and his open embrace of all those on the margins of society. Luke creates a long travel narrative of Jesus' journey to Jerusalem and death (9:51—19:28). Luke also writes a second volume, the book of Acts. Luke-Acts together form a consecutive history of the founding of the Christian movement, from the time of Jesus to the time of the church. Both volumes must be interpreted simultaneously when one evaluates the work of Luke. The focus here, however, will be on the first volume, the story of Jesus, and those special Lukan traditions that illumine Jesus' relation to those in positions of authority. (An excursus will discuss the political views of Luke-Acts in light of recent controversy and scholarship; see below.)

---

82. Paul wrestles with the issue of freedom and submission for the sake of love in Rom. 14:1—15:6 and in 1 Cor. 8–9 on the question of whether Christians can eat meat offered to idols.

83. See above, chap. 2, for further discussion of the contemporary application of this principle.

Prologue and Lukan Infancy Narratives:
Pax Romana *versus* pax Christi *(Luke 1–2)*

Of all the evangelists, Luke exhibits the keenest interest in the historical context of Jesus' ministry. As both historian and theologian, he keeps his eye on the larger world and on how the events associated with Jesus affect that world. While Matthew portrays the birth of Jesus from within Jewish history as a clash of kingships, Luke grasps the events from a more universal perspective. Already in the literary prologue, Luke dedicates his Gospel to "most excellent Theophilus," most likely a Roman official of some status (Luke 1:1-4; cf. Acts 1:1-2).[84] In accordance with the custom of Hellenistic historians of his time, Luke intends to provide the necessary background so that Theophilus might better grasp the events concerning Jesus and all that has occurred. When Luke begins the account of John the Baptist's birth, he dates it carefully to the days of King Herod of Judea (1:5). Of greater weight in the Lukan story are the two references to the imperial setting that form the sociopolitical background for the universal story of Jesus (2:1; 3:1). Here is a clue to Luke's overall purpose: He sets before his readers a contrast between two kingdoms: the *pax Romana* and the *pax Christi*.

Birth of Jesus: pax Christi *(2:1-20)*. The Lukan infancy narratives differ almost completely from those of Matthew. They obviously represent another source known to the evangelist, involving the birth of both John the Baptist and Jesus. Luke, however, has put his own stamp on the material, so much so that at times it appears to be Lukan composition.[85] My interest lies with those themes that reflect Luke's attitude toward the world of politics and with Jesus' coming as the world's savior *(soter)*.

In 2:1, Luke dramatically announces the birth of Jesus within the framework of the rule of the Emperor Augustus and his decree that all the world must be enrolled. According to Luke, this imperial census was administered by Quirinius, the legate in Syria. While there are historical difficulties in dating the census at the time of Jesus' birth (6–4 B.C.E.), Luke's intent is to link world events and this special birth.[86] As a result of the emperor's

---

84. I am aware of the debate on the identity of Theophilus and the numerous questions about the exact meaning of the prologue. Theophilus was most probably a Gentile God-fearer who recently converted to Christianity; at the least he was a devout Gentile, like Cornelius (Acts 10), open to the Christian way. The discussion of Luke-Acts here does not hinge on the identity of Theophilus nor of Luke the evangelist.

85. See Brown, *Birth*, for a thorough discussion of the Matthean and Lukan birth narratives.

86. The Lukan census at the time of Jesus' birth would have had to occur before the death of King Herod (4 B.C.E.) under whom Jesus was born. However, Josephus dates the census at 6 C.E., when Archelaus was deposed and a Roman proconsulship established in Judea and

decree, Joseph and Mary must go to Bethlehem, the royal city of David, where Jesus is born.

At first reading, the significance of Luke's placement of events and naming of the world's figures can be easily overlooked. And familiarity with the simple but eloquently told Christmas story can prevent us from comprehending the social and political realities of the narratives. But the mention of Caesar Augustus, the census, and Quirinius would surely call to mind for Luke's readers the reality of Roman domination and military occupation. The *pax Romana* existed by the power of the sword. Little Judea was but one of many conquered peoples, yet it felt the sword and resisted it more mightily than most until the revolt of 66–70, which ended with the destruction of the city, the Temple, and the nation. The imperial census was especially hated, because it was the basis of paying tribute to imperial Rome. In the census of 6 c.e., under Quirinius of Syria, full-scale resistance broke out in Judea and Galilee, and the Roman legions expended considerable effort and time before it was crushed. Paying the tax to Caesar was the most visible sign of Israel's subjection to foreign powers. Jewish resistance movements and the peasants all agreed in opposing it. Therefore, when we read Luke's opening statement, "in those days" under the emperor and the census, we need immediately to fill in the historical reality of conflict and resentment and hatred against a foreign and tyrannical superpower.

Into this oppressive world Jesus was born. The setting of Bethlehem evokes the royal city of King David and the birth of a potential rival to imperial Rome. But Luke will soon show that the coming of Jesus belongs to another sphere than that of the *pax Romana*. Here again, an effort is required to hear the familiar birth-story with new ears. The birth itself occurs in a decidedly nonroyal setting. A lowly manger places this peasant family among the world's outcasts. The announcement to despised shepherds continues this theme.[87] They are strange messengers of hope for the world that runs against the imperial claims of Caesar. Yet that is precisely what Luke does. Angels appear to shepherds and relate the significance of Jesus' birth for Israel and humankind (2:8-14). This lowly child is savior of the world: the Messiah of Israel and Lord of the nations (2:11). As the

---

Samaria. Because no earlier record of a census exists, this latter date seems more likely, and it also agrees with what we know of Quirinius's tenure as legate of Syria. See Brown, *Birth*, Appendix 7, 547–56, for a thorough discussion of the problem.

87. Joachim Jeremias, *Jerusalem in the Time of Jesus*, trans. F. H. and C. H. Cave (Philadelphia: Fortress Press, 1969), 304–305, 310, shows how shepherds were frequently on the lists of despised or least desired occupations in first-century Palestine. The reasons had to do with their rugged appearance as well as the suspicion that they grazed their flocks on other person's pastures.

world's liberator, he brings the *pax Christi*, the reign of peace on earth (2:14). His coming is marked by great joy, not the fearful sound of marching armies. The angelic choir announces this new era of peace and gives glory to God for setting it in motion. Throughout the birth narrative, one sees how Luke dramatically and deliberately contrasts the reign of Emperor Augustus and the *pax Romana* with the reign of David's royal successor, Jesus, and the *pax Christi*. The one rules by force and arms and census, the other by lowliness and joy and peace. From the beginning, these two worlds are on a collision course, and they will do battle until the very end.

The preaching of John the Baptist (3:1-3). Luke's other significant reference to the imperial setting of his Gospel occurs in relation to the prophetic ministry of John. In effect, John's appearance initiates Jesus' ministry as well. Hence Luke carefully dates these momentous, world-shaking events, beginning with John. He lists all of the political participants: Emperor Tiberius, Pontius Pilate in Judea, Herod Antipas in Galilee, and the high priesthood of Annas and Caiaphas. In this way, the political rulers, both Roman and Jewish, provide the contrasting background to the prophetic movement of John and the one who comes after him. As the Gospel story unfolds, these two worlds remain in tension, the one calling people to repent and prepare for the imminent reign of God and the other consisting of those who rule by pretentious claims to earthly power and control.

Lukan hymns: The Magnificat, *The* Benedictus, *The* Nunc Dimittus. Among the special features of Luke's birth narratives are several hymns or psalms placed on the lips of key figures. Whatever their origin, they give eloquent expression to the hope and joy of early believers over the significance of Jesus' birth. Relevant to the topic at hand are the surprising political themes that arise in this material.[88]

The Magnificat *(1:46-56)*. The psalm attributed to Mary[89] has been much beloved throughout history, yet its political impact has received scant attention. It is a powerful song of praise about a God who reverses the ordinary way of action in the world. In the first half, Mary marvels at the personal favor God has shown to her (1:46-50). Although her own position in life is one of humbleness and insignificance (RSV, handmaiden), the

88. See Brown, *Birth*, 346–55, on the origin of the Lukan hymns, whether by Luke or of pre-Lukan formation. Brown is especially helpful on understanding the Old Testament background of the hymns.

89. Some early mss. have Elizabeth as the speaker. Although the majority still defend its attribution to Mary, many scholars now argue for Elizabeth. See Frederick Danker, *Jesus and the New Age according to Luke* (St. Louis: Clayton, 1972), 42, for the arguments favoring Elizabeth.

Mighty One has raised her up so that all generations will call her blessed. In the second half, the hymn exults in the God who continually puts down the mighty and lifts up the lowly. The key verses are 51-53: God reveals strength in the world by striking down the proud, the powerful and the rich; at the same time, God rescues the lowly and fills the needs of the hungry. The sociopolitical implications of this subversive hymn are immense. It proclaims a God who takes sides in history against the rich and powerful and those who rule, a God who promises to reverse the favored status of those who presently are in control. One can understand why this hymn was rediscovered in our day by liberation theology and by base Christian communities of the poor around the globe and even banned by some dictatorial regimes.[90] All political structures are here placed under the divine judgment. The God of Israel enters the arena of human history to right the wrongs of tyranny and domination and to promise new hope for the poor and oppressed.

The Benedictus *(1:67-79)*. The second hymn in the Lukan infancy narrative is placed on the lips of Zechariah, the priestly father of John. It, too, is filled with sociopolitical implications, and we should hear the hymn in light of the hope for national liberation alive in first-century Israel. What Luke attempts to do is to translate these literal expectations, linked with messianic and prophetic figures, to the coming of Jesus. He shows thereby how Jesus fulfills the promise of salvation through the house of David and through father Abraham (1:69, 73). Yet Jesus' coming as "mighty savior" (1:69) moves beyond national and political hopes to include a new covenant with a merciful God and a new way of peace. Thus we hear echoed throughout the hymn the hope for liberation "from our enemies" (1:68, 71, 74) mixed with the new covenant of forgiveness and era of peace (1:72, 75, 77, 79). Both political and spiritual liberation are inextricably intertwined. Along with the *Magnificat*, this hymn expresses the conviction that the days of deliverance are at hand with the coming of the savior from

90. See Robert McAfee Brown's introduction to liberation theology, in which he relates the fascinating account of a base Christian community in Brazil discovering the "real Mary" of the *Magnificat*, who belongs among the poor (*Theology in a New Key* [Philadelphia: Westminster Press, 1978], 97–100). Liberation theology emerged out of the struggle for justice in less developed lands throughout the world. It attempts to read the Bible through the eyes of the poor and their social and economic oppression. The *Magnificat* was banned by the government of El Salvador during the time of the martyrdom of Bishop Oscar Romero. Bishop Romero, a staunch advocate on behalf of the poor, was assassinated in San Salvador on March 24, 1980, in the very act of speaking the words of institution, while celebrating a memorial mass on Easter eve. Much earlier, the Reformer Martin Luther preached a powerful sermon on the *Magnificat* in which he, too, grasped its potentially subversive impact upon unjust rulers and princes. See *Luther's Works*, vol. 21, *The Sermon on the Mount and the Magnificat*, ed. Jaroslav Pelikan (St. Louis: Concordia Publishing House, 1956), 343–44.

the house of David. How this works out politically, Luke makes clear in the Gospel and Acts. Here Jesus' kingship becomes apolitical, in the sense his rule comes not by earthly power or national claims but through a new community of followers who take up his cause. Nevertheless, Luke shows that, even after the resurrection, there remained confusion among Jesus' closest followers about its political or national effects (Acts 1:6-7).

The Nunc Dimittus: *Simeon and Anna (2:25-38).* The parallel stories of Simeon and Anna, which conclude the birth narratives, reflect the same tension between Israel's hopes for national liberation and the coming of Jesus. The aged patriarch Simeon, described as a "just and devout" saint waiting for the "consolation of Israel" (2:25), sings a hymn of thanksgiving for the long-awaited "salvation" about to be fulfilled through the child Jesus (2:29-32, *Nunc Dimittus*). This salvation will bring liberation to the whole world, both Israel and the Gentiles.

When the matriarchal prophetess Anna encounters the child in the Temple, she, too, praises God for the "redemption of Jerusalem" now begun (2:38). This expected redemption sounds political, and it is. Yet Luke goes beyond this in the Gospel to define redemption in terms of Jesus' preaching of God's rule of mercy and peace now at work in the world. Later, the Lukan Jesus will lament over the fate of Jerusalem because it chooses the way of violence rather than the way of peace (19:41-44).

The birth narratives in Luke demonstrate how closely related are political and religious hopes. Readers not familiar with the story might wonder whether Jesus comes to claim political power and authority. This will finally not be so, but there is the revolutionary claim that a new era of peace and righteousness has dawned for the world. And this new age challenges and threatens the powers of the old age. Jesus, not Caesar Augustus, comes as savior of the world. Jesus, not Tiberius, is the Messiah and Lord. And Jesus inaugurates the *pax Christi,* not the *pax Romana.*

Inaugural Address: Good News to the Poor (4:16-30)

This text is important for understanding Luke's presentation of the ministry of Jesus. Luke structures his Gospel so that Jesus opens his public ministry with an inaugural address in the synagogue at Nazareth. While Luke draws from a similar tradition placed later by Mark (Mark 6:1-5), he adopts it for his own purposes in order to set forth the main themes of Jesus' preaching and activity. The second half of the speech deals with Jesus' rejection and so foreshadows the way to the cross (4:22b-30). It also anticipates the mission to the Gentiles outlined in the book of Acts. But the beginning section announces Jesus' programmatic mission as the Spirit-anointed servant of God (4:16-22a). This opening speech quotes from the

prophet Isaiah (Isa. 61:1-2; 58:6), which the Lukan Jesus then applies deliberately to himself (4:21). Its content proclaims words of good news to the
poor, the captives, the blind and the oppressed, claiming that their time of
liberation has come. One even hears echoes of the ancient year of Jubilee
("the year of the Lord's favor," 4:19), a time that promised release from all
debts and the return of ancestral lands.[91]

What is most intriguing is the fact that the Lukan Jesus quite literally
fulfills the Isaianic prophecy throughout the Gospel. The concretely poor,
sick, blind, outcast, and oppressed are set free (6:20-26; 7:18-23; 12:13-21;
14:12-14; 16:19-31; 19:1-10). Unlike Matthew, there is little spiritualizing of
Jesus' teaching. While there is also the inner dimension of freedom from sin
and its bondage throughout the Gospel (5:21; 15:1-32; 18:9-14; 24:47), social
evils are never forgotten or denied.

If we apply this text to those in positions of power, Jesus appears as the
great liberator of humankind. He comes to defend the poor, release those
imprisoned by debt, and proclaim freedom for all the oppressed. A great
reversal is taking place in which the weak and lowly are raised up and the
mighty overthrown (cf. the *Magnificat*, 1:51-53). A reader hearing this inaugural speech for the first time would doubtless envision Jesus as a prophetlike figure who calls for justice and who challenges all those structures that
oppress humankind. "The political language of the text is unmistakable.
Greco-Roman auditors would associate with the prophetic words the kinds
of expectations that were pronounced at the beginning of an imperial
reign."[92] Perhaps, too, a reader would become aware of the possibilities of
a collision course with the current holders of power, the emperor or his
puppets or those who hold religious office (2:1; 3:1-2). For the moment,
however, Jesus does not confront the authorities but rather an angry crowd
from his own people who question his credentials as the Isaianic prophet
and respond violently to his claim that God loves foreigners as much as
Jews (4:22b-30, Syrians). He escapes momentarily but the wheels of conflict
are set in motion, and they will finally crush him.

91. See Pilgrim, *Good News to the Poor*, 64–71, for a study of this inaugural text. On the
Jubilee year, see John H. Yoder, *The Politics of Jesus* (Grand Rapids, Mich.: Eerdmans, 1972),
64–77, who even thinks Jesus announced a literal jubilee in Nazareth. We find this most
unlikely; yet jubilee themes are present in the Gospel's presentation of Jesus' teaching. See also
Sharon Ringe, *Jesus, Liberation and the Biblical Jubilee* (Philadelphia: Fortress Press , 1985). The
Jubilee year, legislated for every fiftieth year, included requirements for the Sabbath year
(every seventh: debts canceled, fields lie fallow), plus the return of all ancestral lands to the
original owner (Lev. 25:10-24). However, it is doubtful that the Jubilee was ever literally enact-
ed in Israel's history.

92. Danker, *The New Age*, 107.

"Go and Tell that Fox" and the Lament over Jerusalem
(13:31-35//Matt. 23:37-39)

Although the lament over Jerusalem occurs in Q, I have waited until now to discuss it, because Luke has combined the lament with a brief story preserving Jesus' barbed response to his ruler, Herod Antipas.

In the Synoptic Gospels, this text on Herod stands out for its openly critical, if not hostile response by Jesus to one who holds political office— Jesus' own ruler, the tetrarch of Galilee and Perea. Luke displays a special interest in the relationship between Herod Antipas and Jesus. A son of Herod the Great, his lengthy rule was more tolerable than that of his father (4 B.C.E.–37 C.E.). But Herod is responsible for the death of John the Baptist. Although Luke omits the popular story of the Baptist's beheading at Herod's orders, he does make a brief mention of John's imprisonment, due to his denunciation of Herod's adulterous marriage to Herodias (3:19-20). Luke also preserves the account of Herod being disturbed by reports about Jesus' activity and wants to see him (9:7-9).[93] But nothing is said directly about any hostility on Herod's part. Later, in the passion history, Luke alone records the occasion when Herod finally does meet Jesus during his trial before Pilate (23:6-12). Yet Jesus maintains a deliberate silence, so that the encounter ends with Herod mocking and abusing Jesus but returning him to Pilate, acknowledging his political innocence.

The scene in 13:31-33 is unique to Luke. Now for the first time we learn about Herod's hostile intent. Some friendly Pharisees warn Jesus to flee because Herod seeks to kill him. But in response, Jesus issues his sharp retort, "Go and tell that fox . . ." and continues to speak words that defy Herod's murderous intent. The term "fox" implies a critical assessment of Herod and his rule.[94] In both classical and Hellenistic Greek, as well as Rabbinic literature, the term "fox" (Greek: *alopex*) is an epithet for a crafty

93. In the Markan account, Herod's guilty conscience leads him to fear that Jesus is the Baptist returned to life (Mark 6:14). In Luke, Herod asks only who this might be, because John has been beheaded (Luke 9:7-9).

94. A few try to argue that the term "fox" is not a hostile comment for Luke, since later, during Jesus' meeting with Herod, the tetrarch finds him innocent of any political crime (23:6-12); see Philip Esler, *Community and Gospel in Luke-Acts* (Cambridge: Cambridge University Press, 1987), 207. It is true that neither Herod nor Pilate find Jesus guilty of any crime deserving death (23:15). Yet this overlooks the fact that Herod grossly maltreats Jesus with abuse and contempt and mocks his supposed kingship in returning him to Pilate (23:11). This hardly smacks of friendship! Likewise, the term "fox" is always a critical term, never neutral. Moreover, Jesus' boldness in the face of Herod's murderous threat must be viewed as something other than submissive or obedient behavior. It borders on defiance: "Let him kill me if he will—I have better things to do." Nor can this be countered by saying that this may express the Lukan Jesus' critical attitude toward Jewish rulers, like the Herodian family (half-Jew), but not toward rulers in general and especially Roman rulers. Luke makes it clear that all political

or sly character, an epithet still in use. In fact, "fox" can become a term of contempt, something more like "skunk" or "rodent," which parallels the subsequent defiant saying of Jesus against Herod's threat.[95] This much can be said: "Jesus' uncompromising reply makes use of an unflattering term about the tetrarch of Galilee, the holder of political power, summing up his estimate of Herod's character and expressing his defiance of Herod's pretensions."[96]

Not only does Jesus declare his own ruler a "fox," however, but the sayings that follow reveal Jesus' refusal to be cowed by fear of Herod. In the first saying Jesus insists that despite Herod's threat he will continue his healing work until it is finished (13:32). The second saying repeats this theme ("today and tomorrow," for a time yet) but adds the motif of the necessity for Jesus to die in Jerusalem (13:33). This saying places Jesus' death within the context of the rejection experienced by Israel's prophets. A divine necessity (dei, "it is necessary") compels Jesus to suffer and die in the city that stones and kills the prophets (13:33-34). Throughout this passage, Jesus resolutely maintains that he will pursue his mission regardless of Herod's threat. In so doing, Jesus obeys a higher authority than that of Herod or any other Herods of this world.

This is a crucial text for revealing the Lukan Jesus' attitude toward those in power. The passage as a whole is a bold and courageous, if not defiant, response to one in authority. Jesus will not be forced into submission out of fear or respect, even toward his own ruler. Luke presents no meek and mild Jesus, no weak and cowering prophet, but one who lives under a sovereign authority, which no political ruler can challenge or deter.

Luke inserts the lament over Jerusalem, found in Q (Luke 13:34-35//Matt. 23:37-39) immediately after Jesus' provocative response to Herod, linking it to the catchword "Jerusalem" and its mistreatment of the prophets. While it thus becomes a part of Jesus' journey to Jerusalem in Luke (9:51), Matthew places it at the end of the journey in Jerusalem itself. Because it is addressed to the people of Jerusalem, Matthew's placement may more likely reflect its original Q location.

The words of Jesus reflect the profound pathos of the prophet who sees the tragic consequences of a people stubbornly turning away from the path

---

authorities, Jew or Gentile, may become hostile persecutors of Christ and his followers (Luke 21:12; Acts 4:25-27). I take up the disputed question of Luke's attitude toward Rome in the excursus.

95. As a term of contempt see H. W. Hoehner, *Herod Antipas* (*SNTSMS* 17; Cambridge: Cambridge University Press, 1972), 220–21, 343–47. Borg, *Jesus*, 163, suggests the translation "skunk" or "rodent."

96. Fitzmyer, *Luke*, vol. 2, 1029.

of peace. The saying is in the form of a prophetic lament ("Jerusalem, Jerusalem . . . how often I desired . . . you were not willing"). Because of their refusal to change, judgment will fall upon "your house" (13:35). By "house," the destruction of the Temple is probably meant. Although few prophets were actually killed in Jerusalem, the tradition existed of Jerusalem as the persecutor of prophets. A long history of struggle between Israel and Yahweh stands behind these words. And Jesus implies he will soon join the company of persecuted and rejected prophets. They may welcome him into Jerusalem with the cry of pilgrims ("Blessed is the one . . . ," 19:38) but that welcome will be short-lived.

In the midst of the prophetic lament we also find a wisdom-saying filled with tender compassion for Jerusalem and her people. As a teacher of wisdom, Jesus employs the feminine image of a "brooding mother-hen."[97] "How often have I desired to gather your children together as a hen gathers her brood under her wings . . ." (13:34//Matt 23:37). The imagery expresses the passionate longing of mother wisdom to care for those under her charge. But Jerusalem refuses to listen and so faces the imminent judgment.

Altogether, the lament portrays the figure of Jesus as a rejected prophet of peace and a teacher of wisdom. Nevertheless, despite the rejection, he responds not with hatred or counter-rejection but with the agony of the faithful prophet and the sorrow of brooding mother wisdom.

Jesus Weeps over Jerusalem: "The Things that Make for Peace"
(Luke 19:41-44)

Although this Lukan text occurs within the context of the passion history, it is closely linked with the lament over Jerusalem. By placing it immediately after Jesus' entry into Jerusalem, Luke draws a dramatic contrast between the enthusiastic welcome of the crowds and Jesus' weeping over the city that is ominously unaware of its fate.

The key motif is that of peace. Jesus comes as the messenger of peace— a favorite Lukan theme (1:79; 2:14; 13:35; 19:38). But Jerusalem rejects the way of peace. In part, this has to do with its rejection of Jesus himself as the final prophet of God and savior of humankind (2:14). But it includes the rejection of Jesus' teaching as well. Jesus taught the way of love even toward

---

97. On Jesus' relation to the wisdom tradition of Israel and his own claim to be a revealer of wisdom, see Borg, *Meeting Jesus Again*, chaps. 4–5). Wisdom Christology may reflect some of the earliest efforts to interpret Jesus. This fact, along with the feminine imagery, has created considerable interest today among New Testament scholars. Consult further, Elisabeth Johnson, "Jesus the Wisdom of God: A Biblical Basis for Non-Androcentric Christology," *Ephemenides Theologicae Lovaniensis* 61 (1987):261–94; Dianne Bergant, *What Are They Saying about Wisdom Literature?* (New York: Paulist Press, 1984); Elisabeth Schüssler Fiorenza, *Jesus: Miriam's Child, Sophia's Prophet* (New York: Continuum, 1994).

the enemy, the path of peace and reconciliation for humankind (6:27-36), but Jerusalem and its leaders will choose the way of violence and self-destruction. Jesus weeps because they do not recognize "the things that make for peace" (19:42) nor "the time of your visitation from God" (v. 44).

And because Jerusalem rejects the path of peace, Jesus foresees its coming dissolution in grim detail: ramparts, surrounded, hemmed in, children crushed, not one stone left upon another (19:43-44; cf. 21:20-24). Much of the imagery comes from the Old Testament and the plunder of Jerusalem by Babylon in 586 B.C.E. Luke himself writes after the fearful events of 70 C.E.. The Lukan Jesus weeps and the daughters of Jerusalem weep with him for themselves and their children (23:27-28). The city of peace, Jerusalem (*salem*, peace), ironically will become a graveyard of the dead. Despite the prediction, however, Luke is careful not to draw a direct line between the death of Jesus and the destruction of Jerusalem. The rejection of Jesus is but the final act among many in Jerusalem's tragic history of dealing with God's prophets (13:24), but the results still remain open for their final resolution.

Here, once again, Luke depicts the chasm between "the things that make for peace," the *pax Christi*, and all other ways to govern in the world. The other ways, such as the *pax Romana*, depend on the power of the sword. Jerusalem, too, will foolishly choose to resist the oppressor by force and suffer the consequences. The Lukan Jesus weeps, knowing what is hidden from their eyes.

The Two Swords: Enough of That! (Luke 22:33-38)

Although this text is found in the passion history in Luke, its content is fitting for the discussion of the special Lukan pre-passion traditions. Luke creates a table conversation between Jesus and the Twelve following the last supper (22:24-38). The Gospel of John has a similar "farewell discourse," only more extended and reflective of typical Johannine themes (John 13–17). In this post-meal conversation, Luke has drawn on traditions from Mark (dispute over greatness, 22:24-27; predictions of Peter's denial, 22:31-34) and added two from his own source (promises of the coming kingdom, 22:28-30; the two swords).

Past commentators referred to this text as "the two swords," but it is really about the imminent change of conditions caused by the death of Jesus and the disciples' failure to understand. In the dialogue itself, Jesus begins by reminding the disciples how he sent them out without "purse, bag, or sandal." The reference is to the sending of the Twelve (9:1-3), although Luke actually quotes the instructions from the later sending of the Seventy (10:4). When Jesus asks rhetorically, "Did you lack anything?" the disciples respond, "Nothing" (22:35). The hospitality of strangers had provided for them, as Jesus had promised (9:4).

The emphatic "But now . . ." marks the shift from "then" to "now," from present to future (22:36). "But now" things will be different. In the new time coming, it will be necessary to have "purse, bag, and sword" (the sword has replaced the "sandal" of 10:4). Why this dramatic shift from reliance upon the hospitality of others to greater self-reliance and awareness of potential conflict? Jesus explains from Scripture: "He was counted among the lawless" (22:37; Isa. 53:12). Several times in his two volumes, Luke cites Jesus' fulfillment of Deutero-Isaiah's portrait of the suffering servant of Yahweh (Acts 4:27; 8:32-35).[98] In this particular passage, the servant is treated as a criminal and outcast. And if Jesus is so treated, so will his disciples. Thus the need in the "now" time after his death for "purse, bag, and sword." Times of hardship and persecution lie ahead. And Jesus will no longer be with them.

The account ends with the disciples displaying total miscomprehension. They take Jesus' words literally about purse, bag, and especially sword: "Lord, look, here are two swords" (22:38). But Jesus speaks metaphorically and symbolically about the future. Violence or even armed self-protection are not in view. Jesus' reply to the disciples reflects their failure to grasp both these words and its entire mission. The NRSV does not do justice to the meaning ("It is enough"). Much better is the translation, "Enough of that!" "With no little irony, the Lukan Jesus exclaims, 'Enough of that!' His disillusionment is complete."[99]

A few interpreters have attempted to find a Zealot-like Jesus behind this text, who deliberately armed his disciples and who sought to foment an anti-Roman rebellion, but they make the same mistake as the disciples by interpreting the words literally. As we have seen, the Gospel portrait of Jesus is consistently and thoroughly antiviolent and pro-peace.

Jesus' opposition is of a different kind than the way of arms and violence. At Jesus' arrest, when one of the disciples asks, "Lord, should we strike with the sword?" and one actually cuts off the right ear of the high priest's slave, Jesus once more needs to say, "No more of this!" (22:49-51; Mark 26:52). Neither Jesus nor his followers take the path of violent resistance to those in authority. They are not outlaws or revolutionaries in this sense. They may resist those who rule—but not by the power of the sword.

98. Luke's postresurrection traditions especially underscore the role of Scripture in understanding Jesus' death and resurrection (24:26, 44–46). Isaiah 53 is but one of many passages the early church found helpful to explain his death. In his use of Isaiah 53, Luke surprisingly omits the vicarious references to the servant's death, focusing only on its necessity and the humiliation of his suffering.

99. Translation and quote from Fitzmyer, *Luke*, vol. 2, 1428, 1430.

"Enough of this!" and "No more of this!" mark the renunciation of earthly power and force to accomplish kingdom goals. Jesus' disciples are to learn another way.

Unfortunately, the history of the church demonstrates a tragic story of forgetfulness or denial of Jesus' renunciation of political claims and violence. And this text on the two swords has had a long history of misinterpretation.[100] But in truth, this passage denies the use of the sword or any kind of political claims by the church. There will be persecution and suffering for Jesus' followers and the need for self-preservation. But "enough" of playing with the sword of religious and civil power.

The Gospel of John

Christology and Politics in John

". . . And his own people did not accept him" (1:11). How does the Gospel of John portray Jesus' attitude toward those in positions of civil and political authority? In comparison to the Synoptics, John goes his own unique way in narrating the story of Jesus, including his presentation of Jesus' conflict with those in power, especially the religious leaders of Jerusalem. In fact, the Fourth Gospel heightens the conflict far beyond that of the Synoptic Gospels. The Johannine Jesus engages in polemical dialogue and debate with his religious opponents that become a life and death struggle to the end. Far from obedience to the religious authorities, he is constantly on the attack and pressing his claims concerning his true identity, regardless of the consequences.

The prologue, found only in John, sets forth the literary and theological agenda of the evangelist (1:1-18). The Gospel's purpose is the revelation of the preexistent Word to the world (1:14). But the incarnate Word receives a mixed response in the world. Some believe the revelation and become children of God. Yet others, especially among his own people, do not accept him (1:11). This struggle between belief and unbelief, ending in his rejection by the religious leaders, forms the main plot of the Gospel.

John also links the story of Jesus and the Jewish people to the larger picture of God's relation to the world. Jesus' conflict with his own people mir-

---

100. The flagrant misuse of this particular passage is best illustrated by the action of Pope Boniface VIII. In 1302 he issued the papal bull, *Unam Sanctum*, which appeals to Jesus' saying about "the two swords" to declare the doctrine that God has entrusted to the church the two swords of civil and spiritual authority. Although this obviously reflects late medieval interpretation of doctrine and Scripture, it is nonetheless totally contrary to the Lukan Jesus' teaching and intention. This passage, like so many others, denies the use of the sword or any kind of religiopolitical claims to power. No such doctrine of the two swords of religious and civil power exists in the teaching of Jesus.

rors the greater conflict between God and the unbelieving world. "The question of the creator and the kosmos, the world, becomes the question of Jesus and Israel. And when that question is resolved with the full paradox and irony of the crucifixion of the king of the Jews, then at once the world can become the beneficiary."[101]

In the Fourth Gospel, as in no other, the core of Jesus' conflict with his own people is christological, that is, it centers on the question of his identity. From the very beginning of his public ministry, Jesus' true identity as the one sent by God is openly proclaimed (cp. the messianic secret in the Synoptics). Jesus himself testifies to his divine origin and oneness with the Father. At the heart of John's Christology and the point of deepest conflict is the claim to be equal with God. All the Christological titles used of Jesus (Messiah, Son of God, Son of man, Lamb of God, King of Israel, I Am) are intended to make this fundamental assertion.

In response, Jesus' opponents ("the Jews,"[102] Pharisees, high priests) accuse him of blasphemy. And it becomes the source of the intense, bitter, sometimes acrimonious and near-violent debates between Jesus and his critics (chaps. 5–10). In these dialogues, the Johannine Jesus aggressively defends himself and his identity with the Father. He accuses the opponents of deliberately closing their hearts and refusing to believe in him or the Father who sent him. So embittered do things become that Jesus even charges his critics with being children of "their father the devil" (8:44). In turn, "the Jews" adamantly deny both his divine origin and claim to be the Messiah, and they seek his death. Clearly, behind this polemical crossfire in

101. N. T. Wright, *The New Testament and the People of God* (Minneapolis: Fortress Press, 1992), 412.

102. By "the Jews," John coins a new term for Jesus' opponents and those who refuse to believe in his divine origin. While there are different shades of meaning in the use of this term within the Gospel, the majority are found in a polemical context against Jesus' critics and the Judaism of John's day. On one level, "the Jews" is a kind of technical term for "the religious authorities, particularly those in Jerusalem, who are hostile to Jesus" (Raymond Brown, *The Gospel According to John I–XII* [Anchor Bible; Garden City, N.Y.: Doubleday, 1966], LXXI). They bring about his death. On another level, they represent the synagogues of Pharisaic Judaism, who are in bitter debate with the church in the Johannine community. The evangelist attacks them not for their moral and social conduct, as in the Synoptics, but for their refusal to believe in Jesus as the Messiah and their desire to persecute his followers. On yet a deeper level, "the Jews" become symbolic of the world and all those who remain in the darkness of unbelief. Robert Kysar, *John the Maverick Gospel* (Atlanta: John Knox Press, 1976), 55–58, among others, seeks to broaden the definition of "the Jews" in the Fourth Gospel. "They are not an ethnic, geographical, national or even religious group as much as a stereotype of rejection. Any person who refuses to accept the human identity proposed by Christ in the Gospel is for the evangelist a 'Jew'" (58). When we read the phrase "the Jews," therefore, these multidimensions of meaning need to be kept in view and any kind of racial or ethnic implications removed.

John's Gospel is the debate between synagogue and church over Jesus' Messiahship and its all too often hostile results.[103]

In the end, Jesus' death is the result of his Christological claims. But Christology and politics merge, so that Jesus' condemnation as a blasphemer leads to his execution by Rome.

Jesus and the Political Authorities: The Book of Signs (2:1—12:50).[104] The first half of the Fourth Gospel provides only a few glimpses of Jesus' attitude toward the political powers.

The "Cleansing" of the Temple (2:13-22). In striking contrast to the Synoptic tradition John places Jesus' "cleansing" of the Temple during the Passover at the beginning of Jesus' public ministry.[105] I will reserve full discussion on the cleansing until later (pp. 102–107). But this opening scene pits Jesus against the holders of religious and civil power in Jerusalem, in particular the high priests and their control of Judaism's most sacred institution, the Temple. In the Synoptics, the entry and cleansing together will arouse the religious authorities to seek Jesus' death at the hands of the Roman government. In John, it will be the raising of Lazarus (chap. 11) and the fear of Jesus' popularity that leads to the decisive action against him (11:45-53; 12:7-11, 17–19; etc.). But for readers who know the end of the story, the cleansing obviously initiates the series of provocative words and deeds that will cause the religious and civil leaders to force his execution by Rome.

Why this bold, even violent protest at the outset of John's Gospel? No doubt it points to the Johannine claim that Jesus fulfills all of Judaism, including the Temple. Jesus, in fact, replaces the Temple as the locus of Christian worship (2:19-22). It also demonstrates Jesus' opposition to the religious and civil leaders who control the Temple and abuse it for their own purposes.

103. See especially J. Louis Martyn's foundational study on the historical setting of John's Gospel during a period of separation between church and synagogue (*History and Theology in the Fourth Gospel*, rev. ed. (Nashville: Abingdon, 1979), 37–62. Martyn argues that a formal decision by some authoritative Jewish group to exclude from the synagogue Jews who confess Jesus as the Messiah occurred before John's writing (*aposynagôgos*, "excommunicate from the synagogue," 9:22, 34; 12:42; 16:2). Of the various possibilities for this official action, he finds the Rabbinic formation of the Eighteen Benedictions for synagogue prayer, and in particular the Twelfth Benediction against Heretics, to be the most probable (58).

104. Commentators generally agree on a twofold outline of the Fourth Gospel, the "Book of Signs" (2:1—12:50) and the "Book of Glory" (or Passion; 13:1—20:31). See Brown, *John I–XII*, CXXXVIII–CXLIV.

105. For arguments for and against the chronology of John, see Brown, *John I–XII*, 117–18, who thinks the Synoptics are correct but that Jesus spoke a prophetic warning about the Temple's destruction at his first visit on the Passover.

Feeding of the Five Thousand (6:1-15). The second moment of insight occurs in connection with the feeding of the five thousand. The sequence of feeding, and then crossing and walking on the water is paralleled in the Synoptics (Mark 6:30-52). But John's account of the miraculous feeding adds two informative details: the Passover setting (6:4, linked to the subsequent bread of life discourse, vv. 22-71) and the enthusiastic response of the crowds (6:14-15). The Markan story of the feeding offers no explanation for Jesus' abrupt dismissal of the disciples and crowds (Mark 6:45). But John attributes the action to an attempt by the excited masses to take Jesus by force and to make him king (6:15). The stupendous "sign" prompts the multitudes to believe Jesus is "the prophet who is to come into the world" (6:14), a messianic expectation. The same messianic identity is involved in the title "king."[106]

In response to the messianic acclaim, the Johannine Jesus deliberately withdraws from the crowds, thereby refusing to take the path of a political Messiah (cf. Jesus' dialogue with Pilate on the nature of Jesus' kingship, 18:33-38, see below). Although Jesus is the true "king of the Jews," as John's readers will come to see, his royalty is something quite other than earthly rule. Here Jesus disengages himself completely from all popular political movements.

The Sanhedrin Condemnation and the Prophecy of Caiaphas (11:45-57). The third text is found within the setting of the Sanhedrin's actions against Jesus. John concludes the first half of his Gospel with the story of the raising of Lazarus, the seventh and greatest sign (11:1-44). Immediately after the raising, the Sanhedrin convenes to plot Jesus' death. Their discussion revolves around the fear that Jesus' signs might cause a disturbance that would provoke the Romans to "destroy both our holy place and our nation" (11:48).[107] At the opportune moment, Caiaphas, high priest in that year, dramatically intervenes with his unwitting prophecy: "You do not understand that it is better to have one man die for the people than to have the whole nation destroyed" (11:50). Caiaphas's blunt statement is meant as a "common-sense maxim of political expediency."[108] That is, by getting rid of Jesus, a potential troublemaker with the Romans would be gone. Christian readers know that Jesus poses no threat to Rome nor to the Temple and nation. But John points to its inner truth as a death on behalf of Israel and

---

106. See Barnabas Lindars, *The Gospel of John* (New Century Commentary; Grand Rapids: Eerdmans, 1981), 244.

107. The "holy place" most likely refers to the Temple, although it could also mean Jerusalem. See C. K. Barrett, *The Gospel according to St. John* (London: SPCK, 1955), 338.

108. Brown, *John*, 442.

all future children of God (11:51-52). Yet Caiaphas's words prompt the Sanhedrin to seek Jesus' death.

While the debates with the Jewish leaders throughout the Gospel center
on Jesus' claim to oneness with God, here the conflict is broadened to
include the political dimensions of Jesus' actions. As the story unfolds further, both religious and political motives merge to bring about Jesus' death.
Yet the underlying cause remains religious, as the Johannine Jesus fulfills
the "hour" of destiny God has planned and which he willingly accepts.

The Book of Glory: The World's Hatred (15:18—16:4)
and Divine Protection (17:6-19)

The second half of John's Gospel, called the Book of Glory, narrates the
story of Jesus' death and resurrection in its own unique way as the "hour"
of Jesus' departure to the Father (13:1). It consists of the last meal, farewell
addresses to the disciples, and a final prayer by Jesus for his disciples and
the church. The passion history itself is very similar to the Synoptic tradition and so will be included later in the discussion of the passion history.

Even though the public ministry of Jesus is concluded by chapter 13, two
texts in this section are important for our understanding of the Johannine
Jesus' attitude toward those in positions of authority.

The world's hatred (15:18—16:4). In the midst of the farewell address, the
Johannine Jesus speaks of the world's hatred for the disciples. The term
"world," here and elsewhere in John, becomes a pejorative description of
the realm of unbelief.[109] Moreover, we now see how the story of Israel's
relationship to Jesus becomes the story of the world's rejection of the
Father. The disciples are warned that they will experience the same hatred
and suffering as their Master (15:18-20). It will mean hostility and persecution and expulsion from the synagogue (16:2). Those who do these things
will even think they are doing a service to God (*latreia,* "service," "worship"). But amid hatred and threats and potential martyrdom, Jesus assures
them they are not alone. He has chosen them out of the world; they possess
the Spirit/Paraclete from the Father (15:9, 26-27); they have been forewarned of their fate (16:4). The discourse concludes with strong words of
comfort: "I have said this to you, so that in me you may have peace. In the
world you face persecution. But take courage; I have conquered the world"
(16:33).

In this passage, the Johannine Jesus faces his approaching death and the
world's hatred without fear. Through trust in the Father who sent him, he

109. On the concept of the world, see Kysar, *John the Maverick Gospel,* 50–54.

has conquered the world and its hostile powers. Despite opposition and persecution, he promises the same victory to his followers.

"Protect them in your name" (17:6-19). The second text occurs in the farewell prayer that completes Jesus' conversation with his disciples. He prays first for himself (17:1-5) and then for the protection and unity and mission of his disciples. After his departure, the believers must cope with the hostility of the unbelieving world. So Jesus prays for the Father's continued presence: "Holy Father, protect them in your name . . ." (17:11). As Jesus kept his chosen disciples to the end (except one), so he prays that the Father will guard all future disciples (17:12).

The problem remains the world's hatred. Since the disciples are in but not of the world, they can expect the world's opposition.[110] Nevertheless, they are not to abandon the world by ascetic withdrawal or apocalyptic flight. But since the disciples do not belong to the world, they must be protected from it (17:6, 11, 14-15). Here the danger of apostasy (especially return to the synagogue) appears to be a real temptation for the Johannine community. Beyond divine protection, the believers are sanctified (*hagiazō*, "set apart," "sanctified") for the task of testifying to the truth about Jesus. As the Father sent Jesus, so Jesus sends his followers as witnesses of the love of the Father for the world, despite its hatred and unbelief (17:17-19).

According to this prayer, the attitude of Jesus toward the world is not one of hatred or fear or withdrawal, in spite of its unyielding opposition. He trusts in the Father and the divine purpose of his mission. Likewise, the disciples live under divine protection amid a hostile and unbelieving world. So they too can experience the joy and peace and confidence of knowing the Father and the Son and the mission they are set apart to do in the world.

Conclusion

How shall we characterize the attitude of Jesus toward the possessors of political authority in the fourth Gospel? The Gospel by and large concentrates on Jesus' conflict with the religious leaders of Judaism. "The Jews," Pharisees, high priests, and Sanhedrin are especially singled out for condemnation. Jesus' aggressive claims about his identity provoke their rejection and hostility and ultimately lead to his death. The Johannine debates center on the religious leaders because of the dual setting of the Gospel: the ministry of Jesus and his controversies with Pharisaic teaching and the

110. See Ernst Käsemann, *The Testament of Jesus according to John 17*, trans. Gerhard Krodel (Philadelphia: Fortress Press, 1968), for a profound discussion of this chapter and John's theology as a whole.

contemporary setting of the Johannine community's polemical debate with the synagogue. What we find, then, is no ethic of obedience to the religious and civil leaders of Judaism, but one of critical, at times radical distancing from their authority and teaching. Yet the response of Jesus and his followers to the hostility and persecution they experience is not one of hatred or revenge but of trust in divine protection (15:18—16:4; 17:6-19).

Little is said of the political powers in John. Not until the end of the Gospel do the Romans intervene and collaborate in Jesus' execution. But three passages do shed some light on the political dimensions of Jesus' ministry. The first is Jesus' cleansing of the Temple at the inauguration of his public ministry (2:13-22). This bold action affirms Jesus' claim over the Temple and sets the stage for the conflict unto death that ends in his crucifixion by Rome. The second is the action of the multitudes after the miraculous feeding to compel Jesus to become a king (6:14-15). By refusing this path, the Johannine Jesus rejects any kind of political or nationalistic grasp of his messiahship. He is no messianic Zealot, such as the later Simon bar Kochba (132 c.e.; cf. 18:33-37, "My kingdom is not of this world"). The third text is the scene before the Sanhedrin, when Caiaphas warns that Jesus may be a dangerous demagogue whose movement might cause Rome to act against "the nation and the holy place" (11:48-49). The reader, of course, knows this is a false accusation, since Jesus is neither a threat to Rome nor a dangerous troublemaker among his own people.

In sum, the Johannine Jesus is neither obedient to the authorities nor a Zealotlike potential revolutionary. His way is another way of obedience to the Father who sent him and to his glorification on the cross.

The Passion Narratives

It is now time to turn to the final events associated with the life of Jesus, the so-called passion history. Each of the Gospels depicts the life of Jesus as moving inexorably toward the climactic events of his life, his suffering and death in Jerusalem: He "suffered under Pontius Pilate, was crucified, died, and was buried." This memory belongs to the earliest creedal confession of the church. Since Jesus' death is to this extent a political act, it is necessary to review the main outline of the story in our attempt to grasp the Gospel's presentation of Jesus' attitude toward those who hold religious and political office. Most important, this survey will undergird my general thesis regarding the ethic of critical distancing toward those who govern found in the Gospels.

I shall discuss the passion tradition in two sections. The first concentrates on the entry and cleansing of the Temple that precede the passion events proper. I do this because of the singular significance of these two key events for this study. The second section will examine the passion events thematically, beginning with the last meal and the arrest in Gethsemane. In this way, certain important motifs will be lifted up without the need to look extensively at each event. Because the Gospel of John also follows the basic Synoptic outline of events for the passion history, both John and the Synoptics will be interpreted together. Due attention will be given to the individuality of each Gospel as well as the special Synoptic relationship.

Prelude to the Passion: Entry and Cleansing

Two provocative events prepare the way for the passion narrative in the Synoptics: the entry and the cleansing of the Temple (John has the entry [12:12-19] but moves the cleansing to the beginning of Jesus' ministry [2:13-22]). Each of these events is crucial for our understanding of the Gospel's portrayal of Jesus' attitude toward those who possess religious, civil, and political power.

Entry into Jerusalem (Mark 11:1-11, pars.)

Jerusalem is the long-awaited goal of Jesus' activity (Mark 8:31; 10:32; cp. Luke 9:51). What happens here is decisive and final. In fact, the Gospels depict Jesus going up to Jerusalem fully aware of the fate awaiting him.

The entry story begins with Jesus' instruction to two of his disciples regarding the colt, which may hint at some prearrangement (11:1-6; cf. 14:12-16, the Passover meal). Jesus mounts the colt and rides "triumphantly" from the Mount of Olives[111] down through the Kidron Valley and up into the Temple site. The disciples place their cloaks on the colt, while the people throw their robes on the path or strew it with cut branches (only John has "palm branches," 12:13). Shouts and applause accompany him along the way (traditional cries of pilgrims at festival times, Ps. 118:26). Mark makes no specific reference to Jesus' identity, unlike the other Gospels. All one hears is the expectation of "the coming kingdom of our ancestor David" (11:10). The entry ends with Jesus looking around the Temple and then retiring to Bethany for the night with his disciples. The cleansing occurs the next day. Nothing is said about the response of the religious leaders until after the cleansing. But then one learns of their rage and intent to kill him, prevented only by their fear of the people (11:18).

---

111. Many interpreters correctly note the messianic significance of the Mount of Olives in the first century. Some attempts by Messianic pretenders in the pre-70 period to foment political uprisings were quickly crushed by the Romans (see Josephus, War 2.13.5). Is there some kind of messianic expectation in the entry?

Mark leaves no doubt about the provocative nature of Jesus' action. Within the story line of the Gospel, this is the one time Jesus allows, if not solicits, the enthusiasm and support of the people. Otherwise one finds the so-called messianic secret, where Jesus commands silence from those he benefits (1:34, 43-44; 3:12; 5:43; etc.). Here that secret is broken with "Hosannas" from the crowds. Moreover, Jesus enters courageously and fearlessly, knowing full well the danger that awaits him. There is something deliberate and calculated to disturb in Jesus' action. Nevertheless, the symbol of a colt or donkey, as we shall see, carries with it a profound ambiguity that undergirds the whole event. While Mark leaves no clue about the size of the multitude, Matthew expands the tradition so that the whole city is stirred up (Matt. 21:10), and in John "the whole world has gone after him" (John 12:19).

The symbol of the entry upon a donkey[112] holds special importance. That it was young and not yet ridden upon conveys its fitness for sacral use. The donkey was the traditional beast of burden in biblical times. Yet there also existed a royal biblical tradition that portrayed the procession of kings upon a donkey (1 Kings 1). Especially was this so for kings associated with the last days (Gen. 49:1; Judg. 10:4; Zech. 9:9). The other evangelists interpret Jesus' entry out of this royal tradition and in particular as a symbolic action fulfilling Zechariah 9:9 (Matt. 21:4-5, pars.). Mark makes no special reference to this tradition, yet it may lie in the background.[113] What one can say with certainty is that Mark understands the entry as a public affirmation of Jesus, linked with the hope of the coming kingdom of David (11:10; 10:47, "Son of David"). Yet the symbol of the donkey brings with it a built-in tension between other traditional Near Eastern figures of royalty and this king. As Mark has already noted, unlike other Gentile rulers, Jesus does not come to lord it over others (10:41-45). In fact, the rejection and crucifixion that constitute the finale of this king's story subvert all notions of royalty.

Matthew makes explicit the Messianic identity of Jesus (21:1-11; v. 9, "Son of David"). The crowds, however, only recognize "the prophet Jesus from Nazareth in Galilee" (21:11). Above all, Matthew exegetes the entry out of Zechariah 9:9. Jesus' action fulfills this royal prophecy (21:4-5).[114] And Matthew underscores one feature of this king: humbleness or meekness or gentleness (cf. 5:5; 11:29). Thus Matthew's quotation in Zechariah 9:9 deliberately omits the phrase "triumphant and victorious" to concentrate only

---

112. Mark 11:2; Greek, *pôlos*, "colt"; a donkey or an ass is meant.

113. See Sanders, *Jesus and Judaism*, 235, 308, 326.

114. In fact, Matthew depicts Jesus as literally fulfilling the prophecy by riding on both the foal and colt, thereby misinterpreting the Hebrew parallelism (21:7)!

on humbleness: "[Jesus] now also mounts to kingship by means of lowliness and in the midst of deepest humility, without money or bribes, without arms or violence, without demagoguery or propaganda."[115]

In Luke's abbreviated version the crowds are largely the disciples, who praise God for all the mighty works done by the prophet Jesus (19:28-40). They explicitly name Jesus as king, and their words parallel the song of the angels at Jesus' birth (19:38; 2:14; 13:35). For Luke, Jesus is the king who brings peace on earth as in heaven (1:79; 2:14; 10:5-6; Acts 10:36). The contrast with the emperors and the *pax Romana* under which Jesus was born and crucified is all too obvious (2:1; 3:1).

John places the entry within his own setting of the raising of Lazarus, which in his Gospel becomes the reason for Jesus' arrest and crucifixion (12:12-19; cf. the Synoptics, where the entry and cleansing cause the arrest). In John, the crowds address Jesus as "King of Israel" (12:13). One commentator thinks Jesus' entrance on a donkey in John is not a symbol of humility, as in the Synoptics (Zech. 9:9), but emphasizes Jesus' universal kingship to counter a potential political nationalism.[116] This may be so. However, in typical Johannine manner, John notes that only after the resurrection do the disciples grasp the meaning of the event and of Scripture (12:16).

How shall we interpret the entry? For Mark, the entry is a provocative, though nonmessianic action by Jesus interpreting his mission. The other Gospels transform it into a public messianic event. In each, Jesus deliberately and openly enters the holy city of tradition and Temple with the dark shadow of opposition gathering around him. His bold action challenges the religious and civil authorities to respond. In the Synoptics, the Passover setting increases the possibility for the entry and cleansing to be misunderstood as some kind of politically suspicious event linked with resistance movements. And they do cause the religious and political leaders to arrest Jesus and do away with him as a potential troublemaker.

At the same time, the entry on the donkey symbolizes something radically different. The entry "is a virtual parody of prevailing ideas of kingship."[117] Here authority and kingship are reinterpreted in terms of lowliness, service, and peacemaking. Here is kingship without violence or national ambition or imperial dominance. In this sense, the entry provides a paradigm of authority that contravenes all the traditional images, then and now.

---

115. Smith, *Matthew*, 244.

116. See Brown, *John, II*: "It is an affirmation of a universal kingship that will be achieved only when he is lifted up in death and resurrection" (462). While this is attractive, I do not think the symbol of humility is forgotten by John.

117. Borg, *Meeting Jesus Again*, 312.

The "Cleansing" of the Temple (Mark 11:15-19 pars.)
The second and even more provocative action of Jesus preceding the passion history is the cleansing of the Temple. Of all the activities of Jesus in the Gospels, this is the one most overtly hostile to those in authority. In fact, this is the one event that associates Jesus with forceful, if not violent, protest. According to the Synoptics, the cleansing challenges those in power as never before and leads directly to Jesus' arrest.[118] It therefore deserves our careful perusal.

In Mark the cleansing is sandwiched within the cursing of the fig tree (11:12-14, 20-25). In this way Mark interprets the event as a sign of God's judgment upon unfruitful Israel. Mark has Jesus cleanse the Temple on the day after the entry (11:12, 15; cf. Matt. 21:12; Luke 19:45, on the same day; John 2:13, early in ministry). The previous day he had entered the Temple and looked around, but he did nothing (11:11). Now he reenters the Temple and determinedly goes about his bold protest. It seems deliberate and preplanned. Two actions occur: Jesus drives out the buyers and sellers of sacrificial animals and overturns the tables of the money-changers and dove-sellers. Both actions involve aggressive physical force (the verb to drive out, *ekballō*, includes compulsion; the tables and chairs are literally pushed over, *katastrephō*). This is no mere shouting match. Mark implies that everyone was driven out, although the language is imprecise.

It is important to keep in mind that both sacrificial animals and conversion of money were necessary for Temple worship. Both are prescribed in the Law. The animals sold included doves, cattle, and lambs (Passover) along with wine, oil, and salt. The sacrifices were offered to make atonement for sin and other purposes (thanks, purification, Luke 2:22-24; Mark 1:45). Likewise, money-changers were required to convert the foreign currency into the requisite Tyrian coinage. Every Jewish male also paid his annual half-shekel tax to the Temple in the same coinage. Jews themselves did not mint coins except during brief periods of revolt (66–70; 132–135 C.E.; also during Maccabean independence, ca. 165–65 B.C.E.). Therefore, neither activity in itself could be the object of religious protest, if the Temple was to remain vital for Jewish religious life.

The location of the commerce was undoubtedly the Court of the Gentiles on the Temple mount. The Temple itself was a magnificent gift of Herod the Great to the Jewish people, one of the wonders of the ancient world (Mark 13:1; Luke 21:5; Acts 3:2,11). Despite their hatred of Herod, the people were proud of the Temple. The Temple area was divided into four courts, arranged progressively according to their religious significance:

---

118. Sanders, *Jesus and Judaism* 305, states graphically about Jesus' arrest: "The gun may already have been cocked, but it was the Temple demonstration which pulled the trigger."

Court of the Gentiles, Court of Women, Court of Israel (males only), Court of Priests (Holy of Holies, the innermost sanctuary). Thus the cleansing took place in the outermost area, where everyone, including Gentiles, could assemble and pray. To have the merchants and money-changers on the Temple mount was an obvious helpful and convenient service for festival pilgrims.

In addition to driving out the merchants and overturning the tables, Mark alone says, Jesus forbade anyone to carry goods through the Temple area (11:16). By so doing, Jesus objects to using the Temple mount as a shortcut into the city itself, a common practice due to its location. Here Jewish Rabbinic law would agree with Jesus.

But why this dramatic, forceful, angry protest? The Markan Jesus links together two quotes from Scripture: "My house shall be called a house of prayer for all the nations" (Isa. 56:7) and "But you have made it a den of robbers" (Jer. 7:11). The first comes from deutero-Isaiah's grand vision of a time when all nations will be included in God's salvation and worship on Mount Zion (Isa. 56). Although the other evangelists preserve this quotation, only Mark includes the phrase, "for all the nations." This shows Mark's special concern as an evangelist to a Gentile Christian community.

The second quotation arises out of Jeremiah's famous "Temple speech," in which the prophet fearlessly denounces the Temple abuse and prophesies its destruction (Jer. 7:1-15). Only friends in high places save Jeremiah's life. So here, Jesus accuses the religious leaders of turning the "house of prayer" into a "den of robbers." Actually, the translation "den of robbers" does not do justice to the Greek (*lēstēs*). The Greek implies much more than petty thievery or simple dishonesty. "Violent ones" or "bandit's lair" better suggest the meaning, which implies a basic corruption that centers on the institution of the Temple.[119] The same word is used of the political rebels crucified with Jesus (15:27). Thus Jesus aims his attack at the core religious structure itself and claims it has perverted its true intent. The house of prayer has become a den of violent corruption.

Mark ends his account with the decision by the "chief priests and scribes" to kill him, fearful only of his popularity with the people (11:18).

Matthew follows Mark with two exceptions: The cleansing occurs the same day as the entry (21:12), and he omits "for all the nations" from Isa. 56:7 (21:13). But Matthew then adds a relatively long section in which Jesus' heals the blind and lame in the Temple and receives the acclaim of children as "Son of David" (21:14-16). This shifts the focus away from the cleansing itself as a sign of protest against the Temple's corruption. Instead, the healings reveal Jesus qualifying those formerly excluded: the blind and lame (2 Sam. 5:8). While the religious leaders do not object to the cleansing or healings, they do reject the claim that Jesus is the Son of David. But in Matthew, the children recognize the compassion of God at work in the Son of David. Would Matthew replace Temple sacrifice with acts of mercy (9:13; 12:7; 20:28-34)?

Luke's order of events differs: entry, lament over Jerusalem, cleansing— all on the same day (19:28-48). His abbreviated account gives the impression that Jesus' teaching in the Temple matters most of all (19:45-48); Jesus enters and drives out only the sellers. Like Matthew, Luke omits "for all the nations," a surprise, given his universal outlook. After the cleansing, Jesus goes immediately into the Temple and teaches daily (19:47). The authorities plot his death.

John, as we have seen, differs sharply from the Synoptics by placing the cleansing at the beginning of Jesus' public ministry (2:13-22). In John, Jesus forcefully drives out the cattle and sheep and sellers of doves with a "whip of cords" (2:15, only John) and overturns the tables of the money-changers. This violent action is justified with the words, "Stop making my Father's house a marketplace!" (2:16).

When "the Jews" ask for an authoritative sign to validate this provocative act, Jesus responds, "Destroy this Temple and in three days I will raise it up" (2:19). In the Synoptics, this saying is only on the lips of false witnesses (Mark 14:58). The ensuing conversation, so typical of John's literary style, moves from their literal misunderstanding ("forty-six years," "three days") to the christological symbol of the Temple as Jesus' crucified and risen body.

What meaning did the cleansing have for the evangelists?

None of the Gospels presents the forceful protest in the Temple as the culmination of a Zealot-like plot to foment a rebellion against Rome. Whatever the intentions of Jesus, this does not cohere with the evangelist's portrait of Jesus' nonviolent and nonpolitical mission.[120] Similarly, the Gospels do not view the cleansing as an action of Jesus bent on destroying the Temple itself. Although this is charged at the Sanhedrin trial, the false witnesses give the lie to this accusation (Mark 14:58-59).

Nor is the demonstrative action directed against the Temple itself or the sacrificial system, as has sometimes been suggested. Yet, as noted, the selling of animals and the presence of the money-changers were necessary for Temple worship. To oppose these would be, in effect, to attack the

120. See Hengel, *Was Jesus Revolutionary?* and Cullmann, *Jesus and the Revolutionaries*, for a thorough refutation of the portrait of Jesus as a militant revolutionary or Zealot.

whole sacrificial system. But nowhere else in the Gospels does Jesus appear antisacrificial. Rather, he speaks as though sacrifices were self-evident (Mark 1:44; Matt. 5:23-24). Even Jesus' action in Mark of barring access to the Temple as a shortcut into the city upholds its holiness. Moreover, the worship of the earliest believers in the Temple is hardly explainable if Jesus was understood to be anti-Temple or antisacrifice (Acts 2:46; 3:1). Only Matthew's use of Hosea ("I desire mercy, not sacrifice," Hos. 6:6; Matt. 9:13; 12:7) may be considered anti-Temple, although it is best explained along prophetic lines as upholding both sacrifice and mercy; cf. Mark 12:33). The post-Easter church came to grasp Jesus' death as the one great sacrifice for the world and so no other was necessary (Mark 10:45; 1 Cor. 15:3; etc.). And John interprets Jesus' death and resurrection as the creation of a new Temple, with the new community the true worshipers of God (2:19; cf. Mark 14:57-58).

The Synoptics (and John 2:16, "marketplace") interpret Jesus' action as a prophetic protest against the misuse of the Temple. Each appeals to the Old Testament to contrast its original purpose, "a house of prayer," with its present condition, "a den of robbers." But what do the evangelists understand by "den of robbers"? It could refer to nothing more than the dishonesty and fleecing of the people by the merchants and money-changers.[121] Or they could think Jesus was simply trying to purify the Temple mount from all forms of commercial activity, along with the associated noise and traffic, so that the whole area might be more like a "house of prayer." But neither of these purposes seems sufficient cause in the evangelist's story to arouse Jesus to such bold and risky action or to incite the religious hierarchy to a death plot.

A more likely possibility is that behind the charge, den of robbers, lies the awareness of a more profound and systemic corruption associated with Temple worship. Historically, we know that in the time of Jesus, there was a massive system of exploitation by those possessing civil and religious control of the Temple. The high priestly and related families dominated the Temple both religiously and economically. From it they amassed exorbitant wealth, which became the basis for their power and influence. Large landholdings, payment of bribes, palatial dwellings, and political collaboration with the Roman procurator all flowed from this structural injustice and corruption. The people were keenly aware of it.[122] We also know that

121. The historical evidence indicates that the business was carefully controlled by those in charge and conducted with reasonable honesty. See I. Abrahams, *Studies in Pharisaism and the Gospels* (Cambridge: 1917, 1924 [reprinted New York, 1967]), 87.

122. In the Dead Sea Scroll commentary on Habakkuk 2:8, written by the Essene (?) community at Qumran, we read the following: "Concerning the last priests in Jerusalem who

Jewish resistance groups fighting against Roman occupation regarded the Sadducean and high priestly elite as their enemies and as collaborators with Rome. In the revolt of 66–67, when the rebels took control of Jerusalem and the Temple, their first actions were to destroy the record of debts owed to the wealthy and to cease praying for the emperor. They also attacked the nobles and chief priests in the upper city.[123] In light of this, the Gospel's presentation of Jesus' violent action in the Temple may have in view this fundamental injustice by the priestly elite in power. The teachers and sellers were part of a system that needed reform. The Gospels present a Jesus who acts with prophetic protest against the system and its benefactors and soon pays the price. The people would heartily approve, hence their "fear of the people." And Mark's reference to a "bandit's lair" thereby takes on greater weight and force.

Beyond the reference to the Temple's misuse, do the evangelists also understand the cleansing as a sign of its coming destruction?[124] Here we need to consider a number of anti-Temple sayings in the Gospels. In Mark, Jesus predicts its coming destruction (13:1-2). In the passion history, Jesus is twice accused of threatening its demise (by false witnesses before the Sanhedrin, Mark 14:57-58; by mockers at the cross, Mark 15:29-30; cf. John 2:19). At his death the Temple curtain is said to be torn in two (Mark 15:38).[125]

While the Gospels obviously reject any notion of Jesus' animosity toward or personal threat to the Temple, the predictions of its future destruction may indicate that the authors interpret the cleansing as a sign of its fate. Like Jeremiah's act of breaking an earthen pot to symbolize Jerusalem's fall (Jer. 19:10-15), so the cleansing may also be viewed as a prophetic act symbolizing the Temple's destruction.[126]

---

heap up riches and wealth by plundering peoples; but at the end of the days their riches, together with the fruit of their plundering, will be delivered into the hands of the army of the Kittim [Gentiles]; for it is they who are the 'rest of the peoples'" (1 QpHab 9:5-7).

123. Josephus, *War* 2.425-429. Josephus states explicitly that their motive was to gain the sympathy of the poor peasants against their rich debtors.

124. For this interpretation, see Borg, *Meeting Jesus Again*, 31, and especially Sanders, *Jesus and Judaism*, 70–76. See the critique of Sanders's view in n. 127, below.

125. Donald H. Juel, *Mark* (ACNT Minneapolis: Augsburg, 1990), 155, correctly observes regarding the cleansing in Mark: "Jesus' provocative act introduces a polemic against the Temple that carries through to the end of the Gospel."

126. "Like the classical prophets of ancient Israel, he performed symbolic actions: On one occasion he provocatively staged a demonstration in the Temple, overturning the tables of the money-changers and driving out the sellers of sacrificial animals" (Borg, *Meeting Jesus Again*, 31).

The Gospels thus depict Jesus as making a demonstrative, semiviolent protest in the Court of the Gentiles that consisted in overturning the tables of the money-changers and driving out the sellers of animals. The purpose of the action seems twofold: (1) A prophetic demonstration against the religious leaders, the Temple hierarchy and their co-collaborators. For them, the Temple provided a comprehensive system of exploitation. In God's name ("My Father's house . . ."), Jesus is pictured as protesting against this pervasive abuse. In so doing, Jesus threatens the central religious institution of Israel and their control over it. (2) A prophetic symbol of the Temple's coming destruction. Unlike the Romans, Jesus poses no literal threat to the Temple. Yet he foresees its coming fate and represents its violent end by human hands.

Like nothing else in the Gospels, the "cleansing" or, better, "Temple protest" depicts Jesus provoking those in authority. Together with the entry, it leads to Jesus' arrest and death. Jesus' action does not advocate armed resistance or active rebellion against the political and religious powers, but it does represent a bold and prophetic denunciation of social and religious injustice. Each of the evangelists retells the story with his respective emphasis, yet the action remains anchored in the story of Jesus as a testimony to one who could and did respond fearlessly and daringly against the holders of civil and religious authority.[127]

127. Even though my primary interest lies in the evangelists' understanding, recent scholarship on the historicity and meaning of the event can shed helpful light.

1. In his excellent study of the historical Jesus, E. P. Sanders regards the Temple cleansing as the surest starting point for studying the historical Jesus, and his chapter on the cleansing clears the air of much confusion surrounding the event (*Jesus and Judaism*, 61–76). Sanders argues that Jesus envisioned both the destruction and restoration of the Temple, a tradition found in other Jewish literature of the period. Thus the cleansing was an eschatological sign of these imminent events. I nonetheless depart from Sanders's interpretation of Jesus' expectation of a restored Temple: (a) It depends too heavily on his view of Jesus' eschatology, in which Sanders still shares the certainty of past scholarship that Jesus expected the imminent end; this once-assured result is now undergoing thorough questioning. (b) The Jewish literary evidence for a "restored Temple" is much weaker than Sanders proposes (see Craig Evans, "Jesus' Action in the Temple: Cleansing or Portent of Destruction?" *CBQ* 51 [1989], 249–50), who notes the diversity of views regarding a Temple [or none] in the messianic era, and who also objects that no passage suggests the Messiah or God would destroy the Temple). (c) Sanders minimizes the systemic injustice of the Jewish hierarchy who controlled the Temple. The latter is puzzling, since he states that the Temple hierarchy made "huge profits" and so had a "vested interest" in the Temple system (69). Yet he strangely draws no conclusions from it regarding Jesus' action, except to quickly dismiss the possibility.

2. Craig A. Evans, "Jesus' Action in the Temple: Cleansing or Portent of Destruction?" (see above) 237–70, responds in part to Sanders's claim that there was nothing inherently wrong with the Temple establishment in the first century that needed cleansing. Evans provides much evidence that the Temple system was corrupt. After citing the Rabbis, Qumran, Josephus, and other contemporary sources, he concludes: "The evidence of corruption in the high-

The Passion Narratives: Jesus and the Powers that Be:
A Thematic Approach

Instead of a analysis of sequential details, I will approach the remainder of the passion narrative thematically.

Within the passion history itself are at least three general, pervasive motifs. One is the innocence of Jesus. The early Christians were keenly aware of the offensive nature of their claim that the one rejected by his own religious leaders and crucified for insurrection by the Romans was nevertheless the promised Messiah (cf. 1 Cor. 1:22-24). In response they demonstrate that the trials were a gross miscarriage of justice. In no way is Jesus guilty of any political or subversive crime deserving of death. A second motif is the responsibility of the Jewish religious leaders. Primary guilt is placed on their rejection and condemnation of Jesus and only secondarily attributed to Pilate. Whether this represents historical accuracy is open to

---

priesthood is sufficiently attested in diverse sources and is at times corroborated, at least in part, so that we cannot escape the conclusion that the high-priesthood of Jesus' time was in all likelihood corrupt (or at least was assumed to be so) and that Jesus' action in the Temple is direct evidence of this" (263). Evans does agree with Sanders, however, that Jesus' action may also include a warning of its coming destruction.

3. Using a social science approach and moving beyond the problem of Temple corruption, Douglas Oakman provides a more fundamental analysis of the oppressive Herodian social system in pre-70 C.E. Palestine ("Cursing Fig Trees and Robbers' Dens: Pronouncement Stories within Social-Systemic Perspective: Mark 11:12-25 and Parallels," in *Semeia 64: The Rhetoric of Pronouncement*, ed. V. I. Robbins [Atlanta: Scholar's Press, 1994], 253–72). Control by the Judean oligarchy (priestly upper class, village and town nobility, scribal administrators of the system) resulted in a systemic exploitation of the peasants and underclass by the ruling elite (see his diagram on p. 259). Oakman interprets both the cursing of the fig tree and the cursing of the Temple ("den of robbers") as Jesus' protest on behalf of the kingdom. On the Temple system: "The people who controlled the Temple trafficked in goods that the Temple system mandated. Oil and livestock were central to this activity; so was the use and exchange of money. Jesus' action calls all of this into question. His action focuses attention on the visible mechanisms of the Temple and the power of the Temple elite" (265). Oakman agrees that Jesus does not call for an end to sacrifice but rather for a new way to use the Temple to benefit everyone.

4. Han Dieter Betz ("Jesus and the Purity of the Temple [Mark 11:15-18]," [*JBL* 1997], 455–72) agrees that Jesus was not opposed in principle to the Temple or sacrifices but to the increased commercialism that undercut its purposes and to its paganization by the Herodian cult. "In his [Jesus] judgment, we can conclude the proper worship of God was compromised by Herod's subjection of the Temple to the political purpose of glorifying his kingship and by the intrusion of commercialism" (472). Betz provides extensive evidence both for its paganization (or Romanization) and commercialization that leads Jesus to call for a choice between "God and Mammon." But, like Sanders, Betz fails to see the corruption of the Temple by the wealth and power amassed by the Temple hierarchy, although it would fit the "God/Mammon" tension he sees. Against Sanders, Betz finds the theme of a restored Temple and Israel to be the views of the evangelist, not Jesus (459, n. 18).

serious doubt, but its determination is not decisive for this study.[128] A third motif is the use of Scripture. For the first believers, what happened to Jesus occurred "in accordance with the Scriptures." In many ways the passion narratives are meditations on Scripture. From the Scripture they discover its divine necessity and reflect on its salvific meaning.[129]

Beyond these general motifs the passion history offers only a bare outline of events. What we have is not detailed eyewitness reporting but only enough to narrate the key events through the Easter memory of the earliest followers and evangelists. I will now focus on four particular themes in the passion history relevant to our subject: (1) the silence of Jesus, (2) nonviolent suffering, (3) the nonpolitical realm, and (4) the sense of sovereign

128. Historically considered, who was responsible for Jesus' death? There is a pronounced tendency in the passion narratives to increase the guilt of the Jewish leaders (and people) and to exonerate Pilate and the Romans. This can best be explained by the growing conflict between church and synagogue in the first century, along with the desire to accommodate the Roman and civic authorities. Matthew's Gospel, for example, written in time of sharp tension with the synagogue, has the Jewish leaders and crowd push to the extreme for Jesus' execution. Luke, while not as favorable to Rome as some think, has Pilate repeatedly defend Jesus' innocence before his accusers. Does this mean that the role of Pilate has been obscured, if not removed, by the tradition?

Many argue that the Roman governor may have viewed Jesus as a potential troublemaker, if not politically dangerous. I think this possible. A few even want to argue the Romans bear the primary, if not sole, responsibility for Jesus' arrest and crucifixion. But not all responsibility can be shifted to Rome and away from the Temple hierarchy. The Gospels reflect a deep conflict between Jesus and the teachers of the law that is unresolved. Jesus' ministry met with increased opposition religiously and politically. His popularity with the people, like that of John the Baptist before him, may have seemed a genuine threat. His prophetic critique of the Temple and the elite holders of wealth and power, and his advocacy for the poor and marginal, challenged the status quo. His provocative arrival and presence in Jerusalem and the Temple likely sparked the religious authorities to respond. I therefore find a shared responsibility of collaboration between the Jewish leaders and the Roman ruler to be the closest to historical truth regarding Jesus' execution. One historical fact is certain, namely, his death by crucifixion at the hands of the Romans on the charge of political sedition.

I am aware of the tragic history of anti-Semitism to which some misreadings of the passion history have contributed. At this point, therefore, it is important to state that even the Gospels claim that the responsibility for Jesus' death lies not with the Jewish people (or even the Pharisees, who disappear from sight), but with the high-priestly Temple hierarchy and their control of the Sanhedrin.

129. Two recent studies illustrate the wide difference in scholarship on the passion narratives and especially their historicity. The monumental work of Raymond Brown, *The Death of the Messiah: From Gethsemane to the Grave*, 2 vols. (New York: Doubleday, 1994), adopts a historical-critical approach that takes seriously the possibility of a historical core in the passion tradition. But the response of John Dominic Crossan, *Who Killed Jesus? Exposing the Roots of Anti-Semitism in the Gospel Story of the Death of Jesus* (San Francisco: Harper, 1995), at times polemical, assumes virtually no historicity but instead posits a combination of scriptural and early church meditations on the passion. I find Crossan's whole starting point, especially his use of the apocryphal Gospel of Peter, to be historically weak, if not spurious.

authority. Each of the Gospels preserve these themes, even if each has its distinctive emphases.

The Silence of Jesus

The motif of silence is rooted in the two trial scenes before the Jewish and Roman officials. The first trial (or hearing) before Jewish officials, occurs immediately after Jesus' arrest.[130] According to Mark, Jesus is brought before the high priest and Sanhedrin, who seek capital charges against him (14:53-65). When the witnesses cannot agree on the accusations, including the charge of plotting the Temple's destruction, the high priest dramatically intervenes. He stands and demands that Jesus respond to the charges. But Jesus keeps silent (14:60-61). Not until the high priest asks if he is "the Messiah, the Son of the Blessed One" does Jesus finally respond by affirming his messiahship ("I am") and role as the coming Son of Man (14:61-62). Jesus does not speak again, despite his condemnation to death and brutal maltreatment by the Sanhedrin and guards.

Matthew's account also has Jesus silent before his accusers. Jesus speaks only to affirm his identity (Matt. 26:62-64, "You have said so"). Because Luke omits the charges of the false witnesses, the silence motif is also omitted. Again, Jesus responds only when asked about his messiahship (Luke 22:66-70).

With the Gospel of John, however, things are quite different, both here and throughout the passion history. While John follows the Synoptic outline of events, John goes his own way by inserting mini-dialogues between Jesus and his accusers, in which distinctive Johannine themes are developed. John also presents his own theological interpretation of the passion as the "hour" of Jesus' glorification, the moment of his enthronement on the cross as the Incarnate revealer of God (12:23, 32; 13:1). Therefore, at his arraignment before the high priest, Annas,[131] Jesus answers openly and

130. Although my primary interest is not historical, it should be noted that the so-called Jewish trial has caused much recent debate. While some argue it is a creation of the early church in reaction to conflict between the church and synagogue, most think the high-priestly leaders and Sanhedrin did initiate the arrest and charge against Jesus. Paul Winter, *On the Trial of Jesus*, rev. ed. by T. A. Burkill and Geza Vermes (Berlin: de Gruyter, 1974), argues that at most the high priest sought to turn Jesus over to Pilate. But David Catchpole, "The Problem of the Historicity of the Sanhedrin Trial," in *The Trial of Jesus*, ed. E. Bammel (SBT 2 13; London and Nashville, 1970), 47–65, argues for a more active role for the Sanhedrin and the high-priestly hierarchy. Perhaps historically it is best to think of the Jewish leader's action as more of a "hearing" or "grand jury" proceeding in order to determine charges against Jesus.

131. In John, it is the former high priest Annas who questions Jesus and then sends him to the acting high priest, Caiaphas, the son-in-law of Annas (John 18:13; cf. Luke 3:2). John's historical data are correct, with the wealthy and influential family of Annas in charge and bribing the Roman governor when necessary to stay in office. Although the Sanhedrin is not mentioned directly, it seems to be present in the trial before Pilate (18:28-31, "them," "Jews").

boldly when asked about his teaching (18:19-24). In fact, so sharply does Jesus speak that one of the police strikes Jesus on the face for insulting the high priest. But the Johannine Jesus does not back off (18:23). The theme of silence will appear only at the trial before Pilate (19:9).

The second and decisive trial occurs before the Roman governor, Pontius Pilate (Mark 15:1-15). According to Mark, the council brings Jesus to Pilate, who asks if Jesus is "King of the Jews." Jesus replies ambiguously, "You say so." But from that moment on Jesus remains silent, despite accusations, flogging, and condemnation (15:2-5). Mark observes Pilate's awe at Jesus' refusal to defend himself. In the Markan story, Jesus does not speak again until the final cry of abandonment from the cross (15:34).

Matthew follows Mark, only heightening the amazement of Pilate at Jesus' silence (Matt. 27:11-31, v. 14). Luke makes no direct reference to the silence during the trial before Pilate (Luke 23:1-5, 13-25). But he makes important use of it in Jesus' encounter with his own ruler, Herod Antipas (23:6-12). This passage occurs only in Luke. As noted above, regarding Jesus' barbed comment against "the fox," Herod, Herod finally gets his wish to meet Jesus face-to-face during his trial before Pilate. Herod hopes to see some miraculous deeds of Jesus (23:8). But despite Herod's lengthy questioning and the vehement accusations by the chief priests, Jesus adamantly refuses to speak or perform any sign (23:9-10). Disappointed, Herod sends Jesus back to Pilate, yet agrees that Jesus poses no political threat worthy of execution (23:15). In Luke's passion account, Jesus will only speak again to the weeping women of Jerusalem on the way to the cross and the three Lukan words from the cross.

In John, the trial before Pilate involves a dramatic struggle between Pilate and the Jewish leaders, with Pilate defending Jesus' innocence. When Pilate asks Jesus, "Are you the king of the Jews?" a dialogue takes place between them on the nature of Jesus' kingship (18:33-38). The next time Pilate questions Jesus, he remains silent (19:9). But when Pilate claims to have power to release or crucify him, Jesus replies by denying Pilate's power over him (19:9-11). No more will Jesus speak until the three Johannine words from the cross.

In short, the pattern is this: Jesus remains silent before his accusers, except when he makes the good confession of his identity or witnesses on behalf of his cause. What does it mean?

In part, it affirms Jesus' innocence. Before both Jewish and Roman officials, Jesus' silence convicts his accusers. This is "innocent silence before the clear expression of the power of this world."[132] It also belongs to the

---

132. Gerald Sloyan, *Jesus on Trial* (Philadelphia: Fortress Press, 1973), 70.

Gospel's portrayal of Jesus as "the righteous sufferer." By his silence he refuses to lash out with anger or curses or hatred. He practices the nonretaliation and love for the enemy he preached. His silence reveals a person of self-control amid the whirlwind of chaos and violence and death that swirls around him. Moreover, it is also a sign of protest against his accusers. Jesus will not be cowed or pushed into submissive words or actions contrary to his will. His action of silent protest speaks louder than words!

What might be the origin of this motif of silence? No doubt the use of Scripture to interpret Jesus' death played a key role. The "righteous sufferer" in the Psalms (Ps. 38:13-15; Ps. 69) and especially the suffering servant of Yahweh (Isa. 53:7-8), "who opened not his mouth" before his accusers" (cf. Acts 8:32), stamped their image on Jesus' dying. Also, the memory of Jesus' character and readiness to face prophetic rejection and suffering were formative in its creation.

Whatever its origin, the motif of silence bears testimony to Jesus' attitude of resistance to and sovereignty over those who hold political and earthly power. Even before his accusers, he remains silent and unafraid, speaking only to make his good confession at the proper time (cf. Matt. 10:17-20//Luke 12:11-12).

Nonviolent Suffering[133]

A second theme permeating the passion history is Jesus' acceptance of suffering and and his refusal to strike back. This crucial motif appears in all the major events: the arrest, before the Sanhedrin and Pilate, on the cross.

The four Gospels place Jesus' arrest in Gethsemane, following the last meal with the disciples. According to Mark, Judas leads an armed crowd from the Temple hierarchy, who arrest Jesus by force, after Judas's betrayal (14:43-46). The religious leaders are named (chief priests, scribes, elders, 14:43), while those who arrest him are "a crowd," including the "slave of the high priest." Someone takes up his sword and cuts the ear of the slave.[134] In Mark, unlike the other Gospels, Jesus makes no response to the attack.

But Jesus does speak offensive words to his captors. In the ensuing conversation, he protests against the manner of his arrest and chides them for coming out with swords and clubs (14:48-49). By so doing, they treat him as a dangerous rebel or insurrectionist (*lēstēs*; cf. 11:17, "den of violent ones"). Yet they act in ignorance. For the Markan Jesus is no mil-

---

133. The discussion above of the Lukan conversation at the first meal, on the question of the sword, should be consulted (pp. 90–92). Both texts agree in presenting a nonviolent Jesus.

134. A few have seized on the disciples' possession of a sword as evidence of a militant Jesus with armed supporters. The Markan Jesus, however, in no way advocates the use of the sword, the presence of which can be explained as having protective purposes.

itant rebel, no Messianic revolutionary, no secret plotter. He has spoken openly in the Temple, where they could arrest him anytime, if they did not fear the people. On one level, therefore, here is a defiant response to those in authority. At the same time, Jesus distinguishes unambiguously between his mission and way and that of others. He comes in peace and willingly submits without violence or resistance to his arrest. The sword is not his way.

Matthew agrees with Mark, but he inserts a mini-speech by Jesus against the use of violence (Matt. 26:47-56; vv. 52-54). After a disciple draws the sword and severs the ear of the slave, Jesus issues a command to put the sword back. There follows a saying intended for all subsequent disciples: "For all who take the sword will perish by the sword" (26:52). The meaning is clear. Violence begets violence. The sword is not Jesus' way. Moreover, with biting irony, Jesus claims to have twelve legions of angels at his disposal (if a legion was 6000, this would be 72,000!). The Matthean Jesus thereby underscores the nonviolent, nonnationalistic, non-Zealot nature of the kingdom way (cf. 5:5, 9, 39, 43; 11:29; 21:5). He comes not to overthrow the Jewish leaders or Roman government but rather to create a new community of peace and compassion and obedience to the will of God.

In Luke's brief account, Jesus himself reproaches Judas and reprimands sharply the disciple who draws the sword: "No more of this!" (Luke 22:47-53, v. 51). Jesus then heals the servant's right ear and again challenges those who came to arrest him as though he were a dangerous rebel (22:52). The Lukan Jesus then solemnly declares this is his enemies' hour of power, the power of darkness (22:53).

John's narrative goes its own way at several key points (18:1-11). John omits Jesus' prayer in Gethsemane to escape the cup of suffering and apparently has both Jewish and Roman soldiers present at the arrest (18:3, 12). After the dramatic response of the soldiers to Jesus' words, "I am," Jesus severely rebukes Simon Peter for using the sword. The scene ends with the Johannine Jesus saying he must drink the cup of suffering the Father has given him (18:11). Once more, there is no simple or passive submission to political authority. Yet Jesus does submit voluntarily to the divine will for his life. But this way excludes the power of the sword.

In the appearances before the Sanhedrin and Pilate that lead to Jesus' sentence of death by crucifixion, the theme of nonviolent suffering continues. The Synoptics agree that in the Jewish hearing Jesus was charged with blasphemy and then handed over to Pilate (Mark 14:53-65 pars.).[135] After the condemnation, Jesus is spitefully abused: spit on, blindfolded and

135. What constitutes blasphemy? The claim to be the Messiah may be false or presumptuous, but not blasphemy. "The Blessed One" is a circumlocution for God, a Jewish way of

struck, beaten by guards (cp. 2 Cor. 11:24). With slight variations the others agree (Matt. 26:67, no beating; Luke 22:63-65, mocking, beaten only by guards, not assembly). In John, the only act mentioned is the slap by the high priest's guard (John 18:22). Nevertheless, despite the false accusations, the unjust decision for death, and the vindictive physical and moral abuse, Jesus does not respond in kind. He accepts the suffering quietly, nobly, patiently.

The trial before Pilate is much the same. Here Jesus receives the final verdict: guilty of insurrection; punishment by crucifixion. Roman power tolerates little room for suspected sedition or trouble-making. Both during and after the trial Jesus is once more brutally mistreated. Pilate releases the guilty insurrectionist Barabbas and has Jesus beaten and crucified in his place (Mark 15:6-15 pars.). The soldiers who crucify Jesus play the mocking sport of king, with a crown of thorns and royal robe and feigned homage (Mark 15:16-20; Matt. 27:27-31; John 19:2-3). In Luke, Herod Antipas and his soldiers do the mocking (Luke 23:11). But, once again, in spite of the successive rejection and suffering and gross miscarriage of justice that leads to execution, the Gospels depict an innocent and righteous sufferer who accepts in silence the ignominy heaped upon him. No outburst of hatred or anger or defiance against his persecutors crosses his lips.

The picture of nonviolent suffering is completed on the cross. While each evangelist testifies in his own way to the manner and significance of Jesus' dying, especially with reference to the last words spoken, there is unanimity with respect to Jesus' attitude toward his tormentors. In Mark and Matthew, the spectators—the chief priests and scribes and even the two rebels crucified with him—mockingly urge Jesus to save himself, as he claimed to save others (Mark 15:29-32; Matt. 27:39-44). He does not respond in kind. Jesus dies with the cry of abandonment on his lips.[136] While nei-

---

reverencing the divine name. Note that Jesus himself avoids the name of God in his response ("right hand of power," 14:62). According to the *Mishnah*, the rabbinic code of law (late 2d to the 3d centuries c.e.), blasphemy consists only in pronouncing the sacred name. Technically, Jesus does not therefore commit blasphemy. Yet it is likely we should understand blasphemy more generally, as any claim by humans for divine prerogatives or authority (cf. Mark 2:5, "forgive sin"). Such blasphemy is a capital offense normally accompanied by the "tearing of robes." Stoning would be the usual mode of execution. But here Jesus is sent to Pilate for trial and Roman execution.

136. The cry of abandonment appears in Mark 15:34-35 and Matt. 27:46-47). It originates from Ps. 22:1. According to Mark, Jesus' outburst in Aramaic (his mother tongue) causes some to misunderstand and think he is crying for Elijah, the promised end-time prophet. How should one interpret this cry? (a)Some take it in its literal sense as a cry of abandonment, a human response to intense suffering, loneliness, and nearness to death; he feels abandoned by friends, by disciples, and now also by God. Although he had proclaimed the nearness of God

ther Mark nor Matthew explain how, they show that Jesus' way of dying, in contrast to previous crucifixions, convinces the Roman centurion and those with him that Jesus was "truly . . . God's Son" (Mark 15:39//Matt. 27:54).

In Luke, the people watching are moved to beat their breasts, a sign of repentance, as they return home (23:27, 35, 48). The religious leaders and soldiers, however, scoff and mock his claims. Jesus keeps silence in spite of their taunts. And then Luke provides three words from the cross that express Jesus' forgiving attitude toward his persecutors. Jesus first prays, "Father, forgive them, for they do not know what they are doing" (23:34). If the text is authentic, these words express not only forgiveness for his executors but for all his enemies.[137] In the second Lukan word, Jesus welcomes one of the dying rebels crucified with him into the coming kingdom. And then Jesus himself dies by committing his life to God with the prayer of the Psalmist, "Father, into your hands I commit my Spirit" (Ps. 31:5). In so doing, the Lukan Jesus dies as the perfect martyr who puts his trust in God alone (cf. Acts 7:55-60, martyrdom of Stephen).

In John, there is no mocking on the cross, only the protest by the chief priests against the inscription of Pilate, "Jesus of Nazareth, King of the Jews," written in three different languages (John 19:19-22). Pilate refuses to alter the inscription. The soldiers divide his clothes and gamble for his seamless tunic, but they do not mock (19:23-25). The three Johannine words from the cross are different from Luke and Mark and not important for this study.

---

and prayed to God as his personal *Abba* (Mark 14:36), he now comes face to face with Abba's absence in his moment of dying. See Cranfield, *Mark*, 458. (b) Others observe that these words are the opening cry from Psalm 22, which becomes a prayer of trust in God by one who suffers unjustly. Accordingly, they think it is a prayer of commitment amid suffering and it is argued that Christian readers would understand it as such. See C. H. Dodd, *According to the Scriptures* (London, 1952), 97. The first interpretation is more persuasive, since it also fits well with the Markan passion story as a tragedy. See Dennis Nineham, *The Gospel of Mark* (Harmondsworth: Penguin Books, 1964), 427–29, for both interpretations. The historicity remains uncertain. Two systematic theologians present both historical and theological arguments for its historicity. See Hans Küng, *On Being a Christian*, trans. Edward Quinn (Garden City, N.J.: Doubleday, 1976), 340–42; and Jürgen Moltmann, *The Crucified God*, trans. R. A. Wilson and John Bowden (New York: Harper and Row, 1974; Minneapolis: Fortress Press, 1993), 146–47. Moltmann concludes that although it is a post-Easter interpretation, it is "as near as possible to the historical reality of Jesus' death" (147).

137. Some ancient mss. omit the saying, which does appear abruptly in the text, as though inserted. Yet many reliable mss. do have it, and it agrees with the spirit of the Lukan Gospel. Moreover, the story of the first martyr in Acts 7 seems modeled after Jesus' own dying, including these words (Acts 7:55-56, 59-60). See Fitzmyer, *Luke*, vol. 2, 1503, who is unable to decide on its authenticity.

Once more, we see in the Gospel depictions of the dying Jesus on the cross the character and spirit of one who suffers faithful to his cause, with compassion and mercy for all. The agony and pain of crucifixion do not harden his spirit nor lead to impassioned outbursts of hate. Even the cry of abandonment does not contradict this portrait but only reveals the inner depth of the struggle of the one who prayed, "Abba, Father," and who now reaches out in dying to the source and power of his life (Mark 14:36).

Throughout the passion history, Jesus is the model of nonviolent suffering. He refuses the path of violence as contrary to the kingdom way. Nowhere is there a hint of rage or bitterness or desire for revenge. Moreover, this portrait of nonviolent suffering is remarkably consistent with the pre-passion traditions in the Gospels. His teaching on love for the neighbor, love of enemy, and nonretaliation, along with his life for the service of others—all find their culmination in this motif lifted up so prominently in the passion.

The Nonpolitical Realm

By "nonpolitical" I mean that the evangelists do not present a Jesus who intended to liberate Israel from its political subjection to Rome or to create some kind of national entity as in the past or who made any messianic claims to religiopolitical rule over Israel. Already in the temptation account in Q, as we have seen, this kind of claim to earthly power was denied. Yet we need to proceed with caution, because the Gospels show that Jesus did not withdraw from the sphere of politics, as did the Essenes who retreated into the wilderness. Nor did Jesus concentrate only on spiritual matters and the inner life of obedience to the Law in some kind of Pharisaic abdication from political involvement. Nor did he escape into utopian or apocalyptic dreams for the future. Jesus' ministry in the Gospel is political in that he himself seeks to renew the public and social life and by the fact that he calls into being new communities of followers to do the same.[138]

The enigma of Jesus' life and death is that he was "crucified under Pontius Pilate" on the charge of political insurrection. Yet the evangelists and the early church insist the charge was false and the sentence a gross miscarriage of justice. In this sense, Jesus did not seek to establish any earthly realm to replace Rome or any other political structure, Jewish or Roman. This nonpolitical nature of Jesus' mission and identity is underscored throughout the passion history.

---

138. In this sense I am in basic agreement with John H. Yoder, who titles his pioneering study *The Politics of Jesus* and looks for the public and social implications of Jesus' teaching and activity. Of course, many other historical Jesus scholars today take a similar path.

During the last meal with his disciples, Jesus celebrates the Passover (according to the Synoptics) and institutes the memorial meal of his death in view of the coming kingdom (Mark 14:22-25 pars.). The coming kingdom is the promised messianic "age to come," not any earthly kingdom. Before the Sanhedrin, the main charge brought against Jesus is religious (blasphemy), not that he coveted messianic authority to rule over Israel (Mark 14:60-64, pars.).

The trial before Pilate especially contrasts Jesus' claim to kingship with other political claimants. The whole trial centers on the title, "King of the Jews." In Mark, Pilate first asks, "Are you the King of the Jews?" Jesus replies affirmatively, "You say so" (15:2). In what follows, however, it is clear that Pilate does not interpret this politically. He seeks Jesus' release instead of that of Barabbas, twice calls Jesus "king of the Jews" (15:9, 12), and defends his political innocence (15:10, 14). Only persistent pressure from the high-priestly inspired crowds leads to Pilate's submission and decision to crucify Jesus (15:11-15). The reader knows that Jesus is not guilty of insurrection as charged, nor does Pilate think so. Nevertheless, the inscription over the cross states the crime: "The King of the Jews" (15:26). Two other revolutionaries are also charged and crucified—only they rightly so (15:27). In the mocking by the soldiers of Jesus' royalty (purple cloak, crown of thorns, saluting and bowing, 15:16-20) and also in the taunting by the religious leaders on the cross (15:31-32), the issue of Jesus as "King of the Jews" appears one final time. The whole trial is thus bathed in deepest irony: crucified as a pseudo king of the Jews, Jesus dies as the authentic king of the Jews and humankind! By not coming down from the cross, he saves others and liberates the world. His burial by Joseph of Arimathea quietly notes Joseph's hope for the coming kingdom taught by Jesus (15:43).

While Matthew agrees on the basics, he heightens the drama with the disturbing dream of Pilate's wife concerning Jesus' innocence and with Pilate's public washing of his hands to declare his guiltlessness (Matt. 27:19, 24). Both actions confirm the political innocence of Jesus and the guilt of the Jewish leaders and people.[139]

Luke's passion also goes its own way at several points in emphasizing Jesus' nonpolitical understanding of the kingdom. During the post-meal

---

139. Matthew alone has the terrible cry of the people, "His blood be on us and on our children" (27:25). Not only is this a Matthean addition and so unhistorical, but it must be interpreted in light of the growing conflict between synagogue and church in Matthew's time and community. It is not to be understood as a general curse on the Jewish people, as some periods of Christian history have so tragically misused the text. Historically, at most, the Jewish religious leaders share responsibility for Jesus' death along with the Roman governor. A few see in this saying a positive statement: "Jesus' dying [blood] will effect the salvation of us and our children." See Smith, *Matthew*, 321–22.

conversation, Jesus promises his disciples a place at table in the coming kingdom and their role as judges over the twelve tribes of Israel (22:28-30). This refers to the idea of a restored Israel in the eschatological future. In Luke, the trial before Pilate begins with the political charges against Jesus: perverts the nation, forbids taxes to the emperor, claims messianic kingship (23:2). If true, Jesus and his movement would be dangerous to Rome. But Pilate is not fooled. Both he and Herod Antipas agree that Jesus' crimes and claims pose no political threat (22:13-15). Finally, on the cross, Jesus promises the dying rebel a place in the future kingdom ruled over by Jesus (23:43). In none of this do we hear any echo of earthly claims to power or rule.

John's Gospel develops the contrast between Jesus' realm and all human realms most fully and explicitly. This occurs first of all in the dialogue between Pilate and Jesus (18:33-38). When Pilate asks if Jesus is the King of the Jews, a conversation ensues in which Jesus claims his kingship is not of this world. Moreover, the Johannine Jesus goes on to distinguish between the two realms by reference to the use of force. If Jesus' kingdom were of this world (human), his followers would take up arms to defend his cause and resist his arrest. But the fact that they do not battle with swords implies that Jesus represents another way and another realm apart from this world (heavenly). No clearer statement is found in the Gospels with respect to the difference between the two sovereignties! The dialogue ends with Jesus agreeing he is a king ("You say I am") but one born to testify to the truth of another kind of kingship (18:37-38).

The other Johannine way of demonstrating Jesus' distinct manner of royalty involves the dramatic trial scene before Pilate and the Jews (19:1-16). Twice Pilate presents Jesus to the crowds as their king: once dressed in a crown of thorns and purple robe, with the words, "Behold the man!" (RSV), and then before the judgment seat called Gabbatha, with the words, "Behold your king" (RSV; 19:5, 14). When the Jews reply, "We have no king but the emperor," Pilate yields and gives the order to crucify (19:15-16). In this way, John brilliantly and profoundly reflects for his readers on the inner meaning of Jesus' kingship over against the political nature of all other human realms.

The Gospels do not shrink from using the title "king" for Jesus, as we have seen. Jesus is crucified as "king of the Jews." But they take great care to show the world that the act of crucifixion as a political crime was wrong and unjust. Moreover, the evangelists reinterpret the meaning of messianic hopes and royal claims linked to Jesus in nonpolitical terms. Jesus is the true king of humanity, when rightly understood. But his realm involves something other than possession of earthly power and authority. In particular, it rejects the use of the sword. The Johannine dialogue between

Jesus and Pilate reflects Johannine theology, yet it states the issue of competing views of royalty with utter clarity. This-worldly realms exercise their authority by lording it over others with the power of the sword. Jesus' realm is not of this world and so lays claim to another way to form human communities and to shape the world.

The passion traditions' emphasis upon the nonpolitical nature of Jesus' exercise of authority and claims to power are consistent with the pre-passion traditions as well. One can almost hear an echo of Jesus' saying on true greatness in the kingdom, in which those who rule over the Gentiles by virtue of the sword are contrasted with the servant way to rule in the new community of Jesus' disciples (Mark 10:35-45). From the beginning to the end of the Gospels, Jesus makes no earthly claims to power and rule, despite his crucifixion on precisely those grounds.

Sense of Sovereign Authority

The fourth theme in the passion narrative that bears on Jesus' attitude toward those holding religious and political power has to do with what we will call his sense of sovereign authority. Here I note those places where the evangelists show Jesus putting others on the defensive or making paramount claims for himself or acting with autonomous freedom toward his accusers and persecutors.

In Mark, this theme first arises at the arrest. After Judas betrays Jesus with a kiss, Jesus vigorously protests his violent and secret arrest. Nevertheless, he voluntarily submits, in obedience to the Scripture (Mark 14:48-49). The scriptural fulfillment theme occurs repeatedly with respect to Jesus' subordination to political rulers. Before the Sanhedrin, Jesus makes a remarkable claim about his present and future identity. When the high priest asks if he is the Messiah, Son of God, Jesus responds, "I am; and 'you will see the Son of Man seated at the right hand of the Power,' and 'coming with the clouds of heaven'" (14:61-62). This is the one time in Mark that Jesus openly acknowledges his Messiahship. Each of the three titles has its own importance and meaning: Messiah, Son of God, son of Man.[140] But by referring to himself with these titles, and especially as the Son of Man, the Markan Jesus stands before his accusers, the civil and religious authorities of Israel, as their future judge! The irony is not lost on Mark's readers. When Jesus appears before the Roman governor, Pilate, he

---

140. On Christology, see Paula Fredericksen, *From Jesus to Christ* (New Haven, Conn.: Yale University Press, 1988); Martin Hengel, *The Son of God*, trans. John Bowden (Philadelphia: Fortress Press, 1976); Larry Hurtado, *One God, One Lord: Early Christian Devotion and Ancient Jewish Monotheism* (Philadelphia: Fortress Press, 1988); Donald H. Juel, *Messianic Exegesis* (Philadelphia: Fortress Press, 1988).

will acknowledge his kingship but then remain silent in noble dignity until his crucifixion, despite repeated mocking and abuse.

Matthew heightens Jesus' authority at his arrest (Matt. 26:47-56). After Judas's kiss, Jesus tells him to do what he must do. The unwarranted use of the sword by a disciple prompts Jesus to claim he has twelve legions of angels at his disposal (note the Roman military terminology). The Matthean Jesus' authority far exceeds that of Pilate or Caesar or any human power. Yet he submits in accordance with the Scripture (26:53-54). Jesus, too, is obedient to authority, but only to one above all earthly rulers and powers. The other moment where Matthew goes beyond Mark occurs on the cross. When Jesus dies, not only does the Temple curtain tear in two, but a mighty earthquake causes many of the saints to arise (27:51-54). This cosmic event symbolizes Jesus' sovereign power over life and death. Appropriately, Matthew's Gospel concludes with the commission from the risen Lord: "All authority in heaven and earth has been given to me" (28:16). On this basis, the risen Lord commands the disciples to baptize and teach the nations to obey all that he has taught them. True authority and obedience belong to none but God and the crucified and risen Lord.

Luke's passion account likewise strengthens the impression of Jesus' control over the events that happen to him. At the arrest, Jesus first confronts Judas with his betrayal of friendship with a kiss but he then submits to the power of darkness now at work (22:48, 53). Before the council, Jesus responds testily, if not presumptuously, to the high priest's question concerning his messiahship ("If I tell you, you will not believe; and if I question you, you will not answer," 22:67-68), and he then affirms his divine sonship. On the way to the cross, Jesus warns the weeping women of Jerusalem of far more fearful times to come (23:28-30).[141] Upon the cross, Jesus extends a royal welcome into his kingdom to the penitent rebel (23:39-43). Luke's Gospel ends with the resurrected Lord commissioning the disciples to be his witnesses to all nations, beginning from Jerusalem (24:44-49; Acts 1:8). Only they await the "power from on high" to begin the task (Acts 2). As in Matthew, authentic power in Luke comes from God alone (24:49).

It is John's Gospel, however, that once again goes its own distinct way in stressing Jesus' authority. Recall that John presents the passion as the hour of Jesus' glorification, the moment of enthronement. Jesus, as it were,

---

141. The impending crisis is no doubt the destruction of Jerusalem (Luke 13:34-35; 19:41-44; 21:5-36). "Weep for yourselves and for your children" means that Jesus' martyrdom foreshadows their own approaching fate (22:38). The proverb about the "green wood" is difficult to understand. One possibility: "If God allows the innocent Jesus to suffer such a fate as Jerusalem prepares for him, what will be the fate of Jerusalem?" See Fitzmyer, *Luke, II*, 1498, for discussion.

marches as the divine king to his coronation on the cross. Accordingly, Jesus possesses foreknowledge of all that happens and puts his accusers on trial. At the arrest, despite knowing everything, Jesus steps forward and asks the soldiers whom they seek. At Jesus' reply, "I am" (Greek, *egō eimi*), they fall to the ground (18:4-6). A divine epiphany has appeared. When Jesus requests that his disciples go free, it fulfills Jesus' own words, not simply Scripture, as in the Synoptics (18:9).

In Jesus' appearance before Annas and Caiaphas, the high priests, what happens to him fulfills Caiaphas's unwitting prophecy: "It is better for you to have one person die for the people than to have the whole nation destroyed." As noted above, John interprets this christologically in terms of Jesus' atoning death for all people (11:49-53; 18:14). At Jesus' interrogation by Annas, Jesus adamantly insists that he has always spoken openly in the synagogue and Temple (18:19-24). Secrecy is not his way. Jesus then challenges the high priest to ask others about his teaching (18:21; "Don't bother asking me any more, since you obviously won't listen"). Jesus' assertive, almost defiant and hostile response provokes one of the police to strike Jesus on the face and to reprimand him for insulting the honor of the high priest's office (cf. Exod. 22:28).[142] But the Johannine Jesus goes on the attack. He defends himself and, in effect, says he has no reason to apologize for speaking the truth, even before the high priest (18:23). While the scene is uniquely Johannine, in the remainder of John's story, Jesus repeatedly acts with sovereign freedom. Jesus stands supreme above all those in positions of civil and political authority. If we had only John's passion history, Jesus would be a model of holy terror to all human authorities.

Before Pilate, we are told that what happens fulfills Jesus' prophecy of his manner of dying (18:32). Most striking is the active participation by Jesus. He scarcely is silent. As we have seen, mini-dialogues occur with Pilate in which Jesus vigorously defends himself. The first dialogue about kingship and truth is framed by the same question in the Synoptics concerning Jesus' kingship. But in John, Jesus presses Pilate sharply ("Do you say this on your own . . . ?") followed by Pilate's testy response ("Am I a Jew? . . . your own nation and chief priests have handed you over . . . ; 18:34-35). And when the sparring is over, Jesus delivers a monologue instructing Pilate on the two kinds of kingdoms (18:36-38).

The second dialogue is even more combative and revealing (19:8-12). Under pressure from the chief priests, Pilate is afraid. He questions Jesus again, but Jesus refuses to respond. When Pilate arrogantly claims that he has the power to release or crucify Jesus, the Johannine Jesus replies one

---

142. Exodus 22:28 forbids one to revile God or curse a leader of the people. Jesus receives the blow for rudeness, or for his refusal to give a direct answer to the high priest.

final time, "You have no power over me at all except what was given to you from above"; 19:11).[143] The tables are turned and Pilate is under authority. "No power over me!" No other statement in the Gospels rings with such sovereign authority. The Johannine Jesus here declares his absolute authority over every earthly power. Yet he submits in obedience to the will of God. The paradox is profound. On the way to the cross, the Johannine Jesus carries the cross himself, unlike the Synoptics (19:17, a sign of his enthronement?). On the cross, the final words, "It is finished," declare the mission given to him by the Father accomplished (19:30). Jesus bows his head and dies, handing his spirit to God. In the Johannine Pentecost, the risen Jesus appears and commissions his disciples ("as the Father has sent me, so I send you," 20:21) and gives them the Spirit to continue his work (20:19-23).

It is evident that the motif of authority underwent considerable development in the passion history, especially in the Fourth Gospel. However, it is already present in the Synoptics, as is also their portrayal of Jesus' suffering with a sense of freedom and in Jesus' self-claims. The paradox exists between Jesus' inherent authority as Messiah/Son of Man/King of the Jews and his voluntary submission to earthly powers. John draws out this paradox with dramatic profundity. No authority in heaven or earth is greater than Jesus and his sovereign obedience to God alone. Over and against all "this world's" religious and political structures, Jesus stands supreme. Yet he finally submits in obedience to a higher authority and accepts the path determined for him.

Conclusion to the Passion History

The entry and cleansing and the four motifs from the passion history outlined above show Jesus in continual tension with the religious and political authorities. He acts provocatively, subversively, courageously, and independently before both the Jewish leaders and the Roman governor. There is here no picture of meek submission or cowardly fear or blind obedience to those who rule. Yet Jesus does not turn on his accusers in revenge nor advocate armed resistance nor call for the demise of all those in authority. He finally submits to those who rule in obedience to the divine will that determines both his life and his death. The paradox is profound: free yet not free, sovereign yet bound. Here is one who stands far above those who rule, yet is "crucified under Pontius Pilate."

---

143. Translation from Brown, *Death of Messiah*, 822.

Summary: Jesus' Ethic of Distancing in the Gospels

This chapter has surveyed a wide variety of Gospel texts in order to uncover the attitude of Jesus expressed in these traditions toward religious and political structures and those who govern. A number of different emphases have emerged. But amid the differences, consistent themes have appeared.

On the one hand, the Jesus of the Gospels accepts the powers that be, both Jewish and Roman. He is no political revolutionary, no Zealot, no advocate of a theocracy created by human hands or political force. He does not preach the overthrow of the political order or armed revolt. He even permits the payment of tax to Caesar and the Temple hierarchy.

Moreover, in contrast to many of his contemporaries, Jesus chooses the path of reconciliation and peace between peoples and nations. Above all, he teaches a radical love ethic that includes forgiveness and love for the enemy and nonviolent resistance to evil. His journey to suffering and death reveals a willingness to suffer innocently at the hands of the religious and political authorities, without hatred or cries for revenge against his accusers.

On the other hand, the Jesus of the Gospels is no servile subject to those who rule. Although he accepts the political order, his allegiance is to God and God alone. Accordingly, his life from beginning to end is a history of conflict with those in power. It is the *pax Christi* versus the *pax Romana*. Throughout his ministry, Jesus refuses to be deterred by those who oppose his mission, including his own ruler. He criticizes those who abuse and misuse their power, wealth, and position. He allows the tax to Caesar but along with it calls for a higher obedience to the things of God. He persists in his preaching of the kingdom to the very end, despite the growing opposition and hostility from those in authority.

Especially do we see this conflict erupt at the end. By his entry and cleansing of the Temple, the Gospels depict a Jesus who deliberately provokes the religious and civil authorities to respond, and they do. His passion journey to death by crucifixion is filled with sharp criticism of and challenge to those who finally put him to death. He dies faithful to the cause his Abba/God had anointed him to do, the last in a long line of rejected prophets.

According to the Gospels, Jesus' vision of the inbreaking kingdom present in his words and deeds is something other than earthly or political. To echo Johannine words, Jesus' kingdom is "not of this world." It is the community of God's people called and shaped to be disciples of Jesus. This community is not established by earthly power and rule. In fact, life and leadership in this kingdom-community stands in acute relief from all political realms. Here all are welcome, especially the least, and leadership is characterized by humble service. In this respect, the politics of Jesus' community and all other human communities of control and dominance stand opposed to one another.

Jesus' way, therefore, is not that of simple subordination to those who rule. Noticeably absent is any call to pray for rulers or emperors or to honor and respect them as servants appointed by God. No saying to this effect was preserved in the tradition. Thus Paul has no word from the Lord in Romans 13, nor do the other New Testament authors who advocate the ethic of respect and subordination.

But neither does one find overt hostility toward rulers per se nor any description of the imperial state as the demonic manifestation of evil on earth or as the great anti-Christ, as we will find in Revelation. Yet at some points, Jesus' bold challenge to the political authorities appears closer to the view of Revelation than the loyalty tradition in the Pauline and post-Pauline literature. In the Gospels there is no peaceful coexistence between the inbreaking kingdom of God and the kingdoms of this world.

There is a distinct attitude toward the state in the Jesus' traditions of the Gospels, one that differs from both the ethic of subordination and also the ethic of resistance now to be explored.[144] I have called it the ethic of critical distancing. While Jesus accepts the necessary role of those who govern, he stands as a constant critic of the political and religious establishment, even daring ultimately to provoke it to change, at the risk of his own life.

144. Wolfgang Schrage, *Ethics*, 110–15, arrives at similar conclusions on the teaching of Jesus regarding the state, even though he does not finally recognize its distinctiveness in the New Testament. He observes that Jesus is neither a Zealot nor one who rejects the emperor in principle, yet remains a constant critic of the possessors of power (Schrage does not always grasp sufficiently the sharp opposition). "His death on the cross also confirms that any "Yes!" to the structures and institutions of the world is always accompanied by a "No!" *a critical distance and an inner freedom*" (115, emphasis added).

EXCURSUS:
CHURCH AND STATE IN
LUKE-ACTS

THE DISCUSSION OF JESUS' ATTITUDE TOWARD THOSE IN POWER IN THE
Gospels is complicated by the current debate over Luke-Acts. The
question about the Lukan attitude toward the religious and political
authorities has become a hotbed of controversy in contemporary scholarship. The positions range from those who think the evangelist deliberately
writes a pro-Roman apologia (a defense of the empire) to those who argue
that he stands in sharp opposition to those who rule.

This debate is of singular importance because of the significance of
Luke-Acts in our understanding of the early church. Luke's two volumes
include the only history of the origin of the church (Acts), so we must rely
in large measure on his telling of that story. In his attempt to write a founding history, Luke exhibits considerable interest in political affairs and in the
interaction between the early church and the Jewish and imperial authorities. At the same time, we see this relationship primarily through his eyes.
So if we inquire about the stance of the earliest church to the governing
powers, while the Lukan story is our main source, it needs to be checked
against the other New Testament writings, along with what can be learned
from nonbiblical sources. This excursus is intended to survey the controversy over the interpretation of Luke-Acts on this question and to offer a
critical judgment.[1]

---

1. For surveys of the controversy, see Mark Allen Powell, *What Are They Saying about Acts?*
(Mahway, N.J.: Paulist Press, 1991), chap. 4; and Philip Esler, *Community and Gospel in Luke-
Acts* (Cambridge: Cambridge University Press, 1987), 205–7.

Luke-Acts as a Political Apologetic (Pro-Roman Apologia)

Until recently, it was commonplace to interpret Luke-Acts as a document written at least in part to defend Christianity before the eyes of the Roman state. Although it took different forms, the basic argument was that the evangelist sought to demonstrate to his readers that Jesus and the movement founded by him posed no political threat to imperial rule and that Christianity and Rome could live together in relative peace and harmony. Whatever conflict there might be, past or present, could be attributed either to misunderstanding or the implacable hostility of the synagogue.[2] This argument for a pro-Roman apologia has taken two forms.

Luke-Acts as an Apologetic on Behalf of the Church to Rome (apologia pro ecclesia)

The majority of commentators believe Luke has shaped his traditions to defend the new Christian movement as politically innocent for outside readers. What kinds of evidence in Luke-Acts may be adduced?

1. In the Gospel, it is argued that the evangelist seems eager to synchronize political history with divine history (Luke 2:1-4; 3:1-2). Accordingly, in the birth narrative, Joseph responds with "unquestioning obedience to an imperial decree."[3] The entire birth stories appear to portray a close harmony between Roman politics and divine purpose, between the *pax Romana* and the *pax Christi*.[4]

Further, Luke's Gospel places Roman officials in a positive light. A Roman centurion "who loves our nation and built for us our synagogue" is praised for possessing a faith not found in Israel (7:1-10, v. 5). This story parallels the conversion of the Roman centurion Cornelius in Acts 10. For Luke, even soldiers have a place in the coming kingdom (3:14; 23:47, and many examples in Acts).

Of special importance is the role of Pilate during the trial of Jesus. Unlike Mark, Luke declares Jesus' innocence three times (23:4, 14-15, 22). Even Herod Antipas, Jesus' own ruler in Galilee, agrees (23:15). To the very

---

2. See Hans Conzelmann, *The Theology of St. Luke* (New York: Harper and Row, 1960); also Conzelmann, *Die Apostelgeschichte* (HNT VII: Tübingen: J. C. B. Mohr (Paul Siebeck, 1963), 10, who states that the two chief concerns in Acts are salvation history and the political apologetic. So Ernst Haenchen, *The Acts of the Apostles*, trans. Bernard Noble and Gerald Shinn (Oxford: Blackwell, 1971), 693. These scholars were among the first to develop this position from a purely redactional study of the Lukan writings. But scholars before and since have accepted this basic pro-Roman interpretation. For a fuller critique of Conzelmann, see n. 40, below.

3. Esler, *Community*, 202.

4. See the discussion in chapter 3, which takes the opposite stance toward the birth narratives.

end, Pilate finds Jesus innocent of any political crime deserving death. Pilate renders the verdict of crucifixion only after yielding to the insistent pressure from the Jewish leaders in Jerusalem.[5] Luke, in fact, leaves open the question of who actually crucified Jesus. As Luke tells it, Pilate finally yields to "their demands" (23:24) and then hands Jesus over "as they wished" (23:25). These ambiguous phrases appear to shift the blame from the representatives of Rome to the Jewish religious authorities. The Roman centurion at the cross confirms the political innocence of Jesus (23:47; cf. Mark 15:39).

2. The evidence in Acts for a political apologetic seems even more abundant.[6] Interpreters have long noted that Luke creates a familiar pattern in his presentation of Christian evangelists and missionaries as innocent victims. Although the evangelists are normally law-abiding and peaceful, when trouble does occur, it is Jewish agitators who are to blame. Roman authorities, in turn, recognize this and typically exonerate the Christians (Acts 13:44-51; 14:1-7, 19-20; 16:35-40; 17:1-8, 10-15; etc.).

Luke's presentation in Acts also shows Paul proud of his Roman citizenship and carrying out a cooperative and beneficial relation with Roman officials (13:7, 12; 16:19-24, 35-40; 18:12-17; 19:35-41; 21:23-29, 37-40; 23:26—24:23; 25:1-12; 26:30-32). Even Paul's appeal to Caesar exhibits an act of confidence in the just outcome of his trial before the emperor (25:11).

It is also argued that Luke draws a favorable picture of the Roman system as a whole—political, economic, legal, travel, even military. While individual Roman officials may be weak or corrupt, the system itself is fair and upholds law and order. Christians in no way aim at its overthrow, despite some occasional misunderstandings.

Upon the basis of this presumed favorable portrait, some commentators also proposed that Luke explicitly sought a special legal status for Christianity. Like its parent, Judaism, Luke covets a similar position as a legally protected religion (*religio licita*).[7] During the early first century, Judaism enjoyed a special privilege within the empire, which allowed it to practice its ancestral faith without interference. This privilege included keeping the Sabbath, circumcision, nonmilitary service, unhindered worship, and

---

5. E. Jane Via agrees that Luke places the chief responsibility on the Jewish and Gentile leaders (not the crowd), with "the Jewish rulers of Jerusalem most guilty" ("According to Luke, Who Put Jesus to Death?" *Political Issues in Luke-Acts*, ed. Richard Cassidy and Philip Scharper [Maryknoll, N Y : Orbis, 1983], 132).

6. I here follow Richard Cassidy's excellent summary in *Society and Politics in the Acts of the Apostles* (Maryknoll, N.Y.: Orbis, 1987), 145–50.

7. Haenchen was a staunch advocate of this theory (*Acts*), 693. Conzelmann agreed in his first edition but then dropped it in the revised edition, although he still insisted on a pro-Roman apologetic (*Theology of Luke*, rev. ed, 1981).

payment of the annual Temple tax. While Luke wants his Roman readers to distinguish between Judaism and its new offspring, at the same time he seeks to demonstrate that they should be granted the same legal status.

However, this theory has undergone severe criticism.[8] There is no sure evidence that Rome gave legal license to any religion. While it did grant special privilege to Jews, this seem to be based on a tradition of privilege stemming from the emperor, beginning with Julius Caesar, and not on any specific acts of Roman law. Moreover, in the post-70 period in which Luke writes—after the Jewish revolt—there would be no benefit from such status. Jews were suspect. In fact, those Jews who declared themselves as such had to pay the annual half-shekel Temple tax to the support of the pagan Temple in Rome, Jupiter Capitolini.

If this theory has proved untenable, another interpreter has suggested that Luke appeals to Roman respect for ancestral traditions.[9] Rome wisely displayed considerable tolerance for tradition, both in politics and religion. For this reason, it is argued, Luke emphasizes Christianity's historical link with Judaism and presents Christianity as a legitimate ancestral tradition. This coheres with Luke's overall purpose "to legitimate faith in Jesus Christ" as a religious movement compatible with allegiance to Rome.[10] While the ancestral hypothesis has some persuasiveness, the overall argument depends on one's agreement with the pro-Roman tendency in Luke-Acts.

Luke-Acts as an apologetic on behalf of Rome to the Church (apologia pro imperio).

This position is a variant of the theory that Luke writes a pro-Roman apologetic. While accepting the notion that Luke places the Roman government in a favorable light, a few recent commentators argue that Luke aims his apology at the church.[11] This argument reverses the direction of

8. See Esler, *Community*, 211–15, among others.

9. Ibid., 214–16.

10. Ibid., 210. Esler further argues that Luke writes an apology that also includes Roman members of his church (military, administrative), and thus he shapes the tradition to show that Christianity is not opposed to or inconsistent with the Roman system at its best. Individuals may err, but as a whole Rome is beneficial to the church and the church no enemy of Rome. Esler even goes so far as to suggest Luke thinks it permissible for Roman Christians to be present at pagan sacrifices, as long as they do not actively take part. But the Lukan evidence is nearly nonexistent (e.g., the example of Naaman the Syrian, Luke 4:27; see pp. 217-22). Here Esler imports Pauline discussion into Luke-Acts. Although helpful at some points, his overall attempt to identify the community is too precise and the study overlooks or too easily explains away any critical stance toward Rome in Luke-Acts.

11. Paul Walaskay, *And So We Came to Rome: The Political Perspective of St. Luke* (Cambridge: Cambridge University Press, 1983); Robert Maddox, *The Purpose of Luke-Acts*, ed. John Riches (Edinburgh: T. & T. Clark, 1982).

Luke's defense from a supposed outside readership (Roman) to the Christian community. In effect, Luke seeks to demonstrate to his Christian readers that the Roman state is no enemy. Christians need not fear the state, as long as they live peaceful and law-abiding lives. Luke wants to persuade Christians to adopt the best possible attitude toward Rome. Behind this concern, so it is argued, are Christians in Luke's community who have taken a negative or even hostile attitude toward the Roman government, which Luke subsequently tries to combat. While one interpreter thinks this negative stance arises out of apocalyptic enthusiasm over the imminent end, another posits Christians courting martyrdom.[12]

It is plausible that Luke may address his writings more to Christians than outsiders, although he keeps his eye as well on Gentile readers attracted to the church (proselytes, God fearers; Theophilus?). But there is little in Luke-Acts to document an underlying hostility to Rome that needs correcting. Although Stephen represents the first to follow Jesus on the path to martyrdom (Acts 6-8), nowhere do we get a sense that Christians court their ill treatment. Rather, their attitude is one of patient endurance toward suffering (14:22; 20:19, 23). Nor does Luke heighten the end-expectation in his writings. In fact, of all the Synoptics, he is the least apocalyptic, envisioning a time of the church whose duration is unknown.[13]

Luke-Acts as a Critical Apologetic

In strong opposition to the dominant view that Luke writes to promote harmony between the new faith and the political authorities, some recent voices argue that Luke-Acts adopts a nonconciliatory stance toward the state. While it is acknowledged that Luke does not advocate any anti-Roman zealotry, nevertheless both the Gospel and Acts present a political and religious stance that makes no compromise with either Jewish or Roman leaders. The prime advocate for this revised view is Richard Cassidy.[14] This is a thoughtful reexamination of the evidence, with which I basically agree, despite some minor reservations.

12. Walaskay, *Rome*, 65, posits the problem of apocalyptic enthusiasm, while Maddox, *Purpose*, 96, suggests the overenthusiasm of Christians courting martyrdom. With respect to martyrdom, only later, with Ignatius of Antioch (d. 110), does one begin to see this problem emerge. In Revelation (96 C.E.), despite the fear of imperial persecution, there is no trace of eagerness for martyrdom.

13. At this point Esler also agrees there is no basis for either "apocalyptic enthusiasm" (Walaskay) or an "ideology of martyrdom" (Maddox) in Luke-Acts (*Community*, 208-9). While he correctly rejects their key arguments, he finally does agree with their claim that there is no basic conflict between church and state in Luke-Acts.

14. The series of studies by Richard Cassidy: *The Social and Political Stance of Jesus in Luke's Gospel* (Maryknoll, N.Y.: Orbis, 1976); *Jesus, Politics, and Society: A Study of Luke's Gospel*

Luke's Gospel

What of Luke's treatment of the story of Jesus in the Gospel? Contrary to most others, Cassidy finds Luke's portrait sharply critical of those in power and devoid of any pro-Roman apologetic.[15]

1. Social Stance of Jesus. Cassidy begins his discussion by pointing to social patterns and practices of Jesus that contravene the existing social order. These include his concern for the poor, the infirm, women, and Gentiles. Especially significant is Jesus' powerful critique of the rich and the call to give up their "surplus possessions."[16] Moreover, Jesus advocates a new social order based on service and humility. Cassidy correctly sees the dispute over greatness in the kingdom as a key text illustrating the difference between political kingdoms and the new community initiated by Jesus (22:24-27). The "kings of the Gentiles" rule by dominance and power in resounding contrast to the Jesus community, where authority is measured in terms of service and self-giving. The kings may call themselves "benefactors" (sarcasm!) but in truth are oppressors. He finds no softening of the criticism in Luke.

(Maryknoll, N.Y.: Orbis, 1978); *Political Issues in Luke-Acts*, ed. Richard J. Cassidy and Philip J. Scharper (Maryknoll, N.Y.: Orbis, 1983); *Society and Politics in the Acts of the Apostles*, ed. Richard J. Cassidy (Maryknoll, N.Y.: Orbis, 1987).

   Others questioning or countering the mainstream: W. G. Kümmel, *Introduction to the New Testament*, "Acts," trans. A. J. Mattill (Nashville: Abingdon Press, 1966), 115, thinks that there are passages that defend the church against charges of hostility to the state yet finds this at best a secondary concern; C. K Barrett, *Luke the Historian in Recent Study* (London: Epworth, 1961), 63, similarly says that although some texts are intended to defend the political innocence of Christianity, it is absurd to interpret this as a primary purpose of Acts as a whole. Of special weight is the critique of Jacob Jervell, "Paul, The Teacher of Israel. The Apologetic Speeches of Paul in Acts," in *Luke and the People of God* (Minneapolis: Augsburg, 1972), 155–58. Although he concentrates on the trial of Paul in Acts 22–28, Jervell finds good reasons "which must raise suspicions about Luke's alleged political concern" (156). For example, contrary to the view that Luke describes Roman officials as well-disposed toward the church: "It is clear, however, that the Roman officials frequently appear in a somewhat unfortunate light in Luke's work—a curious way of proceeding vis-à-vis the court whose understanding or protection is being sought" (157). Other examples are given. Nevertheless, despite some growing voices, most commentators, often unreflectively, repeat the pro-Roman understanding of Luke-Acts. This needs thorough revision.

   15. My summary of Cassidy's views on the Gospel follow his outline in *Jesus, Politics, and Society*, 20–86 (chaps. 2–6). Esler, *Community*, 207, rightly criticizes Cassidy for unclarity over whether he seeks the historical Jesus or Luke's distinct portrait. However, despite the occasional confusion, Cassidy's overall purpose is to concentrate on the Lukan portrait.

   16. Cassidy, *Jesus*, 25–31. He correctly notes that in Luke the poor are the literally poor and social outcasts and that the Zacchaeus story is Luke's model for the decisive change necessary for the rich to share in the kingdom. See Walter Pilgrim, *Good News to the Poor*, 129–34, on Zacchaeus.

On violence, Jesus rejects the Zealot way. Instead, he opts for nonviolent resistance against unjust practices (not nonresistance). The Temple "protest" (i.e., cleansing) has in mind the economic injustices of the priestly leaders. In sum, the Lukan Jesus espouses a new order of social relations that conflicts with and challenges the status quo and its supporters.

2. *Jesus and the Political Rulers.* Here Cassidy develops the thesis that Luke consistently portrays Jesus as refusing to defer to or to cooperate with those who govern. With his own ruler in Galilee, Herod Antipas, Jesus denies any accommodation with that "fox," a term of scorn toward Herod's destructive and puppet role (13:31-33). Before the chief priests and their allies, who are Jesus' primary adversaries, he responds without fear or deference.

On the question of paying tax to Caesar, Cassidy rejects any kind of dualism of realms. Caesar also belongs to God's realm and so should be obeyed only when Caesar conforms to God's way; otherwise one must follow God rather than Caesar.[17] Jesus freely criticizes those who rule and finds "nothing sacrosanct about the Roman social order."[18]

3. *The trial and death of Jesus.* The pattern of refusal to cooperate with those in power continues in the trial scene of Luke. Before the Sanhedrin, Jesus answers "searingly" and asserts his authority over his accusers (22:67-70; v. 67, "If I tell you, you will not believe . . ."). Before Herod Antipas, Jesus remains resolutely silent (23:6-12).

And what of Pilate? As we have seen, most interpreters find Pilate's threefold insistence on Jesus' innocence to be Luke's way of informing his readers that Jesus and his followers are not a political threat to Rome. Cassidy, however, argues convincingly that the emphasis does not intend to establish Jesus' political innocence and loyalty to Rome "but rather to indicate in unmistakable terms that the chief priests and their allies were the ones primarily responsible for Jesus' ultimate fate."[19] It thus belongs to the anti-Jewish motif present in both the Gospel and Acts.

As for Pilate's surprising declaration of Jesus' innocence, even in the face of the Sanhedrin's accusations and the ambiguity of Jesus' response concerning his kingship, Cassidy says that Pilate knows Jesus is no Zealot, whatever else he may be (23:1-4). This explains Herod's equally surprising statement of innocence (23:15).

Finally, although Luke is at first unclear about who actually crucified Jesus ("they" in 23:26 could mean either the Jews or Pilate), Luke eventually makes it obvious that the Romans and Pilate bear ultimate responsibility (cf. Acts 4:26-27, etc.).

17. Cassidy, *Jesus, Politics, and Society,* 55-60. See the discussion above, pp. 129–31.
18. Ibid., 61.
19. Ibid., 69.

4. Predictions of hostility from Gentiles and Jews. On persecutions[20] Cassidy notes that the Lukan Jesus foresees hostility from religious and political authorities that future generations will suffer (21:12-19). The passage specifically names "synagogues and prisons . . . kings and governors" (21:12). Luke already has the story of Acts in view, where both religious (synagogues) and political (kings, Roman governors) leaders cause suffering and imprisonment and even martyrdom (Acts 4:25-27). No distinction is made between Jewish or Gentile opponents, although in Acts the Jewish hostility will be dominant. Nevertheless, here and elsewhere, both Jew and Gentile (Roman) belong to the social and political environment of opposition to the Christian message.[21]

Was Jesus a danger to the Roman Empire? Yes and no. While he rejected the use of violence and was not a militant revolutionary or any kind of political nationalist, he still posed an ultimate threat to Rome. The Lukan Jesus is not submissive to rulers or a passive citizen of either Herod's Galilee or of the Roman-governed Judea. His introduction of social and religious patterns disruptive to the status quo, along with his refusal to cooperate with the religious and political leaders, depict a Jesus founding subversive communities of followers.[22] And the story in Acts, as we will see, continues this pattern of opposition in the ongoing life of the early church.

Acts

Cassidy likewise argues against a pro-Roman political apologetic in the story of the church in Acts.

1. Acts does not represent Christians as law-abiding and harmless. Controversy continually dogs their steps and Christians determinedly pursue their course regardless of what the authorities say. A key text is Acts 5:29: "We must obey God rather than any human authority" (cf. 4:19-20). Here Peter and the apostles speak for the whole church in the story of Acts.

20. Cassidy, *Society and Politics*, 165.

21. Esler, *Community*, 207, tries to explain away this text by arguing that in Luke-Acts the Roman authorities only adjudicate cases, not prosecute! But such fine distinctions fail. Rather, in both volumes it is the Roman authorities who declare final innocence or guilt and who order and carry out the appropriate punishment.

22. Although I agree with Cassidy's general conclusion (*Jesus, Politics, and Society*, chap. 6), I do not find it overly helpful to compare Jesus and Gandhi. They both have a utopian vision of a new society (Jesus: the kingdom of God) and renounce violence in social relations, but beyond this it is difficult to go. Unlike Gandhi, Jesus does not deliberately initiate a campaign to confront the colonial powers ("Quit India"); in fact a new nationalism is not his goal. Nor is nonviolence the core of Jesus' teaching, vital as it is. Jesus' vision is more God-centered, with the dual love-command its ethical core. Moreover, God's action in bringing about change is more central in Jesus' teaching.

Nothing can hinder their prior responsibility to God, not even orders from the rulers in Jerusalem or any other rulers. Some have tried to restrict this strong statement only to the Jewish religious authorities, since it occurs in the early encounter before the Sanhedrin in Acts. But I agree with Cassidy that "Romans are reading Acts too."[23] This fundamental principle applies to all human authorities, religious and political, Jewish and Roman, in Luke-Acts.

A related episode occurs in Acts 17:6. Here the accusation is made before Roman civic officials ("politarchs") that "these people who have been turning the world upside down. . ." are causing trouble in Thessalonica as well. They are even described as traitors to the emperor, persons who follow a king other than Caesar. Luke plays with irony, since the charge that they act contrary to the decree of Caesar and proclaim another king, Jesus, is false if meant they are political revolutionaries. But it is true in the sense that they do "turn the world upside down" with their social values and with their new kinds of caring communities and above all with their ultimate allegiance to Jesus. The politarchs demand bail before they release the troublemakers and do nothing further to protect the innocent victims, Paul and Silas, who must flee (17:6-10).

2. Paul's attitude toward his Roman citizenship and toward Roman law is highly qualified in Acts. Cassidy agrees that Paul's citizenship does give Paul certain special privileges and protection. But more often than not the protection comes late and after physical abuse and maltreatment (16:35-39; 22:22-29).

Paul's appeal to Caesar is at best ambiguous. Here one must consider the puzzling ending of Acts, with Paul under house arrest, awaiting trial (28:16-31). Under the assumption that Luke knew Paul's fate, why does he remain silent about it (Paul's martyrdom, 60-65 C.E.; Acts, 80-90, C.E.)? If Paul had been released and Luke knew this, to report that fact would vindicate both the apostle and the imperial government. But it is more likely that Paul was martyred, and that Luke was aware of this. Accordingly, Luke's puzzling silence is interpreted by the majority as an attempt to put Rome in the best light and to preserve Paul's political innocence.[24] Once again, Cassidy

---

23. Cassidy, *Politics and Society*, 153.

24. Walaskay, *Rome*, 19–22, thinks that Paul's martyrdom by Nero would not be considered a disgrace or something evil, since even Roman authors saw Nero in a bad light for killing persons like Seneca, the famous philosopher and his own mentor. Walaskay proposes another explanation for Luke's silence: Luke is embarrassed by the fact that fellow Jewish Christians from Asia had a role in Paul's death. To argue this, however, he must use uncertain evidence from *1 Clement* and claim that Luke shifts the blame from Jewish Christians to "Jews from Asia" in his ending. Both arguments are hypothetical. But Walaskay agrees in general that the conclusion is not anti-Roman.

interprets things differently. Luke ends the story of Paul in silence over the outcome, with no favorable verdict in sight. This means that Roman justice is not done, despite Paul's dramatic appeal to the emperor.[25] In fact, Paul's whole trial is a classic case of judicial injustice.

I agree with this revised assessment of the ending of Acts. From the religious point of view, Paul's arrival in Rome completes Luke's vision of the universal mission (Acts 1:8). But from the political perspective, justice is never accomplished—with Paul as with Jesus. Despite the fact that Paul is free to carry on his missionary work and tries with mixed results to persuade Jews in Rome about the messiahship of Jesus, he languishes in prison for two years, with the sword of life or death over his head (28:30).

3. Luke does not portray the Roman system with special favor. Cassidy grants that some military officials are friendly and helpful, but, in general, justice is not the outcome throughout Acts. Paul receives unfair treatment before two Roman governors, who delay any decision in his case and who wait for bribes (Acts 24-25). After four long years of imprisonment and trial, no vindication occurs, and the appeal to Caesar only prolongs the injustice, as noted above. One can easily conclude that Roman law does not assure a just outcome in Paul's case, any more than it did in the case of Jesus.[26]

4. The response of Roman political officials to Christian missionaries in Acts is mixed. On the one hand, there are those who respond favorably: centurion Cornelius (10:1ff.); Sergius Paulus, governor of Cyprus (13:1ff.); Roman tribunal in Jerusalem (21:37-23:30); Felix, governor of Palestine (24:1ff.); Festus, successor to Felix (25:13-22, 30-32); Lysias and Julias, two military officials (27:1ff.). On the other hand, there are those who fail to carry out justice. Herod Agrippa I, a Roman official, although Jewish by race, kills James and imprisons Peter (12:1-5); a magistrate in Thessalonica demands bail and fails to protect Paul (17:8-10); Felix, governor of Palestine, seeks a bribe and delays Paul's trial (24:27). There is a clear recognition by Roman officials that Paul is not guilty of any political crime and could be set free if he had not appealed to the emperor (26:30-32). But the emperor and the system do not bring justice.

Although Cassidy does not appeal to this text, Acts 4:23-31 serves as a kind of leitmotif throughout Luke-Acts for Christians in relation to the political rulers. In this passage, the arrest of Peter and John is interpreted on the basis of Psalm 2:1-2. Luke emphasizes that the community of disci-

---

25. Cassidy, *Society and Politics*, 152.

26. Esler, *Community*, 204, claims that Roman judicial procedure "prevails over corrupt and lying local governors." But where did fair judicial procedure prevail either with Paul or with Jesus?

ples will be repeatedly opposed and persecuted by Gentile and Jewish authorities alike. "Kings" and "rulers" are specially named: Herod and Pilate, Gentiles and people of Israel (4:27). Most important, this passage fulfills the word of Jesus in the Gospel (Luke 21:12). Thus for Luke, both the Gospel and Acts bear out the truth of a church living under the threat of persecution from the synagogue and equally from the empire.

5. Finally, Cassidy alleges that other kinds of data in Acts are damaging to the political apologetic position. The thematic statement that Christians owe allegiance only to God (Acts 5:2) is not only to be applied to Jewish leaders. Likewise, Christians witness without regard to the commands or reactions of civil authorities throughout Acts. Wherever the Christian movement goes it creates public controversy. Cassidy recognizes that Jewish opposition is central, yet whenever Roman authorities get dragged in, the conflict stays unresolved. A Roman reader would not get the impression that Christianity will bring peace and stability but only more trouble, despite the religious nature of the conflict. Cassidy also calls attention to the explicitly double reference in Luke-Acts to the disciple Simon the Zealot (Luke 6:15; Acts 1:13). He finds this a surprising reference in a volume supposedly pro-Roman.[27]

We have indicated our basic agreement along the way with the attempt to demonstrate that Luke-Acts is something other than a political apologetic for Rome. I now want to add some comments and attempt a summary of the Lukan attitude toward those in political power.

Luke's Gospel

1. The infancy narratives. My reading of the birth stories is the exact opposite of those who find a pro-Roman tendency in Luke-Acts. The *pax Romana* and the *pax Christi* are not copartners in bringing peace and hope to the world but two contrary ways of envisioning community and ordering the world. Nor is the census the gift of a benevolent emperor to be unquestionably obeyed but rather the tyrannical instrument for oppressing the nations by the power of the sword. The census is the sign of subjection by taxation to the economic and military imperium that dominates the world. The *Magnificat* announces a God who acts to bring down the

---

27. Cassidy, *Society and Politics*, 155. Walaskay grants that the Zealot reference is anti-Roman, if meant for Roman readers (*Rome*, 13). But his thesis is that Luke writes for Christian ears and so he interprets this reference as a warning to the church against adopting a political revolutionary agenda, rather than keep to its task of witnessing (16). This reading is possible only if one adopts a pro-Roman stance on Luke-Acts, against which I argue. Likewise, the evidence for any problem with "revolutionary Christians" in Luke-Acts seems to be read into the text from outside.

oppressors and exalt the lowly (1:52), whose presence has now drawn near in the birth of the one divine savior and lord of the world (2:11).[28] The difference between the two realms is like that of night and day.

2. *Soldiers.* Luke's attitude toward military personnel is mixed. On the positive side, the Baptist welcomes soldiers, only warning them against extortion and discontent with their wages (3:14); centurions and tribunes play prominent roles (7:1-10; 23:47; Acts 10; 22:25-29: 23:22-23). On the negative side, soldiers arrest Jesus, mock and flog and crucify him brutally. Paul is severely beaten by order of a Roman magistrate (*praetor*; Acts 16:19, 22-23).[29] On the whole, soldiers in Luke-Acts carry out their harsh duties obediently, with the exceptions Luke takes care to note. No hostility to their profession itself seems apparent.

3. *Passion predictions.* The Lukan predictions of Jesus' death add one surprising feature that argues against a pro-Roman bias. In the first prediction, the Synoptics agree on naming the "elders, chief priests, and scribes" as those responsible for his death (Mark 8:31//Matt. 16:21//Luke 9:22). The second prediction mentions only "human hands" (Mark 9:31//Matt. 17:22-23//Luke 9:44). But in the third, Luke alone mentions the Gentiles and omits altogether the chief priests and scribes (Luke 18:32; cf. Mark 10:32-34//Matt. 20:18-19, who name both). From this, one could conclude that the Gentiles, i.e., the Romans, are the main instruments in fulfilling the fate predicted by the prophets. At the very least, Luke does not avoid the role of the Romans in putting Jesus to death.

---

28. In 27 B.C.E. Augustus was acclaimed divine (*divus*) and savior (*soter*) and one who would bring peace to the world. Consult Frederick Danker for excellent background material on the imperial claims, including an illuminating inscription from Priene (*New Age*, 54). Raymond Brown thinks that Luke notes the census either to show how the holy family got to Bethlehem or to contrast the "advent of the *pax Augusta* with that of the *pax Christi*" (*Birth*, 415). Brown and Danker agree that Luke challenges the imperial propaganda, although "not by denying the imperial ideals, but by claiming that the real peace of the world was brought about by Jesus" (Brown, *Birth*, 415); cf. Danker, *Luke*, 24). I agree that Luke challenges the imperial propaganda but I also find Luke sharply opposed to the imperial ideals.

Walaskay thinks otherwise. He admits the piling up of royal titles for Jesus over against Caesar would not evoke a positive response from Roman readers. But it is fine for Christians, for whom, he argues, Luke is writing. "Augustus had a part to play in God's plan for salvation. His edict set the plan in motion. . .and the *angels sang the doxology that the* pax Augusta *was completed (complemented) by the* pax Christi" (emphasis added). Or on the census, which he views positively: "Luke's message to the church is to follow the example of Jesus' parents. Pay taxes to whom taxes are due thus avoiding any suspicion about Christian loyalty" (*Rome*, 26, 27). This interpretation, however, lacks real appreciation for the social-historical reality of the *pax Romana*; it represents also a serious misreading of the text and Luke's purpose in the birth narratives.

29. Gerhard Krodel, *Acts* (Minneapolis: Augsburg, 1986), 309, writes: "The representatives of Roman law and order became the instruments of a hysterical mob."

4. Pilate and the slaughter of the Galileans (Luke 13:1-3). The story of the murdered Galileans occurs only in Luke. As introduced, it sounds as though the event happened within recent memory, but there is no historical certainty of its origin.[30] The massacre attributed to Pilate has to do with some incident within the Temple area in Jerusalem. Most likely it refers to soldiers of Pilate killing some Galilean pilgrims while they were offering their sacrifices in the Court of the Priest. No reason is given for Pilate's action. A few have suggested the Galileans were Zealot rebels or even that the "sacrifices" were Roman soldiers killed by Galilean freedom-fighters.[31] Although the latter is possible, the first explanation is preferable.

It is true that the main point of the event is the call to repentance (13:3; cf. 13:4-5). But the image of Pilate is that of a bloody tyrant, violating the sacred Temple in the midst of the act of sacrificial worship. With this description of Pilate, Josephus would agree. "Luke's picture of this episode is not contradicted by the brutal person depicted in Josephus' writings."[32] If Luke were trying to put Pilate or Roman justice in the best possible light, why would he include this tradition? No positive portrait is given of Roman rule or their puppet representatives.

5. The trial before Pilate. As noted earlier, the trial before Pilate has been used repeatedly as evidence of Luke's apologetic toward Rome. It is true that, in contrast to Mark, Luke has heightened the insistence by Pilate on the innocence of Jesus, particularly with Pilate's threefold assertion (23:4, 14, 22). But one can interpret this in line with Luke's anti-Jewish tendencies rather than as pro-Roman, as Cassidy has done. Pilate's declarations confirm the guilt of the Jewish leaders, and the same can be said for the ambiguity about who actually crucified Jesus (23:24-25). Pilate finally acquiesces to the demands of the "chief priests, the leaders, and the people" (23:13, 24), who thus bear the chief responsibility. But when Luke narrates the actual crucifixion, it is the Roman soldiers who do the ghastly deed (23:36, 47), and Pilate, the representative of Rome, allows the grave injustice to happen.

In the sermons of Acts we find the same mutuality of responsibility between Pilate and the Jewish leaders. Peter's Pentecost sermon accuses Israelites in Jerusalem for causing the death of Jesus by persons outside the

---

30. No similar pre-30 C.E. event occurs in Josephus. Commentators look for its possible origin in other reports about Pilate by Josephus. Most common is the incident of Pilate sending soldiers to prevent some Samaritans from worshiping in their Temple on Mt. Gerizim. The parallels, however, are few, as Fitzmyer points out (35 C.E., not Galileans, not in the Temple, led to Pilate's recall). Fitzmyer lists five possible options hypothesized by scholars (*Luke*, vol. 2, 1006-7). While some event stands behind it, we can no longer determine its origin.

31. Cullmann, *The State*, 14.

32. Fitzmyer, *Luke*, vol. 2, 1007.

law (Gentiles, Acts 2:22-23). Peter's next sermon likewise blames Israelites for handing Jesus over to Pilate and for insisting on his death (3:12-15) A third accuses the rulers and elders without mentioning Pilate (4:5-10). The thematic text interpreting the event from Psalm 2 names Herod and Pilate, Gentiles and Israelites (4:27). Earlier Cornelius Peter says ambiguously, "They put him to death by hanging him on a tree" (10:39). Paul's sermon in Antioch names "the residents of Jerusalem and their leaders" who fulfill Scripture by asking Pilate to have Jesus killed (13:27-28). The pattern is clear. The people of Jerusalem and, above all, their leaders initiate the action against Jesus, but Pilate permits it to happen despite his knowledge of Jesus' innocence. Both are involved, and both share ultimate responsibility. It is also interesting to note how Luke's final sermon is the most precise about those responsible: the Jewish leaders in Jerusalem and Pilate (13:27-28). Pilate is not forgotten.

Acts

Several other motifs or events in Acts oppose a pro-Roman apologetic.

1. *Bold witness and martyrdom.* Throughout Acts, Luke emphasizes the bold witness of those who proclaim the new Way in the face of suffering and persecution. In the first half, the church responds fearlessly in the face of threats from Jewish leaders in Jerusalem. Twice the apostles Peter and John are arrested and brought before the Sanhedrin with explicit orders not to speak of Jesus, but they adamantly refuse (4:13, 19-20; 5:17-32). Meanwhile the believers gather together and pray for courage to continue speaking and healing (4:23-31, v. 29). Stephen becomes the first martyr at the hands of the Sanhedrin and their enraged followers, including Saul, after a provocative speech in which Stephen indicts his accusers for perpetuating the long history of Israel's rejection of the prophets (7:51-53). A persecution then breaks out that initiates the scattering of the church into Judea and Samaria and beyond to Gentile areas (8:1; 11:19). Paul's conversion leads to his persecution by fellow Jews, but Paul responds with fearless witnessing about Jesus as Messiah (9:23-25, 28-30). The Lukan pattern is this: threats and persecution from Jewish opponents, bold witnessing and suffering by the apostles and believers. Gentiles are not yet involved.

In the second half of Acts, Luke concentrates on the story of Paul's missionary travels in Gentile territory (Acts 13-28). Although now in Gentile lands, Luke develops the motif of "Jew first, then Gentile." Accordingly, Paul first enters the synagogue (if possible) and after expulsion he begins to reach out to Gentiles (13:45-52; 14:1-7, 19; 17:1-9, 10-13; 18:1-18, 12- 17). Luke attributes the Jewish hostility that dogs Paul's heels to preaching Jesus as Messiah and to jealousy over converts from Gentile proselytes and God-fearers (13:45; 17:5). In some Hellenistic cities, however, the opposition comes from magicians or persons economically threatened because of Paul's preaching against pagan gods (16:16-24; 19:11-20, 23-41). From the official Roman point of view, Paul's conflicts with the Jews are matters of interreligious disputes and not politically dangerous or illegal (proconsul Gallio, 18:12-16). But this does not lead to Roman justice nor to any kind of defense of the new religion by Roman authorities.

In general, Paul in Acts models the leitmotif of the Christian life as one lived under the shadow of persecution. At the conclusion of his first missionary journey, Paul strengthens the neophyte churches with the word, "It is through many persecutions that we must enter the kingdom of God" (14:22). Discipleship for Luke involves suffering, as Jesus himself had forewarned (Luke 21:12-19). Likewise in his farewell address to the Ephesian elders, Paul states that the Holy Spirit revealed to him, "in every city imprisonment and persecutions are waiting for me" (20:23). In Caesarea, the prophet Agabus symbolically binds Paul and predicts his arrest by Jews in Jerusalem and handing over to the Gentiles (21:7-14, v.11). Paul declares his readiness to die in Jerusalem. The struggle is interreligious, not anti-Roman. Yet, because of it, Paul must suffer along with other Christians. And Roman justice is not done. Although Roman officials may periodically come to Paul's rescue, they will finally do to Paul what they did with Jesus. After his handing over by Jews, they imprison him and put him on trial, with the sentence of unjust execution waiting in the wings. The emperor himself is the implied executioner. Suffering and endurance are the Christian way, with martyrdom from Jew and Gentile an ever-present possibility.

Does Luke write in a time of actual persecution? While there is disagreement among interpreters, I think not. No official or widespread Roman persecution occurs in the first century.[33] The Neronian persecution was intense but limited only to Rome (54 C.E.). The end of Domitian's reign saw some minor persecution in Asia Minor (90–96 C.E.; see chap. 4). Luke knows of sporadic persecution of the early church, including three martyrdoms (Stephen, James, Paul) and he sees the potential for more. So he issues a clear warning for Christians to be ready at any moment to suffer from Jew or Gentile. Above all, he calls for fearless and bold witnessing, in imitation of their Lord and the first martyrs who followed in his steps.

---

33. Conzelmann, *Luke*, 209–10, thinks Luke writes in a time of persecution (*ecclesia pressa*). But there is little evidence, if any, for persecution during the rule of the Flavians in the first century (Vespasian, Titus, 70–90; not until the end of Domitian's reign may some persecution have begun, 93–96). Bo Reicke finds evidence for some trials in Rome from *1 Clement* (1:1; 7:16; 95 C.E.) and for problems in Asia Minor under Domitian (*The New Testament Era*, trans. David Green [Philadelphia: Fortress Press, 1968], 291–302). See chapter 4, below.

2. Death of Herod Agrippa: "The voice of a god" (Acts 12). The case of Herod Agrippa I is especially illuminating with respect to Luke's attitude toward political authorities. Herod Agrippa, grandson of Herod the Great and his Hasmonean wife, Miriamne, hence both Edomite and Jew, ruled by Rome's decree during a transition period in Palestine (37–44 C.E.).[34] According to Luke, Herod takes advantage of the uncertain times to attack the leadership in the Jerusalem church (12:1-4). He first kills the apostle James, brother of John, "the sons of Zebedee" (Luke 5:10; 9:54; Acts 1:13; cf. Mark 10:35-39, prediction of suffering). Then he has the chief apostle, Peter, arrested, with the intention to execute him after the Passover. Luke attributes the persecution to Herod's attempt to court favor with the Jews (12:3). When Peter escapes by divine intervention, Herod orders the prison guards killed, while Peter flees to Caesarea (12:19; some texts have Herod going to Caesarea).

Luke then provides a colorful description of Herod's death (12:20-23). We are told a delegation from the Phoenician cities of Tyre and Sidon attempt a reconciliation with Herod, who is angry with them for unspecified reasons. Luke notes the economic dependence of Tyre and Sidon on Herod's benevolence (12:30). On the day of the official hearing, Herod dresses in royal apparel, mounts the judgment seat and delivers a public oration. The people shout repeatedly, "The voice of a god, and not of a mortal!" (12:22). Immediately, we are told, an angel of the Lord struck him down and he suffered a gruesome death. Luke explains to his readers that he did not give glory to God (12:23). That means Herod's death is divine punishment for his acceptance of the blasphemous acclaim of the crowds. Josephus has a parallel account of Herod's death that agrees on the essentials with Luke, particularly with respect to his failure to repudiate the invocation as a "god."[35]

34. Herod Agrippa was the son of Aristobulus, who was executed by Rome in 7 B.C.E.. His mother sent him to Rome for education and he became a close friend of Gaius, the future emperor. So Gaius granted him rule over the former tetrarchies of Philippi and Lysania and the title king in 37 C.E.; two years later he added Galilee and Perea (after Herod Antipas's exile); under the emperor Claudius, after Gaius's assassination, he also received Judea until his death (41–44). He thus ruled 37–44 C.E.. Afterward, Rome returned Palestine to rule by procurators.

Josephus tells us that Herod was sympathetic to the Jewish cause and even fought boldly to prevent Gaius from erecting his statue in the Temple at Jerusalem. As a part-Jew, Herod courted their favor, which agrees with Luke's story.

35. Josephus, *Ant.* 19.343-352. The two accounts are independent versions. Josephus adds details (e.g., the gorgeous silver robe shining at sunrise; the event occurred on the festival day in honor of Claudius; the death came from natural causes [a sudden pain in his belly lasting five days until he died]). The general story and the main cause for the death, however, are in agreement. To be "eaten by worms" was mentioned by ancient writers as a fitting death for especially despised rulers (e.g., Antiochus Epiphanes, the Syrian tyrant, 2 Macc. 9:5ff.; or Herod the Great, Josephus, *Ant.* 17.168-170).

This is revolutionary thinking about political rulers. Luke does indeed link the death of Herod to his persecution of the church, but there is much more at stake. Jews and Christians, almost alone in the ancient world, refused to deify human rulers. At best, they carry out the will of God through their position or activity. They do not represent "god" on earth but are mere mortals; rulers who make divine claims stand under divine judgment. This is the cause of Herod's death. Furthermore, although king of Palestine, Herod represents the rule of Rome in the world. While his actions against the church arose in response to Jewish animosity toward the new religion, this is not the case with his actions against Tyre and Sidon. Here Herod simply acts like an arrogant and presumptuous, and yes, blasphemous tyrant. Therefore, all rulers like Herod or any other imperial puppet of Rome who may lay claim to divinity, stand under the same judgment. And would this not also be true of the supreme emperors whose coins are stamped *divus Augusti*? There is nothing pro-Roman in this text. In truth, it challenges all political powers who usurp their role and fail to acknowledge the obedience and honor due to God alone.

3. Trial of Paul. While Luke's presentation of the trial of Paul in Acts insists on Paul's innocence of any political crime deserving death, nevertheless, the same trial demonstrates that Roman justice remains a problem for the church and Rome itself a potential enemy.

Commentators frequently note some striking parallels between the trial of Jesus in the Gospel and the trial of Paul in Acts. One common theme is the handing over of Jesus and Paul by Jewish leaders to Gentile authorities (Luke 18:32; 23:1, 24-25; Acts 20:22-27; 21:7-14; 28:17). The narration of events from the time of Paul's arrest to his imprisonment in Rome lays chief blame on Jewish opposition. At his arrest in the Temple, Paul is falsely accused by Asian Jews of bringing a Gentile into the Court of Israel, a violation carrying with it the penalty of death (21:28). Paul is rescued from a furious mob by a Roman tribune, who learns that Paul is not the Egyptian revolutionary who caused a recent disturbance in Jerusalem by 4000 Jewish "assassins" put down brutally by Roman soldiers.[36] After learning of a Jewish plot against Paul, the tribune hurriedly sends him by night under armed guard to Caesarea and writes a letter affirming Paul's innocence (23:12-25, 29).

---

36. Josephus, *Ant.* 20.169-172; *War* 20.261-263. A self-proclaimed Jewish prophet from Egypt gathered followers at the Mount of Olives to wait for the walls of Jerusalem to fall down at his command. Instead, the Roman governor, Felix, attacked with troops, and some of the followers were killed or imprisoned, while the Egyptian escaped. Josephus estimates the mob of followers at 40,000, but Luke's estimate of 4000 seems more probable. Also, Luke uses the term *sicarii* of the 4000, which refers to armed resisters of Roman occupation. This makes the comparison with Paul's peaceful intentions all the more obvious.

The trials before the Roman governors Felix and Festus, King Agrippa, and Berniece all follow a similar pattern.[37] Paul is accused by Jewish leaders of causing public disorder (24:5-6, pestilent fellow, agitator everywhere, ringleader of the sect of Nazarenes, profaned the Temple; 25:7, 25). In turn, Paul defends his political innocence and denies the role of troublemaker, while arguing instead that the conflict is religious (24:12-13; 25:8, no offense against Jews or Temple or emperor; 25:25; 26:32).When Festus requests that Paul return to Jerusalem for a hearing, as a favor to his Jewish accusers, Paul feels compelled to make his dramatic appeal for justice before Caesar (25:8-11).[38] Festus and Agrippa both agree that Paul has done nothing deserving death and could have been set free (26:32). In Rome, Paul once more defends his political innocence before local Jewish leaders and insists it is for the "hope of Israel" that he is on trial (28:20). While the leaders know something about the new religion, they strangely know nothing about Paul.

Nevertheless, Paul's trial in Acts ends with justice never done. Even after two years, Paul is not freed. His evangelistic work fulfills the mission of the risen Lord announced in Acts 1:8, "...to the ends of the earth." Paul remains faithful to the end, "proclaiming the kingdom of God and teaching about the Lord Jesus Christ with all boldness and without hindrance" (28:31). But the silence about his fate is deafening. The emperor, like Festus and Agrippa and Felix before him, does not execute the promised rule of law and order to Roman citizens. No Roman or outsider could finish reading Acts and claim the appeal to Caesar had accomplished its purpose. Rome remains a potential problem for the church. God's will was done in spite of Rome's failure to defend the cause. Like Jesus, Paul, too, must suffer and die, the victim of both Jewish and Roman injustice.

Summary

Contrary to the prevailing opinion, Luke does not write a pro-Roman apologetic, either toward Rome or the church. In the Gospel, the story of

37. Cassidy argues persuasively that one of Luke's primary purposes in Acts is to model Paul as a trial witness before Roman officials. Thereby Christians in Luke's day will be prepared to make their own witness. He notes nine trials of Paul in Acts before officials, which shift the image of Paul as the "great missionary" to that of the "great witness." And he calls the ending of Acts Paul's "summit" encounter with Caesar in Rome (Acts 23:11; 27:24). But the problem remains why Luke then does not describe in full detail the great climactic trial before Caesar. What a fitting climax that would be! In effect, the vision of Paul's witness before Caesar is not fulfilled. While I agree with the thesis of trial and witnessing, other Lukan motives are at work in the ending of Acts.

38. Luke's remark that Festus acted "as a favor to the Jews" (25:9) likely means that Festus was willing to grant the request of the Jews for a trial in Jerusalem, not Caesarea.

Jesus that Luke presents is highly critical of those who hold political office, both Jewish and Roman. Jesus envisions a new pattern of community and social relations that reverses the established order in which the rich and powerful dominate and instead welcomes the poor and marginal. Significantly, much of the critical evidence comes from Luke's own sources or redaction.[39] Where Luke might seem to favor Roman rule (e.g., the trial before Pilate), this can best be explained by his consistent tendency to place the primary blame on Jewish leaders. Therefore I view Luke's Gospel to be in general agreement with the other Synoptics and their portrayal of Jesus' critical distancing from those who rule.

In Acts, it is the same. A one-sided reading may give the impression that Acts is generally favorable toward Roman rule, especially in the story of Paul. But a closer reading reveals a more complex and ambiguous portrait. Both Jewish and Roman officials oppose and persecute the church. Believers obey only God, despite risk of suffering and martyrdom. In spite of periodic rescues of Paul, Roman justice is not accomplished. While the problems of Paul arise chiefly from Jewish hostility to the heretical sect, Rome does not defend the accused or bring about Paul's freedom. The imperial state therefore remains a potential enemy of the church and the missionary enterprise in the Gentile world. Like Jesus, Paul and the other witnesses must be ready to suffer and die at the hands of those who possess the sword. Rome is neither friend nor partner of the church.[40] Subsequent history proved Luke right.

---

39. E.g., the *Magnificat* (1:46-55), the inaugural address to the oppressed (4:16-30), the beatitudes and woes (6:20-26), the "fox" Antipas (13:31-33), the passion prediction (18:32), Pilate's slaying of the Galileans (13:1-2), and Simon the Zealot (6:15).

40. Because Conzelmann's work has been the most influential in the political apologetic debate, Cassidy provides a critique in his study. According to Cassidy, Conzelmann thinks that "Luke portrays Jesus in harmony with, and subservient to, the existing political order" (Cassidy, *Jesus, Society, and Politics*, 120). In response, he raises the following objections (among others): (a) Conzelmann never explains how Pilate could declare Jesus innocent, after Jesus affirms his kingship (23:3-4). (b) Conzelmann: "Thus his [Jesus] kingship does not stand opposed to the Empire on the political plane, yet it implies the claim to supremacy over the world . . ." (188). For Conzelmann, this somehow implies there is no challenge to the existing earthly orders. Cassidy: No, Jesus constantly challenges it. He asks, "What passages in Luke's Gospel indicate that Jesus was concerned about heavenly kingship and submissive to the social order the Romans were maintaining?" (*Jesus, Society, and Politics*, 129). (c) Conzelmann does not treat passages that show Jesus refusing to cooperate with or criticize his political rulers.

E. J. Via agrees with Cassidy that the Lukan Jesus does not defer to authorities and is not loyal to Rome. But she argues that Cassidy misses Conzelmann's main point that Jesus and the disciples are not criminals or deserving of death; rather, the dispute is interreligious ("According to Luke, Who Put Jesus to Death?" *Political Issues*, 138–40). While this point may be granted, it does not necessarily lead to a pro-Roman political apologetic. And Via is wrong on Luke's hope for the church to become an official religion (*religio licita*).

4.
ETHIC OF RESISTANCE

I N THIS CHAPTER I WILL EXAMINE THE BOOK OF REVELATION (THE APOC-
alypse) and its stance toward the state. It quickly becomes apparent that
the Apocalypse takes a position quite the opposite from that of Romans 13
and the loyalty tradition in the New Testament. Nor does its ethic correspond to that of the Gospel's depiction of Jesus' critical response to those
in religious and political authority. In Revelation, the church and political
powers are mortal enemies. Christ and Caesar are engaged in deadly combat, the classic New Testament example of "Christ against culture."[1] There
seems to be little room for compromise or accommodation. As we shall see,
the Christian response toward the state in Revelation is not an ethic of subordination or one of critical distancing but rather an ethic of resistance,
even to the point of martyrdom.

How does one account for this radically new point of view? Among the
primary causes for this changed attitude is the historical setting of the
Apocalypse.

Historical Setting

There is widespread agreement that Revelation was written near the end of
the reign of Domitian (96 C.E.).[2] But there is less agreement on what that
means for understanding Revelation. Earlier commentators by and large
thought that Domitian's rule was a time of official and widespread persecution for the church in Asia Minor. Recent studies, however, have raised
serious doubts about the extent of persecution under Domitian, if any.
Evidence no longer permits the old assumption of officially sanctioned and
extensive persecution by Domitian in Asia Minor. A few even question
whether there was any persecution at all. How, then, shall one deal with the
obvious fear of persecution that permeates the Apocalypse?

---

1. This typological description comes from H. Richard Niebuhr's famous study, *Christ and Culture* (New York: Harper, 1951).

2. E.g., M. Eugene Boring, *Revelation* (Interpretation; Louisville: John Knox Press, 1989), 8–10.

It will not do to attribute this fear solely to the mind or imagination of the author.[3] John writes to genuine Christian communities in Asia Minor who have already experienced some forms of violent hostility: imprisonment (2:10), the martyrdom of Antipas (2:13), potential martyrs (3:10; 6:9), betrayal by the synagogue (2:9; 3:9), and John's own exile on Patmos (1:9). Throughout the book the expectation of opposition from those in political power underlies its message. But if the current hostility is more sporadic than organized, it is apparent that John perceives a grave threat on the horizon. The present conflict looms as a sure sign of the feared future, a future envisioned apocalyptically as a holy war between the kingdom of this world and the kingdom of God.

What more do we know about Domitian's rule that might help us understand Revelation? Unfortunately, neither ancient contemporary or modern historians agree in their assessment. While the early years appear favorable to him, in the later years he met with growing opposition, ending with his assassination. Early-second-century Roman historians and others accuse him of creating an atmosphere of fear and suspicion.[4] He carried out bloody attempts to diminish the influence of the Roman aristocracy. Roman senators and their families were banished or executed or both, and many distinguished poets and philosophers faced exile. Even his own wife joined in the successful plot to assassinate him. Moreover, the same historians accuse Domitian of self-deification. Their indictment includes his aggressive promotion of emperor worship, his insistence on the use of *dominus et deus noster* (our Lord and God) on public documents and at all public appearances. Moreover, coins were minted under his reign with the obverse side depicting Domitian in the form of the god Jupiter crowned with an oak leaf, while on the reverse side Domitian sits enthroned in a palace like the god Jupiter. A mid-second-century Christian bishop of one of the seven churches in Revelation, Melito of Sardis, concurs when he calls Domitian "a second Nero."[5] This sweeping judgment colors all later Christian portraits of Domitian.

---

3. Most recently by Leonard L. Thompson, *The Book of Revelation: Apocalypse and Empire* (New York: Oxford University Press, 1990), especially chap. 11. He agrees that it is written under Domitian, but he attempts a revision of what he calls the popular portrait of economic and political oppression in favor of a broader social location of alienation in which the readers of Revelation understand themselves "as a minority that continuously encounters and attacks the larger Christian community and the even larger Roman social order" (195). While helpful at times, his argument is unpersuasive and insensitive to the concrete rhetoric of the author.

4. Among these are Tacitus, Suetonius, Pliny, Juvenal, Martial, and, a century later, Dio Cassius.

5. Similarly, the second century Tertullian, *Apol.* 5.

Yet, against this apparent damning testimony, some today question the evidence as badly tainted. All the Roman historians belonged to the senatorial or equestrian rank. They had an obvious ax to grind. And Domitian's growing suspicions of their power were partly justified.[6] Despite some truth in these objections, it is nearly impossible to attribute the accusations of eyewitnesses solely to bias or unfettered exaggeration. Domitian's rule provoked an outburst of warranted fear and resistance that finally caused his violent removal. And the case can be made within the Apocalypse itself "that the Revelation is strongly antithetical to the language of the imperial cult as current under Domitian."[7] By this is meant in particular that the titles ascribed to Christ in the Apocalypse correspond antithetically to the divine appellation applied (blasphemously!) to Caesar. Obviously, for the author of Revelation there is but one true *dominus et deus* (Lord and God).

A fascinating exchange of correspondence between Pliny the Younger and the emperor Trajan (98–117 C.E.) sheds further light on the historical setting of Revelation.[8] Pliny, governor of Bithynia, a province bordering the region of the seven churches in Asia Minor, wrote a series of letters to the emperor asking his counsel among other things on how to deal with the obstinate sect of Christians. Some excerpts from the letters:

> In the meanwhile, the method I have observed towards those who have been denounced to me as Christians is this: I interrogated them whether they were Christians; if they confessed it I repeated the question twice again, adding the threat of capital punishment; if they still persevered, I ordered them to be executed. For whatever the nature of their creed might be, I could at least feel no doubt that contumacy and inflexible obstinacy deserved chastisement. There were others also possessed with the same infatuation, but being citizens of Rome, I directed them to be carried thither." . . . "Those who denied they were, or had ever been Christians, who repeated after me an invocation to the gods, and offered adoration, with wine and frankincense, to your image, which I had ordered to be brought for that purpose, together with those of the gods, and who finally cursed Christ—none of which acts, it is said, those who are really Christians can be forced into performing—these I thought it proper to discharge. Others who were named by that informer at first confessed themselves Christians

---

6. See Gerhard A. Krodel, *Revelation* (ACNT; Minneapolis: Augsburg, 1989), 36–37, for detailed arguments.

7. Colin J. Hemer, *The Letters to the Seven Churches of Asia in Their Local Setting* (JSNTSup 11; Sheffield: JSOT, 1986), 5.

8. Pliny, *Epistles* 10.96-97, ca. 112 C.E.

and then denied it; true, they had been of that persuasion but they had quitted it, some three years, others many years, and a few as much as twenty-five years ago. They all worshiped your statue and the images of the gods, and cursed Christ.

From the correspondence we learn the following: (a) Christians as a group are under a cloud of suspicion, assumed to be potential enemies of the state simply by association with the new movement. (b) Under Pliny, some Christians have been brought to trial and executed, if they did not recant their faith; or if Roman citizens, they were sent to Rome. (c) A "test" is given to determine whether persons are Christians or not. The accused must prove their innocence by invoking the gods, offering a pinch of incense and wine before an image of the emperor, taking an oath cursing Christ, and confessing Caesar as Lord (*kyrios kaisaros*). (d) Christians have been accused and tried before Pliny's time. In fact, some claim to have renounced their faith more than 25 years ago (ca. 90 C.E.). (e) The emperor forbids seeking out Christians or relying on slanderous accusations, yet he agrees they are to be regarded as politically dangerous.

The evidence from this correspondence indicates that no general persecution existed in a neighboring province of Asia Minor in the early second century. Perhaps fifteen to twenty years earlier there was even less conflict. Nevertheless, the letters do demonstrate considerable opposition, including trials and possible deaths under Domitian. To be known as a Christian created suspicion and may even put one's life in jeopardy. In this respect the fear of the future present in Revelation seems valid and understandable.[9]

While there was no systematic or universal persecution under Domitian, the cult of emperor worship is well-established. Domitian especially coveted such honors. Asia Minor was a veritable hotbed for the imperial cult. Leading cities competed for the honor. Temples with statues of Domitian existed in at least five of the seven cities of Revelation (Laodicea and Philadelphia are uncertain). Prominent citizens, known as Asiarchs

---

9. Another possible evidence for persecution under Domitian concerns the well-known case of Flavius Clemens and his wife Domitilla. Clemens, a senator and cousin of Domitian, was executed by imperial orders (96 C.E.). His wife, Domitilla, a niece of Domitian, was banished. The charge against them was "atheism" (Dio Cassius, *Hist.* 67.14; third century C.E.). Most interpreters conclude that they converted to Christianity (or Judaism), since atheism for the Romans meant rejecting their traditional gods. A few today dispute this interpretation (Krodel, *Revelation*, 32), but most still think it reliable and so another example of the danger for Christians under Domitian. Robert L. Wilken, *The Christians as the Romans Saw Them* (New Haven, Conn.: Yale University Press, 1984), 5, 25, agrees with the famed Roman historian, A. N. Sherwin-White, *The Letters of Pliny: A Historical and Social Commentary* (Oxford: Oxford University Press, 1966), 695, that Pliny was actually present at one of the earlier trials under Domitian.

(Acts 19:31), established and maintained the cult. John's reference to "Satan's throne" may be his apt description for the imperial cult in Pergamum (2:13).

How might Christians respond to emperor worship? Only Jews and Christians, monotheists in a polytheistic culture, perceived it as a threat. Neither Jew nor Christian could bestow divine honors on any earthly power. But the Jews had received special dispensation from Rome on this and other matters that allowed them to abstain from practices that were contrary to their religious beliefs. As long as Christians were perceived as Jews, there was no problem. When the two groups appeared to be different religions, however, Christians were left without imperial protection. This growing vulnerability of the churches may lie behind the animosity toward the synagogue and "Jews" expressed in two of the letters (2:9; 3:9).

Moreover, for outsiders the refusal of Christians to participate in the imperial cult involved both religious and political sensitivities. To refuse to honor the emperor as the divine guardian of the state was perceived as an act of disloyalty to Rome. Not to join the citizenry in sacrificing a pinch of incense at Caesar's altar would arouse political suspicion. And, since the honor of the emperor was inseparable from the polytheistic worship endemic in the culture, Christians had an insoluble problem on their hands.

Pagan religiosity was everywhere. At civic celebrations or public forums, at sporting events or theater, in the marketplace or the private collegiums of the trade guilds, at weddings or burials or banquets, religion was in the air. Idolatry was the constant temptation facing Jews and Christians. Accordingly, the most difficult questions had to do with the degree of withdrawal from or accommodation to the thoroughly pagan society. This basic issue prompted fierce debate within the churches of Revelation.

It is difficult to assess how strong the pressure to assimilate became for Christians in Asia Minor under Domitian. Pliny's letter gives indisputable evidence that some Christians risked their lives by refusing to practice emperor worship. Probably the majority were left alone to pursue quietly their own livelihood. Persecution could likely be avoided by not attracting attention to oneself. Yet Christians had to walk carefully at best. Open refusal to honor the emperor or respect the deities could and did lead to serious consequences.

Letters to the Seven Churches (Revelation 2–3)

The letters to the seven churches can also help us to grasp the historical setting of the Apocalypse. Within the letters we encounter a variety of problems facing the respective churches. From without, they struggle against hostility from imperial Rome and from the synagogue, and from within they must deal with a growing lack of spiritual vitality and with sharp divisions between their leaders. As the careful reader will note, the context and particular set of issues differ from church to church. Despite the formal similarity of each letter, the author evaluates each church according to their specific needs. The issues are diverse: threat of imprisonment and martyrdom; social and economic isolation from the community; expulsion and/or betrayal by the synagogue; lack of first love and spiritual lukewarmness; false teaching and theological and ethical disagreements. The seer writes to speak the fitting word of encouragement or warning appropriate for each church and for their spiritual health and survival.

Despite this surprising diversity of concerns, however, there is one that holds them all together: faithfulness in time of crisis. Without overlooking the multiplicity of problems and needs pertaining to each community of faith, the author perceives the common threat to arise from a hostile and idolatrous state, a threat that appears to have reached the boiling point. The claims of a totalitarian government with its values competes with the claims of those communities who confess only one Lord. The question of worship so central to Revelation finally become this: Christ or Caesar?

John writes in this perceived moment of crisis. The danger of intense persecution seemed right around the corner and the temptations from an idolatrous and corrupt culture on the move.[10] Like the author of Daniel, who wrote to defy the inroads of the Hellenizing tyrant Antiochus IV (ca.175 B.C.E.), so John writes against the latest imperial tyrant. Under pressure from the political powers centering in imperial Rome, Revelation is

10. Adela Yarbro Collins, *The Apocalypse* (NTM 22; Wilmington, Del.: M. Glazier, 1979), XI, argues that Revelation is written in light of "the expected hostility on the part of Rome" still lying in the future. Although I agree the author sees the graver threat still ahead, persecution has already begun. Elisabeth Schüssler Fiorenza, *Revelation: Vision of a Just World* (Minneapolis: Fortress Press, 1991), 124–27, understands this clearly. She holds that Revelation is written in response to an actual crisis experience of persecution and deprivation; or differently put, "Revelation's . . . rhetorical world of vision can be understood as a fitting response" (124) to their daily experience of vulnerability and suffering.

Another commentator writes: "Though a state-sponsored persecution did not take place in Asia Minor at John's time, as far as we know, nevertheless his visions were credible because idolatry and the imperial cult were real and obvious to any Christian with eyes to see and so were the resultant vices, including Roman exploitation and the suffering of the poor" (Krodel, *Revelation*, 68–69). Although this statement is generally accurate, it understates the real danger: the imperial cult and idolatry are threats only if there is genuine pressure to enforce them. If no one cared about emperor worship, why should Christians worry? John writes because he and the churches are already experiencing harassment and threats and more from those in authority, and he fears the worst for the future.

written to resist the temptation to idolatry and compromise and to encourage believers to faithful endurance. This is Christian underground literature. The Apocalypse offers a message of encouragement, comfort, and protest in the face of social and political and religious oppression.

The Understanding of the State

In the Apocalypse, the political authorities have become the enemy of God, the church, and humankind. Here, as nowhere else in the New Testament, the kingdom of God and the kingdom of the world stand opposed to one another. The state unquestionably belongs to the kingdom of the world, under the dominion of Satan and his rule.[11]

Revelation symbolizes this theme with three provocative images of the Roman imperium.

Beast (to thērion)

In Revelation 13 the seer paints his apocalyptic portrait of the state with the image of the two beasts. There is general agreement among interpreters that Revelation 13 and 17 reveal in apocalyptic manner the historical setting of the Apocalypse. That is, behind the imagery and symbolism of the chapter, including the imagery of the two beasts, lies imperial Rome and its political structures.

The First Beast

This first beast arises out of the sea (13:1). In the ancient world, the sea represents the symbol of chaos, the abyss of demonic forces (cf. Ps. 74:12-15; 89:9-10; Job 26:12-13; Isa. 27:1; Dan. 7:2ff.). But this beast rules on earth. The description centers on two features: its unparalleled authority and its blasphemous arrogance. Its claim to authority is derived from the dragon (Satan), from whom the beast has received absolute power and domination. Thus for John, the beast is the historical manifestation of evil on earth.

In the image of the beast, John has borrowed from Daniel's vision of four beasts, where each represents successive empires opposing God's

---

11. Elaine Pagels has shown how in the late Jewish pseudepigrapha and the New Testament the figure of Satan serves to characterize perceived human opposition to God and God's people or, in the case of the New Testament, to Jesus and his followers ("The Social History of Satan, Part II" [*JAAR* 62 (1994)], 17–58). While she concentrates on the Gospels and the problem of the identification of Jewish opposition with "Satan," she notes that the "author of Revelation graphically depicts the powers of Rome in the animalistic and monstrous imagery adopted from prophetic tradition while simultaneously denouncing certain groups of Jews— apparently those who rejected his claims about Jesus—as the "synagogue of Satan" (20).

people (Dan. 7:2-8). Here, however, one empire constitutes the composite image of the beast. But John adds a striking new feature: the beast "whose mortal wound had been healed" (13:3, 12, 14; 17:8, 11). This oft-repeated reference originates in a rumor that swept over the Roman empire after Nero's suicide in 68 C.E., a rumor that Nero had not really died and that he was about to revenge his death by returning at the head of the Parthian armies, Rome's feared enemies to the East.[12] John not only draws from this "Nero legend" but remakes it into a parody of Christ in that the beast dies and comes back to life ("mortal wound . . . healed"). This frightful beast now holds supreme authority over the earth. Everyone follows this beast with wonder and awe. "Who is like the beast, and who can fight against it" (13:4)? Moreover, the whole earth worships this beast, and they do so in full knowledge that the authority of the beast is in the service of the dragon (13:4). But apparently, overwhelming power proves irresistible to the earth's inhabitants.

Arrogance is the other mark of this imperial beast. Not only does it demand and receive worship, but it bears blasphemous names upon its seven heads and speaks blasphemy. In the height of arrogance it even utters blasphemy against God (13:5-6), while on earth it makes war against the saints and conquers them (13:7). For John's readers, the blasphemous names are transparent as divine titles claimed by the emperor: *dominus et deus* (Lord and God), *soter* (Savior), *divus Augustus* (divine Augustus), or whatever other titles may be used.

There are only two challenges to the supreme authority and arrogance of the imperial beast. One is the divine limit placed on its rule: "It was allowed [by God] to exercise authority for forty-two months" (13:5; cf. Dan. 7:25). The other is the existence of the saints, those few on earth who see through the seductive power of the beast and who refuse to worship any other than God and the Lamb (13:8).

In this image of the beast the seer has created a deliberate parody of Christ: divine names, along with authority over every tribe and people and nation (4:11; 5:6, 12; 19:6-8). This is the great Antichrist, even though John never uses the term. And this Antichrist includes both the empire itself and the individual emperors who rule.[13]

The Second Beast

The second beast arises out of the earth (13:11). This beast, it is made unmistakably clear, acts wholly under the authority of and in the service of

12. Krodel, *Revelation*, 248. Similar rumors occurred following Hitler's suicide.

13. According to Krodel, *Revelation*, 63, "He [John] envisioned the anti-Christ in terms of the totalitarian, self-deifying, all-embracing power of the state."

the first beast (13:12). Later in Revelation it is called the false prophet (16:3; 19:20; 20:10). It, too, is a parody of Christ, with horns "like a lamb" though it speaks "like a dragon" (v.11). Its preeminent task is to create images of the first beast and to enforce worship of the images (v. 14). Those who refuse to do so risk death (v.15).

Who is this second beast? No one can mistake the obvious reference to the cult of emperor worship. John is describing the local and regional representatives of Rome in Asia Minor who promote the cult and related practices and who otherwise serve as puppets of the imperial regime. Along with the forced worship, the seer refers to great signs performed by the second beast (v. 13). Even false prophets can work miracles (cf. Mark 13:22). Like Elijah of old, this second beast makes fire come down from heaven and performs other signs that deceive people on earth (Deut. 13:1-5; 1 Kings 18). And, like the Israelites who built the image of the golden calf, advocates of the imperial cult encourage the populace to erect images for the beast (v. 14). Religious hucksterism is involved. Statues of the images breathe and speak (v. 14). We know from literature of the period about both magical practices and illusory tricks used to cause images of the gods to move and talk.[14] The Jewish apocryphal writing *Bel and the Dragon* pokes fun at pagan priests who use deception to have idols smoke or speak. Simon Magus, known as the father of magic, brought statues to life (Acts 8:9-11; *Ps. Clem. Recog.* 3.47). For John, every effort is being made to promote idolatry in the cities of Asia Minor. And the backing of the state lies behind their attempts.

Beyond the religiopolitical pressure to practice emperor worship, John alludes to economic and social tensions. We are told that the second beast causes all people to receive the infamous "mark of the beast" on their right hand or forehead (13:16-17). Without this mark no one could buy or sell. No doubt the economic survival of Christians is endangered. Their purchase of daily necessities or their membership in local trade guilds may be at risk. Altogether, they experience increasing social and economic isolation from their communities.

What of the "mark of the beast"? Some suggest it refers to the imperial coins which bore the image of the divine emperor and the goddess Roma. This currency was necessary for all economic transactions.[15] This is possible, but one does not literally carry coins on the forehead. A few argue more dramatically that John has in mind a literal tattooing on the forehead or right hand of all cult worshipers. But no evidence exists for this. Others

14. See Steven J. Scherrer, "Signs and Wonders in the Imperial Cult: A New Look at a Roman Religious Institution in the Light of Rev. 13:13-15," *JBL* 103/4 (1984): 599–610.
15. Fiorenza, *Revelation: Vision*, 86.

think John is speaking metaphorically.[16] Those who bear the mark of the beast represent those who give their allegiance to the imperial regime and its idolatrous values; those who worship the living God reject its pseudo-values and give their allegiance to God and the Lamb (14:1). Whatever explanation may be best, it is significant to note that the mark of the beast has its counterpart in the "seal of the redeemed," who bear the Name of God and the Lamb on their foreheads (14:1; 7:2-4). So, too, John deliberately contrasts "all" the people who receive the mark of the beast (13:16, "small and great, rich and poor, free and slave") with the 144,000 sealed by God (14:1; 7:4). Although they may be small in number, they are secure before God.

In effect, the second beast symbolizes the religious and political and social policies and personages of Roman rule in Asia Minor. As imperial puppets, they represent the religopolitical propaganda machine for the state and its pseudo claim for ultimate loyalty.[17]

Taken together, the two beasts represent imperial Rome, depicted "in terms of the totalitarian, self-deifying, all-embracing power of the state."[18] This imperial beast and its regional puppets in Asia Minor expect undivided allegiance. For John and his readers, there appears to be little or no room for compromise. In fact, the demand for worship is a blasphemy that God's people cannot give. Hence the battle lines are drawn, the consequences frightening. Christ and Caesar have become mortal enemies!

Whore (hē megalē hē pornē)

A second image of the imperial state is that of the great whore. This image first appears in Revelation 17, within the vision of the seventh and final bowl of God's wrath (16:17—17:1). It ranks among the most grotesque of the seer's colorful symbols; we need special sensitivity to this image in view of the long history of patriarchal insensitivity and misinterpretation with respect to biblical symbols.[19]

The image itself has roots in the prophetic depiction of Israel or Jerusalem as God's bride, wife, or harlot, most often as an unfaithful part-

16. Krodel, *Revelation*, 256. Why a mark on the right hand? It could relate to the fact that the sacrifice before the imperial image was done by sprinkling incense with the right hand. Others think it could be a deliberate contrast with the Jewish practice of wearing prayer phylacteries (leather pouches) on the left hand or on the forehead.

17. Oscar Cullmann, *The State in the New Testament* (New York: Scribner's, 1956), 76, vividly describes the second beast as "the religio-ideological propaganda authority of the totalitarian state." And he insists that every totalitarian state needs an ideology that is a parody of faith.

18. Krodel, *Revelation*, 63.

19. See below, especially note 25.

ner of Yahweh gone whoring after other gods. The sin of idolatry is bitterly denounced as fornication by the prophets (Isa. 1:21; Ezek. 16:15-21; 23:1-2). But the same image is also used against foreign nations and their capitals, called "harlots and prostitutes" (Isa. 23:16-18). Moreover, it was common practice, then and now, to use female imagery for cities and countries. So John is drawing upon conventional and prophetic language in describing Rome as a great whore.

There is a surprising diversity in female imagery throughout Revelation. There is the great whore who corrupts the whole earth. In one letter we meet a prophetess, Jezebel, and her followers, who are charged with advocating fornication and idolatrous practices (2:20-23; cf. 2:14-15). But the seer always employs counter-images. Thus the woman in chapter 12, clothed with the sun, gives birth to the Messiah (v. 5) and then becomes mother church persecuted on earth (v. 17). And the counterpoint to the harlot and her followers is the bride of the Lamb, the New Jerusalem. The bride is dressed "with fine linen, bright and pure" (19:7-8), while the New Jerusalem comes down from heaven "prepared as a bride adorned for her husband" (21:2). The church as the holy bride is the seer's response to the unholy company of the great whore. As Fiorenza concludes, "John thus uses the image of woman to symbolize the present murderous reality of the imperial world power as well as the life-nurturing reality of the renewed world of God."[20] These images, of course, are metaphorical and have nothing to do with individual women and so are not meant to caricature women as whores or seductresses. Even with the prophetess Jezebel, it is a matter of dispute over leadership and authentic Christian teaching, not over gender. Yet it is surprising to observe how women as women do play a significant role within the life of the seven churches.

There is no doubt that the great whore, like the beast, represents imperial Rome. She is "seated on many waters," the global capital that dominates all the peoples and nations of the earth (17:1, 15, 18). Even the seven hills on which she sits are named (17:9). This is Rome, the eternal city, the invincible conqueror of the world.

The images, however, are fluid. As we shall soon see, the images of the whore and Babylon merge (17:5; 18:2ff.). The "judgment of the great whore" (17:1) becomes the fall of mighty Babylon (18:1-24). Likewise, the image of the whore and the beast interrelate. They remain two distinct images, yet represent one demonic opposition to the Lamb and the faithful. At first, the woman is shown seated on a scarlet beast full of blasphemous names (17:3).This is the same beast of Revelation 13, with seven heads and ten horns (17:3, 7; cf. 13:1) and with another allusion to the Nero legend (17:8, 11,

20. Fiorenza, *Revelation: Vision*, 95.

"was, is not, is to come"; cf. 13:3). So both the beast and the whore refer to Rome's rule. Moreover, both belong to the list of seven kings, the successive series of first-century emperors (17:7-18). But while both symbolize Roman rule, the whore especially portrays the city itself (17:18) and the beast the empire.

In the end, ironically, the city itself is destroyed by the beast with its army of ten kings (17:15-18). Here, once again, the beast is linked to the Nero legend and becomes the vengeful emperor leading Rome's former collaborators against the hated imperial city (17:11-13, 16-18).

In John's vivid imagination, the imperial whore is the great seducer and corrupter of the earth. Mounted upon a scarlet beast, she is clothed with royal purple and scarlet, adorned with gold, jewels, and pearls, and drinks from a golden cup (17:3-4). All the wealth and splendor of the nations is lavished upon her. This is the best the world can offer, and John marvels at her magnificence (17:6-7).

But beyond the appearance is the reality. The beast has blasphemous names (v. 3), the golden cup is full of abominations (v. 4), the kings of the earth have committed fornication with her and become drunk with her wine (v. 2). These metaphorical descriptions point to the ways in which Rome and her vassals have profited from their ill-gained wealth and domination. And they also illumine the worst of the abominations, the impurities of idolatry in the worship of the goddess Roma and the emperor cult. The great whore turns out to be no more than a gaudy prostitute. And on the forehead the seer sees a mystery title: "Babylon the great, mother of whores and of earth's abominations" (v. 5). For John, the whore is the principal source of all earthly evil. The scene climaxes in the most repelling imagery in all the Apocalypse: The woman is "drunk with the blood of the saints and the blood of the witnesses to Jesus" (v. 6).

The seer has chosen every detail with care to express his outrage at imperial Rome. The grotesque image of the state as a whore states his conviction that the imperial government in truth represents the epitome of evil structures on earth. Tacitus, a contemporary Roman historian, described Rome as "the city where all things hideous and shameful from every part of the world find their center and become popular" (*Annals* 15.44). But the charge here is more serious and sweeping. Far from an institution to promote justice and discourage lawlessness, the imperium has become the mother-lode of tyranny, injustice, and corruption. The most obvious sign is its idolatrous claim for allegiance and resultant persecution of the saints (v. 6). But it is guilty not only of the bloodshed of "prophets and saints," but of the bloodshed of all those whom it has forcibly conquered (18:24). The *pax Romana* itself lies under God's judgment. Its unlimited lust for power and wealth will be described more fully in the fall of Babylon narrated in chapter 18. Yet we already glimpse here how its splendor and might have seduced and corrupted the kings and inhabitants of the earth (17:2, 4). For John, the imperial whore and the bride of Christ, the counter-image of the church, belong to two different worlds. For the church of Jesus Christ, there can be no traffic with this whore.

Babylon the Great (babylon hē megalē)

The third image of the state in Revelation is Babylon the great. Babylon is John's pseudonym for Rome, chose, in part because of its link with Israel's past. The time of the exile, when the armies of Nebuchadnezzar carried away the survivors to Babylon, marked the low point in Jewish history. This tragic memory burned deep in their psyche. John revives ancient and painful wounds when he designates Rome as the contemporary equivalent of the old arch-enemy Babylon. Other Jewish and Christian literature written after the fall of Jerusalem also names Rome as Babylon (see above).

In the literary structure of Revelation, the fall of Babylon constitutes the fulfillment of divine judgments upon earthly kingdoms. Only the final battle of Armageddon remains (19:17-31; 20:7-10). Moreover, since Rome represents the epitome of unjust and tyrannical powers (17:5, "Babylon the *great, mother . . .*", emphasis added), John pays full attention to its demise. He carefully prepares the reader for its imminent judgment. Already in 14:8, an angel flying in mid-heaven announces, "Fallen, fallen is Babylon the great!" Again, with the outpouring of the seventh and final bowl of wrath, a violent earthquake destroys the great city Babylon and all the cities of the nations (16:17-21). As in Revelation 17, Babylon is the great whore, whose destruction presages the fall of Babylon (17:1, 5).

After all the premonitions and warnings, the seer finally narrates the fall of Babylon the great. Only one verse actually describes the fall (v. 16, by conquest and fire). Yet all of Revelation 18 revolves around the fall and its significance. The author has composed this section with considerable literary and artistic skill; it can be outlined thus:

- 18:1-3, announcement of Babylon's fall by an angel possessed with great authority
- 18:4-8, call for the saints to come out of Babylon, who is receiving due payment for her sins
- 18:9-20, series of three laments by those who had gained most from Babylon's wealth and power (kings, merchants, seafarers)
- 18:21-24, symbolic action by a mighty angel, with a concluding dirge of remembrance

The description of Babylon in chapter 18 concentrates on its pretensions to unlimited power. Even the repeated use of the term "great" is
meant to parody this claim. With dramatic and moving rhetoric, the oracle opens with a comparison between Babylon, once proud and secure in
its economic and military and political strength, and God's sudden reversal of its fortune (18:1-8). One day mighty Babylon rules the world, proud
as a peacock, saying to herself, "I rule as a queen; I am no widow, and I will
never see grief" (v. 7). Then comes the fall, and the arrogant city lies in
smoking ruins. One day mighty Babylon possesses all the luxuries and
treasures of the world; the next moment Babylon is a haunt and wasteland
of demons and foul birds. One day mighty Babylon glorifies herself as the
eternal city and trusts in her powerful legions; then in a single moment the
eternal city is crushed and leveled. With imaginative power, the seer
exposes the illusions of grandeur and permanence endemic to political
structures.

The central section of the laments is framed by the appeal for God's
people "to come out of her" (v. 4) and to rejoice in God's just judgments (v.
20). The call to come out is a plea to separate themselves from Rome's gross
injustices and idolatries. There can be no compromise with the city whose
evils are "heaped high as heaven" (v. 5). In the laments of those who prospered from their alliance with Babylon/Rome, we learn more about the
sins that God now remembers (cf. the oracles against Tyre in Ezek. 26–27).

The first lament comes from the kings of the earth (18:9-10). Once again
they are accused of committing fornication with Babylon (17:1-2) by sharing in its corrupt rule and idolatry. They are also condemned for living in
luxury. No doubt the alliance with Rome brought extravagant wealth to the
ruling elite, but all that is now over and they weep and wail for their loss.
Each of the laments concludes, like a funeral dirge, with the repeated
refrain: "Alas, alas, the great city . . . for in one hour your judgment has
come" (vv. 10, 16, 19). The "alas" or "woe" is typical of prophetic funeral
laments. The solemn phrase, "in one hour," lifts up the finality of divine
judgment.

The second lament by the merchants provides considerable detail
about the commerce that creates abundant wealth in the empire (18:11-13).
We know that the first century was a time of unprecedented growth in
trade and prosperity. Historians often point out that the economic and
political ties between Rome and its provinces fostered unparalleled stability and growth in wealth. And the merchant class led the way with their
new-found prosperity. Nevertheless, the benefits reached at best only a
few in the empire. "Only the provincial elite and the Italian immigrants,
however, especially the shipowners and merchants, were reaping the

wealth of the empire's prosperity in Asia Minor, whereas a heavy burden of taxation impoverished the great majority of the provincial population. Thus a relatively small minority of the Asian cities benefited from the international commerce of the Roman empire while the masses of the urban population mostly lived in dire poverty or slavery (18:13)."[21] It is obvious that John sides with the poor and oppressed majority. By and large, the churches in Asia Minor belong to the lower class. Hence two churches are praised for their inner health, despite their external poverty (Smyrna, 2:9; Philadelphia, 3:8). But the church in Laodicea is severely condemned for claiming to be rich and prosperous, when in fact it is spiritually dead (3:17). We also find a critique of the rich and powerful elsewhere in Revelation (6:15; 17:4; 18:3).

A look at the detailed catalog of goods in the lament reveals luxuries that only the privileged could enjoy: gold, silver, jewels, and pearls; purple, silk, and scarlet; ivory, bronze, iron, and marble; and various spices. The list highlights "fine" linens and "scented" and costly wood (from African citrus trees, *thuia*). But it also includes the basics needed to feed and maintain the huge empire and its legions: flour and wheat, cattle and sheep, horses and chariots. The merchants exploited the world's resources to feed the empire's insatiable appetite. Yet most telling is the seer's conclusion to this long list: slaves and human lives (v. 13). Here is the real cost to create and maintain and defend the empire. Rome's supercolossus was built on the backs of human slaves. Nothing could be more devastating as a critique of this superpower and all subsequent superpowers. Human lives become objects to be conquered and exploited without mercy. This, one can say, is their true beastliness.

But now all of this splendor is gone forever, and the merchants stand in fearful torment wailing their loss: "Alas, alas, the great city . . . in one hour all this wealth has been laid waste" (18:16-17).

The third lament comes from the shipowners and those who prospered from their trade (18:17-19). Since the bulk of commerce occurred by sea, the traffic was immense and highly profitable. Mention is made of the extravagant luxury that flowed into the city. But now those days are past and all the seafarers mourn the burning of the great city: "Alas, alas . . . in one hour she has been laid waste" (18:19).

Upon conclusion of this lament, a voice from heaven calls upon God's people to rejoice at the judgment of Babylon (18:20; cf. 19:1-8). This is not

21. Ibid., 100. Krodel, *Revelation*, 302, agrees and even speaks of "a new class of business magnate, who gained fabulous wealth throughout the Empire, while the majority of the people lived in poverty and was burdened by taxation."

to be understood as a call for vengeance nor a kind of psychological catharsis of the oppressed against their oppressor. Rather, it is a cry for justice, a
plea for God to put an end to all the suffering of the victimized. The voice
assures the "saints and apostles and prophets" that this judgment of Babylon is on their behalf. John here speaks in solidarity with all the oppressed.

The portrait of the fall of Babylon culminates with a symbolic action
and concluding dirge (18:21-24). A mighty angel throws a great millstone
into the sea, as a symbol of Babylon's coming destruction (cf. Jer. 51:63).
Then, with haunting pathos, the seer portrays the cessation of life in the
city. Six times the refrain "no more" echoes down its silent streets. "The
silence of death hovers over the doomed city."[22] Yet the tone here is more
sympathetic, less harsh, almost regretful at the passing of the once magnificent city. Musicians, parades, artisans, craftspeople, home and family,
bride and groom, all of this "will be heard in you no more." But the reason
remains clear. Rome and its conquering legions have deceived the nations.
The divine verdict that brings judgment is this: guilty of murder. The persecution of God's people and the blood of imperial conquest are on its
soiled hands (v. 24). The blood of the saints and of all the victims of the *pax
Romana* cry out for justice (19:1-8).

Once again, in the image of Babylon the great, John has interpreted the
Roman empire as a malevolent power at work in the world. Its chief sins are
the exploitation of the earth's resources and people and the idolatrous
claims to allegiance. The fall of Babylon is God's just judgment upon a
human institution, the state, that has usurped its authority and become the
enemy of God, the church, and humankind.

These three images—beast, whore, Babylon—all spell out in their own
way John's view of the state. For him, the political structures are neither a
benevolent nor a neutral power. Rather, they act as agents of the demonic
realm opposed to God's people and all humankind. In fact, among the
earthly institutions that affect people's lives, the government has become
the chief instrument for the oppression and exploitation of the earth. In
particular, its claims to allegiance set it against the church of Jesus Christ.

In his pioneering study, Oscar Cullmann described Revelation as the
classic New Testament statement against the totalitarian state. "The totalitarian state is precisely the classic form of the devil's manifestation on
earth."[23] This rings true for what we have learned from Revelation. A totalitarian state, like Rome, with its self-deifying tendencies and all-pervasive
power, demands a loyalty that becomes idolatry. And this is true not only
of Rome but also of its counterparts throughout history. There seems to be

---

22. Krodel, *Revelation*, 307.
23. Cullmann, *The State*, 74.

something inherent in all human structures, and particularly political ones, that tend toward totalitarianism and its abuse of power.

In Revelation, evil has become institutionalized. Revelation sees the power of Satan at work in political, economic, and religious structures. Though cosmic in scope, evil takes visible form in historical or earthly institutions. "Revelation's notion of ultimate evil is best understood today as systemic evil and/or structural sin."[24] This is profoundly true, and this is what makes the evil so difficult to eradicate. Embedded in the authority and power of the government, systemic evil takes on near-superhuman dimensions. That is why in the Apocalypse the historic conflict has its counterpoint in the cosmic conflict between the kingdom of God and the kingdom of the world. Only God can overthrow this kind of tyrannical evil, and only faith in God and the Lamb can enable the saints to survive and resist on earth. In its persecution of the church, the state has in effect declared war on the kingdom of God.

The Church's Response

What then is the church's response to the demonic and oppressive state in Revelation? It finally becomes this: one mighty NO to imperial Caesar and all his idolatrous works and ways! The whole purpose of Revelation centers on this point. It is written to provide encouragement, hope, comfort and strength in the struggle against the tyrannical and destructive powers embodied in the state. We see this profound opposition expressed in several distinct ways.

No to Compromise!

In the face of strong temptations to compromise with the totalitarian claims of the government, Revelation urges a bold stance of uncompromising allegiance to God. This attitude of noncompromise comes out with special clarity in the opening letters to the seven churches (Rev. 2–3). Recent studies suggest that behind the controversy with certain groups—Balaamites (2:14), Nicolaitans (2:6,15), and the prophetess Jezebel (2:20-23)[25]— lies the burning question of the Christian's relationship to the surrounding

24. Fiorenza, *Revelation: Vision*, 307.

25. Jezebel was the infamous wife of King Ahab, denounced for spreading the worship of Baal and Asherah in ancient Israel (1 Kings 16-21; 2 Kings 9-10). Her name became synonymous with idolatry and heresy in later Jewish/Christian writings.

The identity of the "Jezebel" in Thyatira is now lost to us. She obviously had considerable influence and status in several churches. Many recognized hers as a prophetic voice and possibly she herself claimed to speak by the authority of the Spirit. Her message about the freedom of Christians to eat idol meat and to practice emperor worship found many prominent

culture.[26] In several letters, John severely denounces these persons for encouraging other Christians "to eat food sacrificed to idols" and "to practice fornication" (2:14, 20). The conflict may look something like this. The issue of whether Christians could in good conscience eat meat sacrificed to pagan deities was vigorously debated in the early church. Much of the meat for sale in the marketplace had been dedicated to idols. Jezebel, John's pseudonym for a Christian prophetess from Thyatira (2:20-23), may have taken the position that Christians could eat this meat and likewise participate in public functions where it was eaten, whether the event was social or religious. Like Paul, who allowed Christians to eat food offered to idols bought in the marketplace (though he forbade participating in Temple banquets), she may have argued that this was an exercise of Christian freedom, since idols have no real existence (1 Cor. 8:1-6; 9). Such a position would obviously make it easier for Christians to live with their pagan neighbors. In particular, it would allow Christian merchants and craftspeople to take part in their respective trade guilds, even though such involvement admittedly included prayers and a pinch of incense to Caesar and the gods.[27]

---

followers. John views her as a formidable opponent. Women played key roles in the churches of Asia Minor already in Paul's time (e.g., Lydia, a professional business person and house church leader, Acts 16:14-15). In fact, women as a whole experienced considerable freedom and influence in the Greco-Roman province of Asia Minor.

Fiorenza rightly calls attention to the way in which the "vitriolic rhetoric" of John against this woman has contributed to the subsequent creation in Western thought and Christian memory of an archetype Jezebel as the embodiment of both heresy and "the sexually dangerous woman" (Fiorenza, *Revelation: Vision*, 135). This archetype needs to be recognized and changed. Yet, on the whole, Fiorenza finds Revelation's attitude toward women separable from patriarchal and oppressive views. For every negative female image in Revelation there are counter-images of faithful and holy figures that consistently arise. For a contrary position, see Tina Pippin, *Death and Desire: The Rhetoric of Gender in the Apocalypse of John* (Louisville: Westminster/John Knox Press, 1992). Walter Wink essentially agrees with Pippin (*Engaging the Powers*, 99). Pippin regards the Apocalypse's portrayal of women as irredeemably patriarchal, but she can do so only by ignoring the weight of the positive counter-images and by a literal reading of numerous symbolic passages. Of special note is the observation that even Jezebel is not denounced because of her gender. Rather it is her prominence as a prophetic and charismatic leader that is the source of John's concern.

26. While there may be differences between these groups, most interpreters today are inclined to treat them as representing the same general theological and ethical positions the seer so harshly condemns. This is an intramural conflict between Christians, even though John views them as outside the realm of faithful teaching and practice—in fact, as a pernicious danger from within. They, however, no doubt see themselves as still within the loyal community of followers.

27. "They may have argued that the divinity of the emperor is a constitutional fiction for promoting the civil unity of the Roman Empire. For them, participation in Roman civil

Against such a willingness to compromise, the seer seeks to draw a clear line between Christian and pagan. He fears any tendency to blur the line will only result in further compromise and therefore insists that Christians cannot eat such meat without betraying their identity and fellowship in Christ.

No to Emperor Worship!

Undoubtedly this matter proved to be the most crucial of all.

Here the prophetess and her followers may have been even more daring. John's charge of "practicing fornication" should not be understood literally.[28] Instead, it is directed against those Christians who participate in the imperial cult. The prophetess may have insisted that this too is a question of Christian freedom. Christians know the emperor is no god, despite their divine pretensions. Hence Christians should be permitted to take part as a sign of loyal citizenship. Of course, the argument continued, this is only lip service, since Christians know better in their hearts and reserve their highest allegiance for God. Moreover, as almost everyone knows, respect for the imperial cult is more a matter of politics than religion. It might even be that Paul's counsel to pay taxes and honor those in authority was known and cited (Rom. 13:7). Even the words of Jesus could be so interpreted ("Give to the emperor the things that are the emperor's . . . ," Mark 12:17). Therefore not to pay taxes or respect those who rule is religious fanaticism at worst or simply plain foolishness.

Other commentators suspect that behind the debate may lie theological views similar to early gnosticism. John accuses his opponents of teaching "the deep things of Satan" (2:24). While this may only be cutting irony (i.e., what they call "deep things of God" is really of Satan), there may be more intended. Perhaps they taught that Jesus rules only in the spiritual sphere of life and so in the inner self they are free to serve God. Hence what they do outwardly matters little and no emperor cult or idol meat or pagan society can corrupt them. If so, the seer vigorously accuses them of falling prey to theological illusion and falsehood.

---

religion needed to be understood in political terms, as part of one's civic duty. . . . Why resist paying ceremonial respect to the image of the emperor? Why not make a compromise with the imperial powers and cults of Asia Minor and Rome?" (Fiorenza, *Revelation: Vision*, 133). Here one may anticipate the discussion of the Confessing Church in Germany under Nazism (below), where the loyalty oath to Hitler and the Third Reich provoked the same kind of arguments pro and con.

28. A few want to see ethical libertinism at work as well. But at least in the latter part of Revelation, fornication is always linked to the imperial cult, as we saw in our discussion of the image of the whore and Babylon the great.

Social class may also play a role in the dispute. In the letters, as we noted earlier, John has nothing but praise and encouragement for the literally poorest of churches (Smyrna, 2:9; Philadelphia, 3:8). But those communities that appear to be prosperous are most severely condemned (Sardis, 3:1; Laodicea, 3:7). The seer may thus be the spokesperson for the marginal and suffering communities, while the prophetess may represent the more wealthy and influential persons, with more at stake socially and economically.

If this is the position of the compromise party in the churches, John's response to their arguments is a thunderous NO. For the seer, such accommodation with the imperial cult would dangerously blur the difference between Christian and pagan, between loyalty to the one God and all other loyalties.

Recall that in Revelation 13 the two beasts focus their efforts on universal worship. And they are successful, except for the saints (13:8). For the author of Revelation, the matter of worship gets to the heart of things. Worship involves one's ultimate loyalties and trust. Therefore the key issue is finally this: Whom does one worship? Or, put differently, To whom do we owe our pledge of allegiance? The temptation to idolatry is always knocking at the door.

In the magnificent vision of the throne room of God and the Lamb that opens the Apocalypse proper, readers are introduced to the Creator and Redeemer of the cosmos (Rev. 4–5). No other is worthy to receive human worship. To God alone belongs the glory: the Pantokrator, the Alpha and Omega, the one who was and is and is to come (4:8, 11; 1:4, 8). To the Lamb alone belongs the victory: the one who was slain to liberate humankind, who creates a new community to serve the living God (5:9-10; 1:5-6). The throne-room vision reaches its grand climax when the whole creation joins in singing the hymn: "To the one seated on the throne and to the Lamb be blessing and honor and glory and might forever and ever!" (5:13). A great "Amen" then echoes throughout the universe (5:14).

Where God and the Lamb are acknowledged as the true sovereign of the cosmos, there can be no worship of Caesar. Any claim by the imperial state for anything approaching ultimate allegiance is arrogant and blasphemous, and must be resisted to the point of death. Here Christ and Caesar are locked in mortal conflict. Hence John's challenging NO to any compromise with the haughty and idolatrous beast. For the seer, the danger of idolatry lies close at hand. He finds the followers of the prophetess already compromised—they are traitors of Christ, cowards in the face of danger, now exploring the "deep things of Satan" in their efforts at self-justification. In contrast, he appeals for an unqualified worship of and obedience to the living God, regardless of consequences. He knows the threats and danger firsthand. He does not seek martyrdom for its own sake. But in view of the temptation to compromise in perilous times, Revelation calls for an unyielding resoluteness against all perceived forms of compromise with an idolatrous culture. Above all else, Revelation thunders a NO to the worship of Caesar, the political and historical incarnation of injustice and evil on earth.

In addition to the refusal to compromise with the idolatrous manifestations of the Roman state and culture, Revelation provides words of hope and encouragement for Christian communities in their ongoing struggle for survival. This positive affirmation is expressed in at least three ways in the Apocalypse.

Faithful Witness

A key word describing the activity of Christians is *martys*, along with its cognates *martyria/martyreō*. The literal meaning of the Greek *martys* is witness. Whenever possible, this literal meaning should be retained, since its does not yet have the restricted connotation of one who dies for the faith, although it is moving in that direction.

The church in Revelation is called to be a witnessing church, one that testifies to "the word of God and to the testimony (*martys*) of Jesus Christ" (1:2, 9; 22:16). The model for its witness is Jesus Christ, named in the opening greeting as "the faithful witness" (*ho martys ho pistos*, 1:5). We hear in this description a reference to Jesus' own courageous and steadfast loyalty to God, even in the face of opposition and death. Moreover, John himself shares with them in "persecution" (*thlipsis*) as well as "the kingdom and patient endurance" (1:9). They have a common solidarity in suffering with one another and with Jesus Christ. Like his, their own witness may include the necessity of suffering.

In the seven letters to the churches, and throughout the Apocalypse, there is the constant challenge to imitate the faithful witness of Jesus. In Pergamum we learn about Antipas, who is put to death for his testimony and who thereby receives the same title as Jesus, "the faithful witness" (2:12). In the vision of the souls under the altar who cry out, "How long, O Lord?" they are identified as those who died for the word of God and for the testimony (*martyria*) they had given (6:9). In Laodicea, an unfaithful church, the message to wake up comes from Jesus Christ, "the faithful and true witness" (3:14). In Revelation 11 there is the appearance of the enigmatic two witnesses (*martyria*, 11:22), whose fearless preaching in the beloved city leads to their death and subsequent resurrection (11:7-12). They likely represent the witness of the suffering church on earth. Later, the souls of the beheaded raised to life at the millennium are identified as those martyred "for their testimony (*martyria*) to Jesus and for the word of God" (20:4).

The Apocalypse reserves a special place of honor for those witnesses unto death, those we today name the martyrs (see below). But they are by no means the only faithful witnesses. Everyone who perseveres in the faith belongs to the company of the faithful. All the saints are called to imitate Christ by their uncompromising life and witness. "Be faithful unto death and I will give you the crown of life" (2:20) is both challenge and promise to all of God's people. In difficult and fearful times, John appeals for constant and bold witness to the gospel of Jesus Christ. Contrary to the opinion of many, the matter of evangelism is not yet a dead issue in Revelation.[29] In fact, the darker the hour, the brighter the light may shine. Neither threats, nor isolation, nor imprisonment, nor exile, nor death, nothing can hide the light of Jesus Christ and his faithful witnesses.

Patient Endurance

Even though the Apocalypse insists upon the church remaining a witnessing church, the overarching struggle has to do with sheer survival. Under pressure from an oppressive state and hostile society, the marginalized Christian communities in Asia find themselves hard pressed to stay alive. Faced with this kind of urgent crisis, the necessary word is simply, "Hang on, don't give up, the time is short!" Behind this encouraging admonition is the resolute confidence that despite all contrary appearances, the true sovereign of the earth is God and the Lamb.

Patient endurance (*hypomonē*) constitutes the core ethic in Revelation.[30] "Rather than faith or love, *hypomonē* becomes the main Christian virtue in Revelation." The Greek word can be variously translated "patience, endurance, fortitude, steadfastness, perseverance."[31] Underlying *hypomonē* is the strong sense of reliance upon God, a willingness to wait with patience

---

29. Many accuse Revelation of sharing the apocalyptic mentality of giving up on the world, which undercuts the motive for evangelism or for care of the earth. This can happen, but it does not seem to be the mood of Revelation, where witness remains alive. Admittedly, it takes place mostly under stress, given the historical context of Revelation. But the controversy over authentic Christian teaching in the letters shows that evangelism remains a significant issue for John and the churches.

30. Fiorenza, *Revelation*, 51. Allen Verhey, *The Great Reversal: Ethics and the New Testament* (Grand Rapids: Eerdmans, 1984), 147, fittingly titles his reflection on Revelation "Patient Endurance." Also Eduard Lohse, *Theological Ethics of the New Testament*, trans. by M. Eugene Boring (Minneapolis: Fortress Press, 1991), 192–97, names his chapter, "Steadfastness and Loyalty."

31. BAGD, "*hypomonē*."

in the sure hope of God's fulfilling what God has promised. In Revelation this is the certainty that the future belongs to God, that the victory over Satan has already been won in heaven (12:7-12) and on earth by virtue of Christ's death on the cross (1:5-6; 5:9-10), and that soon the struggle will be over and the cosmos will belong to God and the Lamb and all the redeemed in the new heaven and earth (1:3; 21:1—22:5).

We can trace the theme of patient endurance running like a golden strand through the Apocalypse. It begins when John announces his solidarity with the seven churches: "Your brother who shares with you in Jesus the persecution and the kingdom and the patient endurance" (1:9). All that follows underscores their mutual sharing in "persistent steadfastness." In the seven letters this becomes the motif that binds together their differing messages. John writes to prepare them for the coming crisis and to urge their unyielding loyalty to God alone. In each of the letters, "Revelation emphasizes the 'works' of the churches. Especially commended is 'patient endurance'; especially censured is any lack of loyalty to the cause; especially commanded is repentance and faithfulness."[32] Formally, each letter not only commends patient endurance but each ends with the promise "to those who conquer" (*nikein*). By his death, Jesus Christ, the conqueror par excellence, has liberated a people to serve God, a people who form a counter-kingdom on earth to that of imperial Rome. This Lamb who was slain is alone worthy of imperial honor and glory and blessing (5:5, 6-10). But through his victory, those from every tribe and language and people and nation who follow him belong to the company of conquerors. John even promises "they will reign on earth" (5:10). By concluding each letter in this formal way, John intends to encourage his fellow Christians in Asia Minor to be among "those who conquer."

Within the letter we find frequent admonitions to faithfulness. The opening letter to Ephesus strikes this theme: "I know your works, your toil and your patient endurance" (2:2, 3). To the church in Thyatira: "I know your works—your love, faith, service, and patient endurance" (2:19). The readers are urged to "be faithful unto death" (2:20), to hold fast and not to deny the faith (2:13, 25; 3:11), to keep the word and not to deny Christ's name (3:8, in v.10 "kept my word of patient endurance"). Even the church in Laodicea, despite its harsh condemnation, receives the promise "to the one who conquers . . . just as I [Christ] myself conquered" (3:21).

The centrality of *hypomonē* emerges at other places in the Apocalypse as well. In the vision of the two beasts in chapter 13, the call to endurance arises abruptly and unexpectedly. After John has introduced the imperial beast/Rome, who makes war upon the saints and before whom all the

32. Allen Verhey, *Great Reversal*, 148.

inhabitants of the earth bow down and worship, the scene is interrupted with the words, "Here is a call for the endurance and faith of the saints" (13:10). Similarly, in chapter 14, after a warning to those who worship the beast and its image, the refrain is repeated, "Here is a call for the endurance of the saints, those who keep the commandments of God and hold fast to the faith of Jesus" (14:12).

This necessity to hang on, however, requires patience and fortitude. When the martyrs under the altar cry out, "How long, O Lord?" they are told to rest a little longer, since other deaths will follow (6:10-11). No doubt patience comes hard in stressful times. Yet repeatedly the saints are assured the time is short. Their patience will be rewarded. The end is near. In chapter 12 the seer describes a war in heaven which results in the dragon and his angels being thrown down to earth (12:7-9). This means that for the moment Satan is alive and well on planet earth. But in the midst of the warnings to those on earth, comes the assurance that his time is short (12:12).

The fervent eschatological hope of the Apocalypse is that the end-time is near. Crisis times raise fervent expectations for believers. Like other apocalyptic visionaries, Jewish and Christian, John looks for the fulfillment of God's future right around the corner (1:1, 3; 22:6, 10, 12, 20). What makes his expectation profoundly Christian is his conviction that the past victory of the Lamb on the cross is the surety of the final triumph of God and the Lamb. The Apocalypse thus ends with the promise of Christ, "I am coming soon" (22:7, 12, 20). In response, the faithful pray with patient endurance, "Amen, come Lord Jesus" (*maranatha*, 22:20).[33]

Resistance

Revelation also issues a powerful appeal to resist the demonic and oppressive political structures that control the first-century world. I want here to examine this topic more fully, especially in view of the conflicting interpretations of the theme.

For a long time, apocalyptic literature has been regarded as essentially escapist literature; that is, a perspective that has all but given up on this present world. For the apocalypticist, so the argument goes, evil powers have so deeply corrupted this world and gained domination over it that the only solution is God's judgment upon the old order and recreation of a new one. Moreover, since the world is fundamentally unsaveable, there remains little or no motivation to care for it. From this perspective, apocalyptic eschatology involves a flight from history and responsibility, undercutting any kind of this-worldly ethic. This negative assessment of apocalyptic ethics

33. This Aramaic prayer probably originated within the eucharistic setting of the early church (cf. 1 Cor. 16:22).

has remained near-orthodoxy among scholars until recently.[34] But the whole assumption needs to be questioned and a more accurate understanding of apocalyptic ethics developed.

It is true that in apocalyptic literature, including Revelation, the present age is dominated by demonic powers and their earthly embodiments. The end result will be God's destruction of these powers and the creation (or recreation) of a new world order. Yet abandonment of this old world is not the basic attitude, nor any kind of otherworldly passivity. Rather, God's people are called to responsible, faithful, courageous, even heroic, life and action, despite crisis times.

Recent studies point out how the previous understanding of apocalyptic was caught between two apparent contradictions. On the one hand, it viewed this literature as abdicating both history and ethics under the pressure of trying historical circumstances. On the other hand, it recognized the near-fanatical inspiration and incentive this literature effected in the Jewish struggles for survival and freedom. Surprisingly, apocalyptic literature heightened the desire and willingness to resist the alien powers and battle for justice and independence. Accordingly, a new understanding is emerging that overcomes this contradiction and better grasps the link between apocalyptic and ethical action. Jewish apocalyptic, both biblical and nonbiblical, continued the classical prophetic tradition of critical opposition to rulers, both Jewish and pagan. The book of Daniel, for example, launches a vigorous protest against the Seleucid regime and their attempt to wipe out the Jewish religion and culture ca. 167–64 B.C.E. Daniel urges a heroic loyalty and resistance, even to death. The same is true of other apocalyptic writings originating during the intertestamental period (200 B.C.E.–200 C.E.). They all advocate opposition toward those who rule, whether apostate Jewish leaders or alien imperiums. Furthermore, their hope is not some pie in the sky, as a facile reading may suggest. They expect a restoration of the land, political and economic and religious freedom, and a new time of peace and justice and prosperity here on earth or a renewed heaven and earth. Jewish resistance movements in pre-70 C.E. Palestine were motivated to a considerable degree by such apocalyptic writings and beliefs. "Far from an 'abandonment of historical responsibility' and 'a retreat into a vision of the higher reality,' apocalyptic visions and literature attempt to make sense of and to respond to concrete historical situations of oppression and even persecution. Far from providing an

---

34. So Walter Schmithals, *The Apocalyptic Movement: Introduction and Interpretation*, trans. by John E. Steeley (Nashville: Abingdon, 1975), 108: "Like the gnostics the apocalypticists know no ethic." Similarly, Jack T. Sanders, *Ethics in the New Testament: Change and Development* (Philadelphia: Fortress, 1975), 114.

escape, apocalyptic visions apparently helped people to remain steadfast in their traditions and to resist systematic attempts to suppress them."[35]

The same kind of vigorous opposition to the Roman empire and its repressive structures is generated by the Apocalypse. This is underground literature meant to create faithfulness to God and the Lamb in times of harassment, suffering, and persecution. This is resistance literature that defies the emperor and his propaganda machine, and unmasks the illusions of power and invincibility as the "great lie." This is subversive literature that refuses to say yes to the imperial cult and proclaims another as "Lord and Savior." This is martyr-producing literature that models bold and unflinching commitment to God and the Lamb, regardless of cost. This is revolutionary literature that creates counter-communities of Christian resistance in the midst of the enemy's domain.[36]

How is such resistance possible? At bedrock is the firm conviction that this world belongs to God, who will ultimately determine its destiny. In the Apocalypse, as noted above, the final victory over the alien powers has already been fought and won. This is the triumph of the Lamb who was slain (5:9-10). But the struggle is not yet over, as the Dragon and his earthly counterparts mount their counter-offensive to preserve their dominion over the world. Tough times lie ahead for the people of God. Nevertheless, they hold firm. "This brutal suppression ought to cut the nerve of Christian resistance. Instead, the Christian movement grows under repression. Jesus' followers seem to expect nothing less from the system that crucified their leader."[37]

Perhaps this is the appropriate moment to look at the role of the martyrs in Revelation. I am now using the term in the restricted sense of one who dies for a cause. Martyrdom plays a significant role in the Apocalypse. Although past interpreters greatly exaggerated the threat of persecution under Domitian, it remained a menacing shadow. Only one martyr is named, Antipas of Pergamum (2:13), yet exile and imprisonment and martyrdom constitute the threatened future for the churches in Asia Minor

35. Richard A. Horsley, *Jesus and the Spiral of Violence: Popular Jewish Resistance in Roman Palestine* (New York: Harper & Row, 1987), 139. Chap. 5 of his book provides the best current discussion of this topic, focusing especially on Jewish resistance in Roman Palestine. Similarly, Paul D. Hanson, *Old Testament Apocalyptic* (Nashville: Abingdon, 1987), 83, protests against the escapist charge by saying, "Nothing could be further from the truth." To the contrary, it provided "The means by which the strength to resist was kept alive and the idiom by which revolutionary strategies were enveloped and promulgated." He cites the black spirituals and the German martyr Dietrich Bonhoeffer as contemporary witnesses.

36. ". . . it [the church] understands itself as already God's empire, God's kingdom in Domitian's empire a counter-empire" (Verhey, *Great Reversal*, 149).

37. Wink, *Engaging the Powers*, 322.

(2:3, 9-10, 13; 13:3, 5, 10). The stirring appeals for endurance, the ringing promise to the conquerors, the conflict with the synagogue, all have potential persecution as their background.

In the vision of the martyred under the altar, the seer sees "the souls of those . . . slaughtered for the word of God and for the testimony they had given" (6:9). To the cry, "How long?" until their deaths will be avenged, they are told to wait a little longer, "until the number would be complete" of those still to die (6:11). Some argue that this text proves a large number of Christians had already suffered martyrdom when Revelation was written. John no doubt has past and present martyrs in mind, including the victims of Nero, the apostles Peter and Paul and James, as well as possible deaths in the churches of Asia Minor. Yet it is unlikely we should take this passage as any indication of numerous martyrdoms. The vision is part of the "great persecution" (3:10) the seer envisions right around the corner. More than one martyrdom may have occurred in John's time, yet wide-scale persecution does not happen until the mid-third century. Nevertheless, under the harassment and pressure the churches were already experiencing, John felt the urgent need to equip the churches for the ultimate resistance, if necessary.

The martyr-witness may also be present in the vision of the 144,000 sealed (7:9-17). Those who are sealed represent the multitude of the redeemed from every nation. In response to the question, "Who are these . . . ?" the elder explains, "These are they who have come out of the great ordeal; they have washed their robes and made them white in the blood of the Lamb" (7:14). The great ordeal (*thlipsis*) is apocalyptic imagery for the final period of conflict between God and Satan, a period of intense suffering for the faithful, along with chaos in the cosmos (Mark 13:14-26, Rev. 3:10). John sees that time drawing near. And, in light of its approach, he exhorts the believers to persevere to the end and win the glorious reward. Among the conquerors clothed in white are doubtless the literal martyrs.[38] Their lives become the model for their partners in the Jesus resistance-movement.

We find the martyr-church elsewhere in Revelation as well. After the devil is thrown down to earth, a heavenly song trumpets the victory of God's people here on earth. That victory was won not by their own power or might but by "the blood of the Lamb," that is by their faithfulness "even in the face of death" (12:11). Or again, the two witnesses who are killed and raised to life for their Christian proclamation represent the martyr church at work (11:4-13).

---

38. A few think the whole group represents the martyrs who pass through the great tribulation (George Eldon Ladd, *A Theology of the New Testament* (Grand Rapids: Eerdmans, 1974), 627.

Even more explicit about the martyr-witness is the end-time period known as the millennium (20:4-6). There is no need here to enter the controversy over this disputed passage. According to John, after Satan is bound and thrown into the bottomless pit, Christ and the martyred rule on earth for a thousand years. John makes it clear that those who come to life and rule with Christ are "the souls of those . . . beheaded for their testimony to Jesus and for the word of God" (20:4).[39] Thus this "first resurrection" (20:5) becomes a special reward for the faithful martyrs. They are promised a reign on earth as a result of their costly service. The seer thereby raises up the martyr profile for his readers as a potent symbol of resistance and hope.

This motif of the martyr-witness also permeates the Christology of Revelation. Its central image is the "Lamb who was slain." This distinctively Christian portrait of the Messiah becomes both the source of divine liberation and the sign of faithful obedience. For John, the crucified and risen Lord is the first of God's faithful witnesses (1:5) and the saints are urged to follow in his steps (14:4).

The theme of martyrdom is indeed pervasive in the Apocalypse, and there is no glossing over its harsh possibility or reality. Yet nowhere do we find any encouragement to seek martyrdom. Nor does Revelation assume most believers will be asked to make the ultimate sacrifice. Rather, all Christians are called to be ready. And the few who follow Christ's own way to death are held up for praise and reward. Their deeds follow them as they now rest from their labors (14:13).

Perhaps the memory of Nero's earlier persecution remains vivid, when for a moment the imperial beast broke out in great wrath. Fiery crosses and tearing to pieces by wild dogs are not easily forgotten. Only twenty years after the writing of Revelation, in the neighboring province of Bithynia, as noted above, Pliny the Younger relates how quickly the virus of hatred and fear and prejudice against religious minorities can turn into matters of life and death. Some had died simply because they refused to curse Christ or to offer a pinch of incense before the image of Caesar. A generation later, Polycarp, Bishop of Smyrna (d. 155), one of the seven churches, bears the hatred and fury of a populace and government demanding he renounce his allegiance to the one true Lord of the universe. His dying words are enshrined in Christian martyrologies: "I have served him eighty-six years and in no way has he dealt unjustly with me;

---

39. A few argue that in this passage all the saints are raised to life. But to do this one must find two groups in 20:4, "those beheaded" and "those who had not worshipped the beast and its image." This forced exegesis negates John's main point that the millennium is a special reward for the martyrs.

so how can I blaspheme my king who saved me?"[40] Justin Martyr follows shortly, in 165.

Against this martyr background one can best understand the list of vices in the Apocalypse. These lists may stem from Jewish antipagan propaganda, but John adapts them to his specific purpose. At the top of the list are "the cowardly, the faithless, the polluted . . ." (21:8). These are persons who do not resist, who compromise the faith, who do not hang on regardless of cost. Accordingly, they are consigned to the lake of fire, the place of eternal punishment (21:8). The other brief lists single out those who practice abomination and falsehood (21:27; 22:15). Here, too, the temptation to idolatrous compromise with imperial Rome is uppermost in mind.

Revelation thus advocates an ethic of resistance toward the prevailing culture and particularly toward an idolatrous and unjust government. Christians belong to another sovereignty than Caesar's. They pledge allegiance to only one Lord and refuse to participate in the "civil religion" of imperial Rome. Rather than teach an escapist ethic that abandons history, Revelation challenges Christians to act openly, daringly, even subversively for their faith. It intends to stir up and empower God's people to work against the evil and demonic structures that dominate this world. The certainty that this world belongs finally to God and the Lamb frees them to live with fervent hope and confidence. Revelation does not engender passive or weak-hearted saints but people of strength and courage. Far from a flight from history or responsibility, the Apocalypse arouses the strength to resist and to live with hope for God's promised future of justice and shalom already begun.

In this sense, Revelation is protest literature. It is written to protest against oppressors and to console the oppressed. To the imperial government's demand for idolatrous accommodation, Revelation says, "Resist!" To the culture's lure to compromise one's faith and values, Revelation says, "Resist!" To social pressures to conform one's ethical standards to the prevailing norms, Revelation says, "Resist!" Moreover, Revelation teaches active resistance to the beast and its dominion.[41] It dares to name the beast as imperial Rome and its collaborators. It condemns Rome's unjust and

40. William R. Schoedel, "The Martyrdom of Polycarp," VIII.9.3, in *The Apostolic Fathers*, vol. 5 (London: Thomas Nelson, 1967).

41. Here I disagree with Schrage (*Ethics*, 346), who fails to grasp the counterculture dynamic of apocalyptic in general and especially Revelation when he emphasizes the passive character of its ethic (e.g., by saying that Revelation does not call for revolt "but for non-violent passive resistance" (346); or again, "they [persecuted believers] should not even try to shake off the demonic and despotic regime" (347). While I agree there is no call for rebellion or a holy war, there is public and heroic protest, and confidence in God's imminent judgment of the oppressive superpower.

inhuman conquest by the sword and its exploitation of the peoples and resources of the earth. It even prays and works for Rome's collapse. It seeks to form communities of protest and resistance, where the will of God is done on earth, not the will of Caesar. And it encourages fearless testimony to the Lordship of Christ over every earthly power, regardless of cost.

Nevertheless, there is one decisive point at which the Apocalypse draws the line on its ethic of resistance. This is Christian literature, and Christian resistance is a special kind. Revelation does not preach hatred, violence, or even revenge. Nor does it rely on the power of the sword. There is no appeal to political or armed revolution, no conscription of Christian legions or armies of crusaders. Neither do we hear the cry for a holy war in the name of God, such as inspired the Zealot resistance against Rome and resulted in the disastrous rebellion of 66–70 C.E., which left Jerusalem and the Temple in ruins. For John, God and the Lamb alone conquer. The followers of Christ know they may suffer at the hands of those in power. The Apocalypse prepares them to accept their suffering with patience and courage. But, like the Lamb, their victory comes by way of suffering love. Their response to hatred and violence is not more of the same, but the willingness to suffer for the cause of Jesus Christ, without hatred or bitterness. Here we encounter once again the radically new ethic toward one's enemies exemplified in the life and teaching of Jesus.

One passage, in fact, appears explicitly to forbid any violent retaliation by Christians, a text that occurs in the midst of the vision of the imperial beasts in Revelation 13. After describing the first beast "who makes war on the saints and conquers them" because they refuse him their worship (13:7-8), the seer pauses to speak words of encouragement: "Let anyone who has an ear listen: If you are to be taken captive, into captivity you go; if you kill with the sword, with the sword you must be killed" (13:9-10a).[42] These words are best understood as a strong word of admonition to Christians faced with persecution. They are told to accept whatever happens. If they face imprisonment or even martyrdom, they are told not to retaliate with violence. But if they take the sword, they are warned that the authorities will respond in kind. It is possible that we have an echo of the saying of Jesus against taking the sword (Matt. 26:52). Once again, we find that Christian resistance, even amid Revelation's powerful protest against unjust and tyrannical governments, is of a special kind. It does not advocate evil for evil. In its place, it responds with suffering love, as did its Lord. Christians

---

42. The text is uncertain. Cf. G. B. Caird, *Commentary on the Revelation of St. John the Divine* (New York: Harper and Row, 1966), 169, who argues convincingly for the reading in most translations, including the *NRSV*. John here reworks the Jeremiah 15:2 text from a threat to an admonition to hold firm.

conquer by the sword of the Word (2:12), by their endurance and faith, and by their mighty NO to the idolatrous claims of Caesar. Only in this way can the cycle of violence be broken and the power of tyranny overcome.[43]

Does Revelation inculcate justice—or vengeance? My contention that Revelation does not preach hatred or violence or revenge against enemies and oppressors needs further consideration. Friends and critics have been troubled by what appears to be a vindictive spirit boiling beneath the surface. Not only does the central apocalyptic section focus on the divine judgment of demonic powers and their earthly partners (chaps. 5–21), but one also hears frequent cries for vengeance intermingled with depictions of divine action in violent and oft-repulsive imagery. One critic went so far as to describe Revelation as "the Judas of the New Testament,"[44] that is, a writing contrary to the spirit and teaching of Jesus.

In part, the concentration on divine judgment is typical of all apocalyptic literature.[45] In Revelation, at least, its purpose is not to show God's vindictiveness against evil. Rather, it demonstrates God's promise to liberate this world from hostile powers and to bring it to its divinely intended purpose. In Rev. 11:15-18, the seer interprets history as a battleground between two kingdoms. In the visions of judgment the kingdom of God is at work overthrowing the kingdom of this world. Here God is busy reclaiming the cosmos. And since the powers of evil are strong, it is a mighty battle to the finish.

Perhaps this much we can understand. But what especially bothers discerning readers are the scenes that plead for divine vengeance and portray God's judgments with seeming delight. For example, the martyrs under the altar ask, "How long . . . before you judge and avenge our blood on the inhabitants of the earth?" (6:9). Again, those tempted to worship the beast

43. So Caird, *Revelation*, 170: "Only if the victim absorbs the wrong and so puts it out of currency, can it be prevented from going any further." Another interpreter puts it this way: "To be sure, this resistance movement, this counter-empire, does not take arms to achieve power. They do not plot to seize economic and political control. But even in the style of their resistance, they are to give testimony to the victory of the Lamb that was slain and to the transformation of economic and political power wrought by him. They are to defend the Lord's claim to an earth corrupted and abused by its alliance with Satan and the emperor. They are to live courageously and faithfully, resisting the pollutions of the cult of the emperor, including its murder, fornication, sorcery, idolatry, and especially its lie that Caesar is Lord" (Verhey, *Great Reversal*, 154).

44. D. H. Lawrence, *Apocalypse* (Heinemann: London, 1931), 13: "And just as inevitably as Jesus had to have a Judas Iscariot among his disciples, so did there have to be a Revelation in the New Testament." Lawrence possessed considerable knowledge of the Bible, despite his sometimes biting critique.

45. See D. S. Russell, *The Method and Message of Jewish Apocalyptic* (OTL; Philadelphia: Westminster, 1964), for the best study of apocalyptic, including the theme of judgment.

are warned about the eternal torment of the damned, whose hellish smoke arises forever before the throne of the Lamb (14:9-11). And God's wrath is imaged as a great winepress filled with all the wicked, whose blood flows a horse's bridle-height for over 200 miles outside the holy city (14:17-20). An avenging angel declares that God's bloody judgments upon the persecutors are deserved and the dead under the altar agree (16:5-7). Finally, the lament at the fall of Babylon begins with a heavenly voice taunting once-mighty Babylon and declaring double-punishment for her sins (18:5-6). And, after Babylon's fall is complete, a great multitude in heaven shout, "Hallelujah! . . . he has avenged on her the blood of his servants." The scene ends with the twenty-four elders and four living creatures before the throne saying, "Amen. Hallelujah!" (19:1-4).

This is troubling material that cannot be dismissed with ease. Unfortunately, some popular commentators revel in the fact God will one day get even with their enemies and take a secret (or not so secret) delight in God's promised destruction of this old world. Other, more sophisticated interpreters try to understand the mind-set of apocalyptic writers. They suggest that in situations of perceived crisis or social deprivation, the authors project their feelings of aggression and hostility outward to the cosmos, where God now acts on their behalf. In this way, their longings for vengeance are relieved.[46] Neither of these responses seems adequate. What then?

Some of the vindictive language can be attributed to the historical setting and to the nature of apocalyptic imagery. Crisis times evoke passionate outbursts of feeling and cries of desperation (cf. the imprecatory Psalms: 35; 69; 137). Moreover, nearly all of Revelation's language has biblical or Near Eastern parallels (e.g., divine wrath, plagues, holy war, messianic woes, combat myth between Yahweh and monsters of chaos, Babylon, cosmic upheavals). Further, this language needs to be understood symbolically or metaphorically, not literally.

But of greatest importance is the need to recognize that this language is fundamentally a cry for justice. What the seer wants to affirm is not vengeance but vindication. And therein lies a world of difference. Justice is God making right what is wrong with the world. Behind the cry for justice is the confidence that some day evil will be punished and good prevail. Without justice, the universe is at the mercy of the powerful and strong. What Revelation promises, along with the rest of Scripture, is that in the end God's just judgments will be done. And this promise is given to those who need it most. For Revelation addresses persons experiencing innocent suffering and grave injustice. It speaks from the underside of history, from

---

46. Adela Y. Collins, *Crisis and Catharsis: The Power of the Apocalypse* (Philadelphia: Westminster, 1984), especially chap. 5.

the vantage-point of the marginalized and dispossessed. Accordingly, "the outcry of Revelation for justice and judgment can be fully understood only by those who hunger and thirst for justice."[47]

We should also observe that in the Apocalypse it is only God and the Lamb who execute divine judgment. There is no call for a holy war by the saints. Never do the people of God become co-executors of God's punishment upon the wicked. Even at the end-time battle of Armageddon, the saints do not fight for or with God (16:12-16; 19:17-21; 20:7-10). Here Revelation differs sharply from some apocalyptic literature of the period, where the elect join in the conflict.[48] The saints in Revelation trust God to do the work of justice and judgment.

Finally, there is a surprising note of universal salvation that sounds throughout Revelation. Beyond the fearful visions of judgment, there are glimpses of God's purpose to save the whole creation (5:13; 21:24-26; 22:2).[49] These unexpected moments demonstrate that judgment is only the penultimate word. Redemption is God's ultimate hope for the world.

Is the spirit of the Apocalypse the spirit of Jesus Christ? Has the Jesus who taught love for one's enemies now been transformed into the avenging Lamb? Is Revelation the Judas of the New Testament? I think not. At the center remains the figure of the Lamb who was slain. This paradoxical image of victory through suffering love forms the heart and soul of its

47. Fiorenza, *Revelation: Vision*, 139.

48. E.g., in I Enoch 91:12-19, the righteous elect use the sword to execute judgment upon their Gentile oppressors. This coheres with the harsh attitude toward the Gentiles found in some later Jewish apocalypses, where the Gentiles either become servants of Israel in the last days or they are condemned to eternal punishment or annihilation simply because they are Gentiles. See D. S. Russell, *Method*. The Essene community at Qumran also foresaw participation by the righteous in the coming war against the nations (*Rule of Community*, 1QS). In fact, the War scroll (1QM) describes in minute military detail the final apocalyptic battle between the sons of light (elect from the tribes of Levi, Judah, and Benjamin) and the sons of darkness. It is a joint action of angelic armies and the elect people of God. While the priests do not take part, they exhort the elect army to battle. "The War scroll demands of the community that they take an active part in the final overthrow of wickedness, in a manner similar to the Jewish military activists of the period, the Zealots." So Christopher Rowland, *The Open Heaven: A Study of Apocalyptic in Judaism and Early Christianity* (New York: Crossroad, 1982), 41. He even argues the War scroll is not apocalyptic since the War takes place in history by human involvement.

Nevertheless, as a whole, the apocalyptic literature believes the endtime comes by divine action, not human. And "By large the apocalypses do not countenance participation in an armed struggle as part of the lot of the righteous." (Rowland, *Open Heaven*, 42; also Russell, *Method*, 269). Rather, they counsel "patient pacifism" as in the Apocalypse of John.

49. See the article by Walter E. Pilgrim, "Universalism in the Apocalypse," *Word and World* 3 (1989), 22–30; also Boring, *Revelation*, 112-19; Mathias Rissi, *The Future of the World: An Exegetical Study of Revelation 19:11—22:15* (SBT 2/23; Naperville, Ill.: Allenson, 1972).

Christology. And suffering love marks the authentic followers of the Lamb.

Yet one must be careful, lest the images of vengeance and violence overshadow the images of transformation and renewal. The Apocalypse pleads for divine justice on behalf of the oppressed and victimized on earth. But beyond judgment lies the new heaven and earth and the promise of divine mercy and healing for humanity, embracing even the nations and kings of this world (21:24; 22:2).

Summary

The Apocalypse adopts a stance toward the state that is radically different from the two other New Testament traditions. Here we find an understanding of the political structures as demonic, historical embodiments of injustice and evil. In response, the church is encouraged toward an ethic of uncompromising resistance.

Why this dramatic change in attitude? In part, it can be explained by the historical setting of potential persecution and intensified pressure on behalf of the imperial cult, most likely under Domitian. John sees the churches in Asia Minor facing a time of crisis from a hostile state and culture, in which their survival will be sorely tested. He therefore writes to ensure loyalty to Christ above loyalty to Caesar and the idolatrous temptations at work. While this historical setting plays a major role in shaping John's attitude, it does not explain everything, since other (and later) New Testament writers face similar hostilities and yet counsel quiet and peaceable submission to those in power (see chap. 5). No doubt a fierce debate engaged Christians within the churches of Asia Minor and elsewhere over the appropriate response to a tyrannical and oppressive government.

Revelation employs three apocalyptic images to depict the state as the prime historical representative of evil on earth: the two beasts, the great whore, and Babylon the great. While imperial Rome is the particular embodiment of the unjust and anti-Christ government, John's images apply to all such political structures. The chief accusations against the imperial authorities are idolatry (the emperor cult, claims to allegiance) and misuse of power and wealth (17:5-6).

In reply, the seer calls for three kinds of responses: faithful witness, patient endurance, and active resistance. Revelation, I argue, does not teach an escapist ethic of irresponsibility toward history. Instead, it intends to motivate and encourage action toward greater justice on behalf of suffering believers and all humanity. And though it advocates resistance, it is nonviolent resistance patterned after the suffering of the Lamb who was slain, the central Christological image in Revelation. Finally, the disturbing images of vengeance and retribution were interpreted as expressions of longing for divine justice.

How shall we interpret this ethic of resistance in relation to the other New Testament responses? Does not Revelation give us a more realistic portrait of political institutions and their self-deifying tendencies? Should the ethic of resistance be the norm for the church's attitude rather than the ethic of subordination? A few have thought so. Or is Revelation the product of an apocalyptic worldview that turns everything into a cosmic struggle between good and evil, right and wrong, and so represents an extremity not to be taken seriously or at least constitutively? And how can one square the attitude of Revelation toward the state as the chief historical representative of evil on earth with the understanding of the state as the divinely appointed instrument for preserving the common good among peoples and nations?

Two positive points deserve emphasis. First, Revelation represents a critical assessment of political structures that needs full consideration alongside the two other New Testament traditions. All stand within the church's canon. Second, the Apocalypse provides the best insight into the reality that evil is not merely personal but systemic.[50]

Political structures can and do become instruments of demonic injustice and profound abuse of power and wealth. We forget this at great cost, as this tragic century reminds us. Moreover, the state can and does become a source of misplaced loyalty and blasphemous idolatry, even for the church. To trust any other than God or to give allegiance to any other than Christ, constitutes the sin of idolatry for John.

Two major problems remain. One has to do with Revelation's obvious tendency to demonize the state. How does one deal with the apocalyptic mentality of seeing everything as good or evil, divine or satanic, just or unjust, with few or no shades of reality between? While this can alert readers to demonic evil that may lurk behind the scenes and to which they may be blind, it seldom describes reality. At the same time, to see only shades of gray can lead to paralysis or failure to recognize radical evil when it is present. Perhaps we need apocalyptic seers to warn against idolatrous ideologies at work in political institutions. They can spur us to insight and action and resistance. But can we live by this vision? And how do we assess when the state has become demonic?

---

50. Krodel, *Revelation*, 65: "In the place of the Pauline perspective of a divine order of creation John introduced the apocalyptic perspective of opposing powers. In so doing, he raised the consciousness of his churches to the presence of radical evil within political power structures."

A second and related problem: Is Revelation an appropriate response "for all seasons" or is it best reserved for times of crisis? Revelation and other apocalyptic writings, both Jewish and Christian, have originated in settings of persecution in order to bring hope and comfort in tough times and to urge bold and heroic resistance. Are these then the proper "times and seasons" to draw on Revelation for the church's response to the powers that be? Many think so. They argue that this was true for the crisis faced by the churches in Asia Minor and that it has proved to be true down through the centuries.[51] This argument is persuasive. But if it is so, this means the use of Revelation with respect to the state is limited in other historical settings. It also means that Revelation is most profoundly understood by Christians experiencing systemic evil and living under political and economic oppression and persecution. Other interpreters, however, find this too limiting. They underscore the potential for evil embedded in all human institutions, and especially political ones, as history so acutely proves.[52] Therefore, they see Revelation as a necessary warning against all governments who may be tempted to usurp their authority and purpose.

Chapter 5 will discuss these and other issues more fully. For the present, I make the appeal to give the ethic of resistance in the Apocalypse an open and honest hearing. It has all too often been neglected, to the detriment of both the church and humanity.

51. For example, two twentieth-century commentaries on Revelation were written under tyrannical governments: Hanns Lilje, *The Last Book of the Bible: The Meaning of the Revelation of St. John*, trans. by Olive Wyon (Philadelphia: Muhlenberg, 1957) during his imprisonment under Hitler; and Alan Boesak, *Comfort and Protest: The Apocalypse from a South African Perspective* (Philadelphia: Westminster, 1984), under the recent apartheid state of South Africa. See chapter 5 for further discussion of this question regarding the "fitting time" to appeal to Revelation.

52. See William Stringfellow, *An Ethic for Christians and Other Aliens in a Strange Land* (Waco, Tex.: Word, 1973); or Daniel Berrigan, *Beside the Sea of Glass: The Song of the Lamb* (New York: Seabury, 1978).

5.

CHURCH AND GOVERNMENT FROM THE NEW TESTAMENT TO THE PRESENT

IN THIS FINAL CHAPTER I SEEK TO DRAW TOGETHER THE RESULTS OF THE foregoing New Testament survey and offer some suggestions concerning their use by the church today.

Summary Statements

Diversity in the New Testament: From Subordination to Resistance
Contrary to what some may think, there is no single, unified attitude toward political structures in the New Testament. As we have seen, the views range from the ethic of subordination to that of staunch opposition. The conclusions of this study can be diagrammed as follows.

Ethic of subordination	Ethic of critical distancing	Ethic of resistance
Christ and Caesar	Christ and Caesar?	Christ against Caesar
Pauline, Pastorals, 1 Peter, Hebrews	Jesus and the Gospels	Revelation

The above diagram provides a concise summary of the primary attitudes toward the state in the New Testament. Many questions arise. How do we account for this surprising diversity? How should one deal with the contradictory views so obvious? Which attitude, if any, is normative for the Christian response to the state? How might one decide? Or might all three have their role to play, dependent on historical or other circumstances in which the church finds itself? Again, how should one decide? In this chapter I will attempt to answer some of these difficult questions so as to provide a basis for contemporary reflection on church/government issues.

How can we explain the surprising, apparently contradictory range of attitudes within the New Testament itself? While some clues have emerged in the previous chapters, the matter needs further discussion. One thing we cannot do is to ignore the diversity. This may happen if we concentrate on only a single view or decide prematurely (on theological, political, or ethical grounds) that one view is normative or at least the most important. Unfortunately, this approach has occurred repeatedly and continues to occur, all too often with harmful, even tragic consequences. We must keep the whole range of the New Testament attitudes in view.

Some try to explain the differences on basis of the degree of opposition experienced by the Christian communities. Accordingly, the more threatened the churches or authors perceive their situation, the more intensely they oppose those who hold power.

But this common assumption does not necessarily hold true in the New Testament or the early church. In fact, it is probably a mistake to assume that pronouncements favorable to the state cannot be written in times of threat or persecution. The Christian theological assessment of the state was not "dependent upon the degree of comfort in which Christians were permitted to live."[1] Even when facing considerable hostility and alienation, as in 1 Peter or Hebrews, Christians sought to demonstrate their loyalty as good citizens and respect for the emperor. At the turn of the century, the author of 1 Clement, as well as the second-century Christian apologists, did not become enemies of the state or call for resistance to Rome, despite increased persecution.[2]

Nevertheless, there is an obvious link between persecution and resistance. In Revelation we find a Christian author who perceives the threat from the state as fundamentally hostile to Christian existence and therefore calls for heroic resistance and noncompromise with the demonic and unjust and idolatrous state.

Another possible way to explain the range of attitudes is to take a chronological approach. Here one seeks to trace in the New Testament writings a record of growing conflict in the first century between church and state. The writings of Paul are the earliest, and come from a time of relative peace with Rome (50–60 C.E., before the Neronian persecution in 64), and so are positive toward those who rule. The Gospels appear between 70–90 C.E., still a time of relative peace and quiet, but now with complica-

1. See C. K. Barrett, "The New Testament Doctrine of the State," in his *New Testament Essays* (London: SPCK, 1972), 18. He calls this an "illusion," often overlooked by New Testament scholars. According to Barrett, "The incidence of persecution did not greatly affect their [Christians'] attitude to the state."

2. See chap. 2, above, on the loyalty tradition in early Christianity.

tions caused by the events of 70 c.e. (the Roman conquest and the fall of Jerusalem), along with growing problems in local communities between nonconformist Christians and the traditional religions and customs. Finally, Revelation is written at the end of the first century under Domitian (96 c.e.), in a time of increased conflict with Rome and regional persecution in Asia Minor, linked especially to the cult of emperor worship. Hence Revelation's vehement denunciation of Rome as the epitome of satanic evil on earth.

There is undoubtedly some truth in attempting to grasp the history of the relationship between the church and Rome from the generally tranquil period of Paul to the more threatening setting at the end of the first century. Nevertheless, there is no straight line of development, as is all too often assumed, and this approach, in fact, presents a host of problems. Among them: (a) The Neronian persecution in 64 interrupts this chronological scheme. (b) The Pauline tradition of obedience to the state continues within the New Testament itself until the end of the century (Pastorals, 1 Peter). (c) The questionable assumption continues that increased conflict with the state means increased opposition from Christians (see above). (d) Although Revelation responds to a growing threat in Asia Minor with the call to resist the godless state, other writings addressed to Christians in neighboring regions about the same time (the 90s) call for acceptance of the suffering without hostility to Rome (1 Peter, 1 Clement [to Corinth], Epistle of Polycarp). (e) In the second century, despite increased persecution and tension (e.g., in Bithynia, Asia Minor, 112), only a very few Christian authors, all with apocalyptic mindsets such as Revelation, call for opposition or name Rome as the devil incarnate.[3] In brief, while the chronological explanation might seem full of promise at first glance, it is finally unable to explain the wide difference of views toward the state in the New Testament.

No single theory adequately explains the diverse attitudes toward political authority within the New Testament. Therefore, it is best simply to recognize the main attitudes present in the New Testament, as I have done, amid all their historical and theological and ethical differences.

Before giving a general summary, I make two preliminary observations. One, in addition to the traditional view of subordination toward those who govern, the Jesus tradition in the Gospels preserves more critical material with respect to those in power than is commonly recognized. Second, the witness of the book of Revelation needs to be taken into full account as well. In fact, this is the one New Testament writing that has as

---

3. See the discussion of the loyalty tradition in chap. 2.

its background the church's relationship to the sociopolitical structures of the time and as its purpose to define that relationship. Of all the writers, it is the author of the Apocalypse who grasps most clearly the potential gulf between church and state. We may raise questions concerning his response, but it needs to be taken seriously by the church in every age.

Is There a Normative View of the State in the New Testament?

The above is no easy question to answer. How should one choose between the response of subjection or that of resistance or something in between?

"For those who call Caesar "Lord" the matter is simply handled. For those who call Caesar "Satan" the matter is just as simply handled."[4] This quotation succinctly defines the complexity of the matter. There is no simple rule of thumb that can provide an answer appropriate for all occasions.

On the whole, Christian interpreters have tended to find the norm in the response of subordination to the state. This has grown out of the conviction that the government is one of the earthly institutions established by God for the good of the human family. "The primary New Testament conviction about the State is . . . that it is one of the provisions made by God for the well-being of his creation."[5] This view, repeated in numerous ways, remains the bedrock for most interpreters even today.

At the same time, the awareness of a persistent history of abuse and misuse by governments of their God-given authority, most recently and devastatingly in the twentieth century, has kept alive the other biblical responses to the state. Many practice a cautious response to the political structures, withholding their support at crucial points (e.g., the tradition of conscientious objection). Some find most governments and their claims to power and loyalty bordering on idolatry. A few courageously refuse to honor or support what they perceive to be unjust or tyrannical authorities. Christians belong to all of these groups, and each can find New Testament sanction for their beliefs and actions.

Is there a normative view of the government in the New Testament? In what follows I will draw some general conclusions from this study that can help provide a framework for answering this question. My response will be both yes and no to the question: yes to the divine intention for the state; no in light of its inherent failure to live up to its providential purpose. This means that the church's response in every situation will depend on its evaluation of the degree to which the particular government fulfills its divine mandate.

---

4. Fred Craddock, *Luke* (Interpretation; Louisville: Westminster/John Knox, 1990), 236.
5. Barrett, "The New Testament Doctrine," 19.

Results

Ultimacy of Obedience to God

There is biblical agreement on one matter: the ultimacy of obedience to God. God and God's sovereignty alone are worthy of human worship and unconditional obedience. For Christians, Jesus Christ alone is Lord. The inbreaking kingdom of God inaugurated by Jesus has priority over all other loyalties. All human authority is subject to God. Caesar is not *dominus et deus* (Lord and God). All divine pretensions of human rulers are therefore rejected. "We must obey God rather than human authority" (Acts 5:29). There is no compromise on this theme in the New Testament.

This insistence on prior obedience to God raises the possibility of conflict whenever human institutions as the state infringe on the loyalty due only to God. The New Testament and the subsequent history of the church provide a continuing record of this conflict in all its ebb and flow. Prior obedience to God also rejects any notion of two independent but equal realms of loyalty, one to God and the other to the state. Christian loyalty to the government, whatever that might be, remains subservient to loyalty to God and Christ.

The State's Mandate

The state's mandate is to serve the public good. The New Testament in general does not view the government as an autonomous human structure but rather as an earthly institution ordered by God to enhance the welfare of the human community. Here the Pauline and post-Pauline tradition is especially significant, but it finds support throughout the New Testament (with the exception of Revelation).

The divine intention for the state is to preserve the civil good. On the positive side, it does so when it promotes peace and justice and equality and freedom and community for its own people and among the nations of the world. On the negative side, it does so by preserving law and order, by deterring the aggression of the powerful, and by punishing offenders of the public good (the power of the sword, Rom. 13:3-4). The Barmen declaration, although written in urgent protest against the totalitarian claims of the Nazi regime (1934), nevertheless acknowledges that "the state has by divine appointment, the task of providing for justice and peace. . . ."[6]

If this is so, the church upholds the state and supports it as it seeks to fulfill its divinely intended purpose. One can speak here of some kind of mutual partnership between the Christian community and the government. At the same time, the church supports the state only to the extent

---

6. See the text of the Barmen declaration in Arthur Cochrane, *The Church's Confession under Hitler* (Pittsburgh: Pickwick Press, 1976), appendix 7, 237–42.

that it intends the common good. Here is where the limits of church-state coexistence or partnership arise. Nevertheless, it should be clear that the church is not inherently an enemy of the state or hostile to political structures per se.

The State as Problem: The Idolatrous Potential of the State

This study has made obvious the fact that the political structures remain a persistent problem for the church. According to the New Testament, the state can become demonic, opposed to God, the church, and the common good.

In the Gospels, the political authorities are in constant opposition to the divine will embodied in Jesus; they finally use the power of the sword to commit the gross injustice of crucifixion. Jesus stands as critic of the old order of dominance and power and representative of the new order of service and self-giving. In Revelation, the state's opposition reaches demonic proportions in the demand for absolute loyalty and idolatrous conformity. John perceives the depth of the conflict as no other in the church, before or since. The question raised by the Apocalypse must be faced by Christians in every age: At what point has the state become an idolatrous power that one must resist? Whom finally do we worship?

In the New Testament as a whole, the portrait of the government is not that of a benevolent power at work in the world but a problematic, often hostile, potentially unjust and tyrannical human structure. Christians need to be constantly on the alert against its temptations and abuses. When necessary, in fact, the church must be ready to oppose the state and bear the consequences.

The Uneasy Tension between Church and State

The end result of this study is that the church and state live together in uneasy tension. On the one hand, they can be mutually supportive of one another, as long as the government fulfills its beneficent role as administrator of the common welfare. On the other hand, the church is obligated to discern the temptations to idolatry from the state and its lack of concern for the good of the human communities it serves.

The church rejects all idolatrous claims of the state as demonic. Some of these claims are relatively easy to discern: emperor worship, twentieth-century tyrannical governments (Nazism, Stalinism, Maoism, apartheid). Other idolatrous claims and injustices are more subtle: reliance on military power, unjust wars, economic exploitation, violation of human rights, racial/gender inequalities, ecological abuses. It is the task of the church, as God's representative in the world, to discern the particular temptation or injustice at work and then to take its stand based on its biblical, theological, ethical, and prayerful grasp of the times and situation (see also below).

The Present/Future Tension of the Church in the World

From the New Testament perspective, the tension between church and government belongs to the more fundamental tension between the "already/not yet" of the kingdom's presence. The kingdom is already present in Christ and the church, through the power of the Spirit, but the kingdom is not yet here in its fullness. The kingdom of God and the kingdom of the world share life together in this interim time. The state belongs to the structures of the old age that are passing away. The church belongs to the new age now begun, even while it lives in this old aeon. Therefore the church can live "free" of the state, while at the same time it seeks to live responsibly in it (1 Peter 2:16-17).[7]

A Proposed Paradigm for the Church's Response Today

From the First to the Twenty-first Century

A preliminary word needs to be said about the problem of bridging the gap between now and then. Any attempt to apply the New Testament to our own time must be aware of the yawning gulf between the first and the twenty-first centuries, with respect to both the changed historical settings and the changed relationships between political structures and the church. Although I will have in mind especially the distinct historical context in the United States and Canada (and similar Western democracies), I am also aware of the increasingly global context in which we live. Some differences between then and now are:

1. The New Testament communities were insignificant minorities in the Greco-Roman world. Although they spread quickly from Jewish to Gentile locales, they never possessed the kind of political or economic or religious

---

7. Oscar Cullmann, in his seminal study of church and state in the New Testament, argues that this basic theological stance provides the underlying unity to the apparent contradictory attitudes toward the government in the New Testament. On the basis of this "provisional" understanding of all earthly life and institutions, the early church neither rejected the state as such, nor gave it uncritical acceptance (*The State*, 3-5, 86-92). While I am in fundamental agreement with Cullmann, I find that his actual discussion of the different New Testament positions tends to downplay their distinctiveness in favor of finding a theological or theoretical unity that holds them together. Thomas Strieter, from whom I will draw a helpful paradigm for understanding the church and state today, also argues for the heart of the New Testament view (and Luther's) in the dualism of two governances under God, with the fulfillment still in the eschatological future ("Two Kingdoms and Governances Thinking for Today's World," *Currents in Theology and Mission* [February, 1989], 29-35).

influence that could alter the social structures. One interpreter finds this social reality to be the dominant reason for the Pauline counsel of "political quietism" toward imperial Rome. It was also true that the divine legitimacy of those who ruled was for most "an unquestioned axiom."[8]

In contrast, the church today exists as a part of the social fabric, both corporately and individually. Whether one sees this presence as waning or not, the history and culture of the West has been and still is decisively shaped by its Judeo-Christian heritage. This means that the church can and does have a vital role to play in the debate on the nature of good government and on what constitutes a just and healthy society. Not only can the church speak and act corporately through its various denominational entities, but it also finds its greatest leaven at work in the daily vocations of the laity.

2. Until the eighteenth century, governments by and large were authoritarian in structure and character and linked to the idea of the divine right of rulers. The New Testament church emerged in such a setting, of which imperial Rome and its local representatives were the chief embodiment. Throughout subsequent history, some governments have been more benevolent than others (even the church tried unsuccessfully to rule!), yet their essential authoritarian structure remained.

We are heirs to a relatively new experiment in political structures and nation-building: the democratization of society. With democracy, the focus shifts from the rights of those who rule to the rights of those ruled. The welfare of the citizens and their collective life together become the norm for what constitutes good and proper government. While it is true that past governments and rulers have been judged by their concern (or lack of it), for the public welfare, democracy brought something new to the relationship between the governed and those who govern. Democratic traditions allow persons and groups to exercise influence and power on political structures, to pass judgment on their performance, and to hold them accountable in numerous ways. In this respect, the democratic process also permits and encourages the church and individual Christians to become a lively partner in the public arena.

3. Along with the democratization of nations and governments in the West, there has occurred an exploding pluralism of beliefs and ethnicity, particularly in the United States and Canada. In such a society, all religions as well as secular beliefs and values claim and receive equal status before the law. Amid the plurality of voices, no one group is to receive preferential treatment.

8. So James D. G. Dunn, *Romans 9-16* (WBC; Dallas: Word, 1988), 772.

This social reality ideally allows for a free exchange of competing values and core convictions. Yet, at the same time, it means the church is only one voice among many. And as the plurality increases, that voice becomes even more diminished or marginalized. Moreover, the Christian community itself is deeply divided on many basic ethical and political questions. Its adherents run the full spectrum of moral and political judgments, from the far right (for example, the Christian Coalition) to the far left (for example, social critical movements such as some forms of feminism, environmentalism, gay and lesbian movements). This fragmentation of the church's witness in a pluralistic society dramatically lessens its ability to speak with persuasion to society or those in political power. To the question, "What does the church say?" there are no apparent answers on many issues; there is only a cacophony of competing voices.

4. A unique feature in the United States and Canada is the political separation of church and state.

Ancient societies were based on the essential unity between politics and religion. Rooted in the Old Testament, Israel envisioned itself as a theocracy, in which God alone would rule through appointed representatives. Obviously, this rule encountered opposition from the current world powers, so that much of Israel's history is a struggle for survival and resistance against outside conquest. In the first century, most Jews regarded Rome as an alien power, a foreign oppressor, with no religious or moral right to rule. The Zealots and others who resisted to the tragic end only put into more militant action the theocratic vision.

The New Testament, on the other hand, never shared in the theocratic vision of church and state. The New Testament writers experience the political structures as outside powers—not "us," but "them." Nor do they look toward any future time when God will rule the nations through "Christian" rulers. Moreover, their vision of the church, the new community inaugurated by Jesus, broke away from the traditional ties to ethnicity and nationhood (Israel, land). They understand the church to be an inclusive community that transcends all ethnic and political and gender boundaries (Galatians 3:28, Jew/Gentile, slave/free, male/female).

Nevertheless, from the time of Constantine (325 C.E.) to the Reformation (the sixteenth century), the history of Christianity could be described politically as one persistent struggle between church and state for control and dominance in earthly affairs.[9] Sometimes the state co-opted the

9. Eventually the alliance of church and state in the West became the Holy Roman Empire. Many now date Charlemagne's coronation by the Pope on Christmas Day, 800, as the beginning of the Holy Roman Empire. But the actual name "Holy Roman Empire" did not begin until Christmas Day, 962, with the coronation of Emperor Otto I by the Pope; the entity lasted nominally until 1806.

church; at other times the church ruled the state. The Reformation marked a political break with the Holy Roman Empire, but the Reformation churches soon lined up with Protestant princes as their protectors and advocates. In modern Europe, the alliance of church and state has greatly changed, yet most European nations still have some form of historic linkage, along with democratic and pluralistic social and political institutions.

In deliberate contrast to this unbroken but troubled history of church-state alliances, the U.S. Constitution (and the Canadian) mandate the separation of church and state. On the one hand, this means that the state remains free from direct involvement in religious affairs and gives no preference to any one religious tradition or denominational affiliation. On the other hand, the state guarantees to its citizens the freedom to practice their own religion without undue hindrance or opposition. How this separation works pragmatically within the various institutions of society (government, schools, family, public and social realm, church) has been and remains a constant source of tension and testing. Views range all the way from the radical left's doctrine of the absolute separation of church and state and the attempt to make all public institutions "secular," to more moderate views of separation but with the recognition of religious values and beliefs in the public sphere, to the radical right's attempt to make public institutions "Christian."

I will enter this debate only at a few points. However, I offer one proposal from a mainline Protestant church, the Lutheran Church in America, which upheld the separation of church and state while also affirming the legitimate role of faith communities and religious beliefs and values in our social and public life. This proposal affirms two basic points: institutional separation and functional interaction.

> By "institutional separation" we mean that church and state must each be free to perform its essential task under God. Thus we reject those theories of relationship which seek the dominance either of the church over state or of state over church. "Functional interaction" describes a process which takes place in areas in which church and state, each in pursuit of its own proper objectives, are both legitimately engaged. We believe such interaction is appropriate so long as institutional separation is preserved and neither church nor state seek to use its type of involvement to dominate the other.[10]

Other denominations may express their views differently. Disagreement on the various expressions of church-state relations are many and pro-

---

10. *Church and State: A Lutheran Perspective,* (Adopted June 21–29, 1966), 1–2, Lutheran Church in America Social Statements.

found. Yet whatever attempts are made to define this relationship in the U.S. and Canada, they must work within the boundaries of the constitutional separation of church and state.

A Contextual New Testament Ethic

Now we must face a key question of interpretation. I have outlined in some detail the three main attitudes toward the state within the New Testament. In light of these different, even contrary responses to the state, how can we decide which is the appropriate response? Or, to put it another way, how can we decide which is the most appropriate in a given situation? Here I already assume that no one approach is normative, but that each may have its fitting occasion. Even if one essentially agrees with the ethic of subordination to the government as established by God for the public good, it is obvious that particular governments do not always do or intend the best (to put it mildly). What then? I noted earlier Paul's "deafening silence" on the problem of unjust or demonic authorities (chap. 2). From the opposite side, even if one is convinced that most governments are tyrannical and corrupt to the core and so find an ethic of resistance most fitting, what does one do in the face of evidence to the contrary? And how does one deal with the New Testament's affirmation of the relative importance of human structures in the present age (marriage and family, vocation, church, government)? No one attitude toward the state is a given for every situation, as the New Testament itself bears eloquent witness by its own varying response.

This means in effect that we must adopt a contextual ethic in our approach to determining the right response appropriate to the particular time and setting. By contextual ethic we mean something like this: an ethic that uses the New Testament resources we have examined, along with other Christian theological, ethical, and historical traditions, as the basis for interpreting the contemporary political situation under which a church lives. Accordingly, in mutual and prayerful discussion, the church is given the necessary responsibility to decide which New Testament response seems apropos to its current setting, with freedom for those who may (even profoundly) disagree.

All three attitudes toward the state are New Testament attitudes: subordination, critical distancing, resistance. No single norm prevails for all occasions. Rather, the church in a distinct social setting must decide what is right in light of its own particular historical and political context. This may differ for churches in dissimilar national and global settings, even though they share the same calendar year. Perhaps here the ecumenical church can assist the national and regional churches in evaluating their context and providing support for their actions, as has been done in recent times (e.g., the South African churches under apartheid). Whatever the response, a biblical, contextual ethic is essential.

Paradigm for the Church's Attitude toward the State
I now offer a paradigm for the church's response to governments that coheres well with the major results of our New Testament survey. This helpful paradigm was developed by Thomas W. Strieter.[11]

A Paradigm for Church-State Relations

- A critical-constructive stance *is appropriate when the powers that be are attempting to achieve justice*
- A critical-transformative stance *when authority errs, but can be realistically moved to salutary change*
- A critically resistive stance *when the powers are responsible for demonic injustice or idolatry and refuse to be responsible to change*

Two general observations are important. First, this paradigm assumes, along with the New Testament as a whole, that governments have been instituted by God for the benefit of the human community. Second, this paradigm insists at the same time on a "critical" stance of the church over against all political authorities, without exception. This, too, is consistent with the New Testament.[12] Even the Pauline injunction to subjection, as we have seen, is not unconditional or blind loyalty. The church may be a faithful supporter of good governments, but the relationship is always an uneasy one so that, contrary to the often tragic and embarrassing history of alliances between church and state, there should be no co-opting of church by state (or the reverse) nor marriages of convenience. The church and Christians as representative of the kingdom of God, faulty as that may be, remain at critics-length from the state.

This critical attitude toward those in positions of power has its roots in the prophetic tradition.[13] The legitimate prophets were not subservient to

11. Thomas W. Strieter, "Two Kingdoms and Governances Thinking for Today's World," *Currents in Theology and Mission* (February 1989), 35. His article is based in part on his unpublished Th.D. dissertation, "Contemporary Two-Kingdoms and Governances Thinking for Today's World: A Critical Assessment of Types of Interpretation of the Two-Kingdoms and Governances Model, especially within American Lutheranism," Lutheran School of Theology at Chicago, 1986. I am grateful to Dr. Strieter for permission to use his paradigm in this work.

12. Cullmann, *The State*, 91, likewise agrees: "That means: it [the church] must remain in principle critical toward every State and be ready to warn it against transgression of its legitimate limits."

13. One who explores this subject in depth is Walter Brueggemann, *The Prophetic Imagination* (Philadelphia: Fortress Press, 1978).

the monarchy but remained free to speak and act as Yahweh's spokespersons for justice and peace. They ridiculed and opposed the royal pseudo-prophets, who merely mimicked the will of the king. Jesus and the New Testament are heirs of this tradition, as they proclaim ultimate loyalty to God alone and become advocates for the righteousness of the kingdom inaugurated by Jesus.

I now consider more fully the three relationships proposed by this paradigm.

1. "A *critical-constructive stance* is appropriate when the powers that be are attempting to achieve justice."

This stance coheres well with the ethic of subordination to the state. It affirms the divine will for governments to enhance the public good, preserve justice, and maintain peace and order. When the church perceives that the political powers are essentially on the side of justice, it will accordingly respond with loyalty and support. In fact, the church will encourage and assist the state to do its beneficial work and to do it to the best of its ability.

This is not a call to perfection or full justice on the part of the state. The New Testament tradition of loyalty and obedience to the powers that be did not require a superior or impossible standard of justice (or even Christian rulers or Christian nations!). In fact, the call to obey was present in times of acute suffering. But behind the Christian ethic of subordination lay the conviction that the emperor and his representatives are God's instruments to promote peace and justice and to prevent civil chaos and disorder. When this intention is missing or flagrantly violated or the state turns deliberately against the church and the public good, however, then the church has no option but to adopt a strategy to resist those in authority.

In democracies, such as the United States and Canada, it is presumably easier for the church to influence the government toward greater justice. This requires active participation by Christians in civic affairs, careful study of issues, moral discourse between Christians and others, and awareness of social injustices. To the extent that Christians agree that a particular government is subject to critique and not bent on serious mischief or aggressive self-assertion, the church can therefore provide the "critical-constructive" stance of patriotic loyalty and encouragement toward the greatest good.

This affirmation of the role of government and the church's positive response to its efforts is underscored in almost all contemporary church statements. Among them are the following: (a) "Human society can neither be well-ordered nor prosperous unless it has some people invested with legitimate authority to preserve its institutions, and to devote themselves as far as necessary to work for the good of all. These, however, derive their authority from God, as St. Paul teaches in the words, "Authority comes from God alone."[14] (b) "Presbyterians give thanks to God for the gift of civil government, which is intended to bring order to our world, to provide a framework in which we can live together in peace and search for fulfillment. We believe in saying 'yes' to the overall role that government plays, even though we may also be called to say 'no' to the government in a particular time and place."[15] (c) "The distinctive mission of the state is to establish civil justice through the maintenance of law and order, the protection of constitutional rights, and the promotion of the general welfare of the total citizenry."[16]

2. "A *critical-transformative* stance when authority errs, but can be realistically moved to salutary change."

This stance finds its closest counterpart in the ethic of critical distancing from the state, present especially in the Gospels. Like the critical-constructive view, it still regards the political powers as necessary earthly institutions and as representative of the divine will. There is no call to oppose the authorities per se nor a wholesale rejection of their social and political status.

Jesus' own prophetlike ministry, as we have seen, can be viewed as a putting-into-practice of the critical-transformative stance toward those in power. Toward the religious establishment, the preservers of the "sacred tradition," he called for repentance in light of the coming kingdom; he challenged the "politics of holiness" based on exclusivism and welcomed

14. "Peace on Earth, Encyclical Letter of Pope John XXIII, 1963," in *Peace on Earth: An Encyclical Letter of His Holiness Pope John XXIII* (New York: Ridge Press/Odyssey Press, 1964), 141. Beyond the common good, the encyclical places great value on the safeguarding of human dignity by those in public office: "For the safeguard of the inviolable rights of the human person and to facilitate the fulfillment of his duties, should be the essential office of every public authority" (141).

15. *God Alone Is Lord of the Conscience.* Policy Statement, 200th General Assembly, 1988, Presbyterian Church (U.S.A.) (Louisville: 1989), 63.

16. *Church and State: A Lutheran Perspective,* 2, Lutheran Church in America Social Statements. In its historic confessions the Lutheran church insisted that civil government is good, contrary to those who had concluded the state was inherently corrupt and evil. "It is taught among us that all government in the world and all established rule and laws were instituted and ordained by God for the sake of good order, and that Christians may without sin occupy civil offices or serve as princes and judges, render decisions and pass sentence according to imperial and other existing laws, punish evildoers with the sword, engage in just wars, serve as soldiers, buy and sell, take required oaths, possess property, be married, etc." (Article 16 of the Augsburg Confession).

the unrighteous and sinners;[17] he took the side of the poor and marginalized and announced God's reversal of status in the coming kingdom; his entry provoked the priestly elite to confront his message before it was too late; his cleansing of the Temple symbolized its systemic corruption and imminent destruction. Toward the political establishment, Jesus felt free to oppose his own ruler, Herod Antipas, as well as the Roman governor, Pontius Pilate.

Did Jesus expect to transform the religious and political authorities? According to the Gospels, he worked and prayed for their renewal, yet finally came to realize his voice would not be heard (Mark 14:25; Luke 19:41-44; 13:34-35). The chain of events from arrest to crucifixion demonstrates that prophetic protest may result in suffering and persecution. The passion history itself vividly illustrates the problem of trying to transform religious and political institutions. And the crucifixion stands as a potent symbol of political authority abusing its power and stubbornly refusing to change, in spite of knowing it has committed a grave injustice. Yet the Gospels picture Jesus willing to stay the course for the greater cause of the kingdom. And he does so without a call to his followers to take up the sword or overthrow those who misuse their political status, unlike the leaders of the other resistance movements in Palestine.

For our time, the critical-transformative stance may be necessary when the church recognizes serious problems with the state, and thereby attempts to call attention to the need for significant change. Some familiar examples from our own recent U.S. history: (a) the problem of racial injustice in law and practice and the civil rights movement it spawned; (b) the question of the justice of a particular war (Vietnam); (c) the use of congregations as "places of refuge" for illegal immigrants who were political victims in their own countries (Latin and South America); (d) the problem of nuclear weapons and nuclear deterrence in light of their potential to cause unprecedented global destruction; (e) the range of issues dealing with the protection of the environment on a fragile and limited planet Earth (nuclear waste, species preservation, sustainable use of resources, population explosion); (f) the problem of economic justice and concern for the poor and underprivileged; (g) the identification of U.S. policy in Latin America and throughout the world with dictatorial and brutal regimes; (h) the breakdown of the family unit in our society and the need to find more effective ways to renew the social fabric; (i) the problems linked to the increase of violence.

17. See Marcus Borg, *Jesus: A New Vision* (San Francisco: Harper Collins, 1987), chaps. 5–6. By "politics of holiness," Borg means the central thrust of the sacred tradition in Jesus' time that was to separate persons and groups by their perceived standards of righteousness.

Other examples could be cited. Here the challenge is not directed to the government as a whole but to specific matters of importance. In particular cases, Christians may think it necessary to adopt a public stance of protest that may even oppose the "law" of the land: discriminatory racial laws; conscientious objection to the Vietnam war; immigration laws against harboring "illegal immigrants"; refusal to pay taxes that support nuclear weapons;[18] pro-life abortion protests. In these instances, the church or group of Christians both seek to change the perceived "unjust law" and, at the same time, are ready to accept the possible consequences of their actions.

Here problems arise on which Christians may be in considerable disagreement on the rightness or wrongness of certain laws or political policies. The protesting group of Christians may represent a minority within the Christian community, at least for a time. The majority view on ethical issues—even within the church—is not necessarily the right or biblical view. History has proved this repeatedly (e.g., slavery, civil rights, women). Jesus goes alone to his death, abandoned even by the community he formed.[19] Therefore, when Christians in good conscience believe their stance is right, they are to be respected and sustained in their effort to do what they think best. At the same time, the mind and judgment of the larger church need to be kept in view as a check against Christian enthusiasm or fanaticism.

What about those urgent moral issues looming today which threaten to divide our society and upon which there is equally profound disagreement between Christians that, for the moment and possibly long-term, seem unresolvable (abortion, homosexual rights, euthanasia)? On these, also, the

18. A personal example witnessed by this author was the decision by Archbishop Raymond Hunthausen of the Archdiocese of Seattle to withhold a portion of his income tax to protest the nuclear arms policy of the United States. He announced his decision in a Pastoral Letter to the Archdiocese in 1982: "I have decided to withhold 50% of my income taxes, as a means of protesting our nation's continuing involvement in the race for nuclear arms supremacy...." In response, the government each year seized an equivalent amount of his wages. His decision caused much controversy within his own diocese and the larger U.S. Catholic church, as well as opposition from other persons who condemned his actions. The Board of Regents of Pacific Lutheran University, Tacoma, my own university, on April 15, 1991, refused to accept the unanimous faculty recommendation of an honorary doctorate for Bishop Hunthausen as a public spokesperson for peace and justice because of his controversial political/moral stance. And this despite the support of the faculty and the recommendation by the three Synods of the Evangelical Lutheran Church in American who corporately own the university.

19. One interpreter writes with respect to Jesus' agonizing and haunting sense of abandonment: "One can hardly imagine a heavier demand on a person: called to obey God, not simply in the face of political wrath but without the support of the community of faith" (Craddock, Luke, 37).

Christian community needs to respect the conscience and judgment of all its members, whatever side they take. Moreover, the church ought to become a place that initiates and supports the kind of Christian moral discourse that leads to a clearer understanding of and empathy with one another, even if no consensus can be reached. Within the political sphere, the implications of persistent division between Christians themselves obviously leads to confusion and conflict. The more deeply one believes in the rightness of one's cause, the more potential for conflict, particularly when the courts or popular opinion take opposing views. On these difficult and sensitive issues, it is ethical to affirm the conscience and goodwill of all persons, to avoid demonizing the other side or persons, and to seek a better understanding of the opposing position and their arguments. Perhaps profound disagreement ought also to lead to greater humility and charity toward both sides of the debate and to search for the common ground on which both can work together for the social and moral good.

By and large, the social statements of Christian denominations in the United States recognize the critical-transformative stand toward those in authority. None advocates total or unconditional obedience to the state (unlike the bumper sticker during the Vietnam War: "My country—love it or leave it!"). Two examples: (a) After stating plainly that "a government is accountable to God for the way it uses, abuses, or neglects to use its powerful civil "sword," one statement goes on to say, "The constant need of the state, therefore, is not for the church's uncritical loyalty and unquestioning obedience but for the prophetic guidance and judgment of the law of God, which the church is commanded to proclaim, in order to be reminded of its secular limits and potentialities."[20] (b) The Presbyterian (U.S.A.) publication *God Alone Is Lord of the Conscience* affirms boldly the priority of allegiances as does the statement noted above, "We may be called to say 'no' to the government in a particular time and place." "We believe that we should stand guard as sentries and cry out against abuse, but never forget that the church must always claim independence for itself and never seek to undermine the independence of the state."[21]

On questions of war and peace, while the majority of churches uphold the "just war" tradition, they also support both selective and full conscientious objection to war. The U.S. Catholic bishops' pastoral letter of May 3, 1983, "The Challenge of Peace," takes the following positions: (a) The opening preamble states, "We agree with the Council's (Vatican II) assessment:

20. Lutheran Church in America Social Statements, *Church and State: A Lutheran Perspective*, 2.

21. *God Alone Is Lord of the Conscience: A Policy Statement*, 200th General Assembly, 1988, Presbyterian Church (U. S. A.) (Louisville: 1989), 63.

the crisis of the moment is embodied in the threat which nuclear weapons pose for the world and much that we hold dear in the world."[22] (b) Nuclear deterrence, while morally permissible as a provisional measure, is granted "strictly conditional moral acceptance."[23] (c) On the value of nonviolent witness in the church, allowance and encouragement is given to pacifist and conscientious objection: "In the light of the Gospel and from an analysis of the Church's teaching on conscience, it is clear that a Catholic can be a conscientious objector to war in general or to a particular war."[24] On pacifism, as is well-known, the historic peace churches adopt a pacifist position that also objects to the possibility of "just war." Here they seek to translate the core "love your enemy" ethic into the political realm.[25]

On other moral issues, the churches run the spectrum from the radical right to the radical left, among which there are fundamental ethical, theological, and political differences. In general, the more conservative churches emphasize personal morality more than social issues, because they believe that the way to change society is through changed individuals, while the more liberal churches place more weight on social agendas and the reforming of perceived social injustices. But this can be a caricature. For example, the Catholic church may espouse both a conservative personal ethic (abortion, sexuality, euthanasia) and a liberal social stance on economics and human rights. The U.S. Catholic Bishops' pastoral letter of 1986, *Economic Justice for All: Catholic Social Teaching and the U.S. Economy*, frequently alludes to the biblical "preferential option for the poor," reminds all readers that the poor have the single most urgent claim on the conscience of a nation, and concludes with a challenge for "a New American experiment" of greater justice for all.[26] Certain evangelical movements similarly combine personal piety with the advocacy of radical social justice

22. The complete text of the U.S. Bishops' Pastoral letter of May 3, 1981, "The Challenge of Peace: God's Promise and Our Response," under the auspices of the National Conference of Catholic Bishops, is found in *Biblical and Theological Reflections on the Challenge of Peace*, ed. John Palikowski and Donald Senior (Wilmington, Del.: M. Glazier, 1984), 181–295. The opening summary from which the quote is taken is found on p. 185 in the above text.

23. Ibid., II.B, 167–99.

24. Ibid., 111–21, esp. 118. The above quote comes from an earlier pastoral letter of the U.S. Bishop's, October 1971 (p. 76), the stance of which is continually reaffirmed here.

25. On pacifism consult G. H. C. MacGregor, *The New Testament Basis of Pacifism* (New York: The Fellowship of Reconciliation, 1936); Peter Brock, *Twentieth Century Pacifism* (New York: Van Nostrand, 1970). On the just war tradition see Paul Ramsey, *Speak Up for Just War or Pacifism* (University Park, Pa.: Pennsylvania State University Press, 1988); U.S. Catholic Bishops' Pastoral Letter, *The Challenge of Peace*, 3. The Just War Criteria, 80–110 (in Palikowski and Senior, *The Challenge of Peace*, 1984).

26. *Economic Justice for All: Catholic Social Teaching and the U.S. Economy*, U.S. Catholic Bishops' pastoral letter (Washington, D.C.: NCC Publications, 1986), 24, 52, 86, etc.

in the economic, sexual, feminist, and environmental areas (e.g., *Sojourners* magazine).

In the United States today there are organized religious movements with competing political and ethical visions. On the one side, the Christian right, are conservative Christian groups such as the Christian Coalition.[27] Founded in 1989, it attempts to organize Christians to lobby for issues such as school prayer and against abortion, sex education, and homosexual rights; it also seeks to find and elect conservative political candidates. Recent coalition efforts concentrate on forging coalitions with other like-minded persons, including Catholics and evangelicals. The coalition also has a distinct notion of a "Christian" nation that it seeks to promote. Those who oppose it argue that its definition of a "Christian" nation is not shared by the majority of Christians, much less the rest of society. They also note its lack of concern for social justice and often uncritical patriotism. Most important, they fear a growing divisiveness and intolerance amid our diverse and pluralistic society and a dangerous crossing of the line between religious belief and a partisan political agenda. Yet those who support its vision fervently believe our nation has lost its moral foundation and not allowed the beliefs and convictions of the majority to be heard.

On the other side, the Christian left, are the voices of a few mainline churches and a wide variety of more radical issue-centered groups and causes, who join with both religious and secular advocates of what they consider to be a more just and humane society. Although not as unified in their political efforts, they seek to approach the burning social questions on human sexuality, abortion, gay rights, euthanasia, capital punishment, women and feminist concerns, and environmental and economic matters in an open and inclusive spirit, mindful of our pluralistic setting. Those who oppose this vision accuse it of an all-too-easy accommodation to the prevailing culture, a selling out to the secular spirit of our age. They also believe this viewpoint has dominated the religious and political establishment in the past and led to the spiritual and moral crisis we now face. Its proponents, however, insist that this perspective is most faithful to the biblical vision of love and justice and human dignity that enables an increasingly diverse society to live together in reasonable harmony.

---

27. See the cover story, "The Gospel according to Ralph," in *Time* magazine (May 15, 1995), 28–36. Founded by Pat Robertson as an offshoot of the Moral Majority, the Christian Coalition quickly grew into an influential conservative religiopolitical movement under the leadership of Ralph Reed. See his recent book, *Active Faith: How Christians are Changing the Soul of American Politics* (Free Press, 1996). Reed has since resigned, and new leaders have emerged. For a critical review of the Coalition, see James Killen, "The Political Confusion of the Christian Coalition," *The Christian Century* (August 30, 1995), 816–17.

Between these two visions and all of those somewhere in between, there is a continuing religious and cultural tug-of-war. Most mainline Protestant and Catholic churches belong to neither extreme of the religious spectrum. As a result, efforts are being made to develop and promote alternative visions of the relation between faith and politics than that of the right or left.[28]

The problem is further complicated by those voices that would exclude religious claims from the public realm or at least minimize their influence. For these persons, the constitutional separation of church and state becomes a dogma that too easily becomes antireligious and hides their own agenda.[29] Two concerns arise. First, in the name of protecting the rights of the minority, the religion of the majority may be pushed to the margins and not allowed a significant role in public affairs, except by default. Second, the exclusion of the religious or Judeo-Christian perspective from the public realm not only leaves out what is central to the lives of many citizens but in effect turns the public sphere into a secular arena with its own ideologies and beliefs. Here the naked public square becomes captive to visions other than the Judeo-Christian.[30]

How ought the church and other persons of faith combat the effort to exclude religious claims and values from public life? Obviously, the home and church remain the primary institutions for nurturing and preserving the faith-traditions and their role in shaping the moral character of persons and cultures. Here, too, the witness of Christians in their daily vocations should be encouraged and strengthened. Beyond this, the church can and should seek to be the public conscience at work in society. How this takes effect will differ, from the enunciation of basic biblical principles, such as

---

28. Two recent attempts are (a) a pamphlet, *Political Responsibility*, published by the U.S. Catholic Conference, Washington, D.C.; (b) a study guide, *Recovering the Evangel: A Guide to Faith, Politics, and Alternatives to the Religious Right*, published by *Sojourners*, Washington, D.C. The latter calls for a new political vision and seeks to demonstrate that being "Christian" is not to be equated with "right wing."

29. The American Civil Liberties Union offers a case in point. Its absolute position on the separation of church and state in schools and other public institutions in effect works to exclude religious beliefs and practices in these institutions. While there are Christians and Jews in the ACLU who support their stance, they usually do so either to protect religious freedom (i.e., they advocate strict separation) or to prevent the legal dominance of any one religious tradition.

30. On this much-debated topic, see Glenn Tinder, "Can We Be Good without God?" *Atlantic Monthly* (December, 1989); Richard John Neuhaus, *The Naked Public Square: Religion and Democracy in America* (Grand Rapids, Mich.: Eerdmans, 1984; Mark Noll, *One Nation Under God? Christian Faith and Political Action in America* (San Francisco: Harper & Row, 1988); Robert Benne, *The Paradoxical Vision* (Minneapolis: Fortress Press, 1995); Stephen L. Carter, *The Culture of Disbelief* (New York: Basic Books, 1993).

human dignity, justice, and compassion, to direct pronouncements or advocacy on specific ethical issues.[31]

With regard to public schools, some argue for school prayer, but the problem of respect for the multiplicity of religious (and nonreligious) convictions has led most churches to oppose it.[32] Others search for ways to teach the major religious traditions in the schools without partisanship or advocacy (European nations follow this path, with admittedly mixed results in combating secularism). Celebration of religious holidays, along with knowledge of their religious significance, seems reasonable to many. Open recognition in textbooks and teaching of the crucial role of religious faith in shaping history and the modeling of religious figures (e.g., Martin Luther King Jr. and Mahatma Gandhi) would reflect reality. Finally, many advocate public financial support for all schools, including the private religious sector. Throughout the debate, the assumption is made that religious institutions and faith commitments need to be recognized as vital for the common good and to be welcomed more fully into the public debate on the character and future of our national life.

To summarize, the churches in general agree on a critical-transformative stance toward those in political authority at particular times and places, and the need to support the right of those who challenge what they perceive to be serious failures of justice or morality. In this respect, Christ and Caesar live in constant tension and uneasy peace.

On those divisive questions where Christians themselves are grappling to know the will of God and have no clear witness to make, it seems best to speak and act with mutual respect, seeking to discern more fully the mind of Christ and the public good. Perhaps on this Christians can agree: Jesus' way is that of love and justice and service, with the good of the neighbor, concern for the least, and the care of creation the goal. How this works out in the political realm remains the task and opportunity of God's people as they reach out to all those who seek the greater good.

---

31. Robert Benne develops and evaluates a fourfold classification of the ways the church becomes involved in political affairs, moving from the noncontroversial to the highly controversial: (1) Ethics of character—indirect and unintentional influence. Here the church is involved in the formation of biblical character. (2) Ethics of conscience—indirect and intentional influence. Beyond character, this aims at conscience formation on specific issues. (3) Church as social conscience—direct and intentional influence. Here the church seeks to shape public policy by persuasion (U.S. Catholic Bishops' letters on peace and the economy). (4) Church with power—direct and intentional action. Here the church uses forms of political power to realize its goals. This alternative is most controversial and risky (the church can become a partisan body, with its distinct mission weakened), yet it may be appropriate at particular times (civil rights, Latin America abuses). From "The Church and Politics: Four Possible Connections," *This World* (Spring, 1989), 26–37; see also Benne's *The Paradoxical Vision*, 181–224, on indirect and direct connections.

3. "A *critically resistive stance* when the powers are responsible for demonic injustice or idolatry and refuse to be responsible to change."

This position agrees most fully with the ethic of resistance toward the state found most clearly in the book of Revelation. Governments can become demonic and idolatrous, opposed to God and the church. And they can become perpetrators of systemic injustice and so fundamentally hostile to the civic welfare.

When the church understands this to be the case, it has no choice but to stand in opposition to the political powers. In these moments the church needs to take a bold stance against the idolatrous ideologies and their propaganda, refuse to compromise on essentials, and do battle against the core injustices. And if the governments refuse to change, Christians will find themselves seeking to remove them from power.

This stance obviously takes courage and wisdom and trust in God. It marks the Christian community as a perceived "enemy of the state" and therefore subject to isolation and hostility and various kinds of suffering and persecution. It requires a willingness on the part of individual Christians and the church to accept the consequences of their resistance, whatever that may be, in the confidence they act out of prior obedience to God.

Does the church in fact become an enemy of the state when it opposes radically unjust and totalitarian governments? To put it another way, can such governments forfeit their role as divinely willed instruments for good? Some interpreters think not. "At its worst the State is a disobedient and rebellious servant. . . ."[33] But the author of Revelation never calls idolatrous Rome a "servant of God," even if rebellious. Indeed, the seer believed that Rome had forfeited its right to rule. Hence for Revelation, particular governments do function outside of the divine mandate. Yet even Rome and all such evil empires are subject to God, who will end their rule in God's good time. One can say, therefore, that while Christians are not enemies of the state per se, they may and do resist particular governments who are incorrigibly corrupt and idolatrous.

For our time, the critically resistive stance toward the state may be appropriate at crisis moments when those in political power lay claim to the church's allegiance and become enemies of the civil order (nationally

32. E.g., the National Council of the Churches of Christ in the U.S.A. (NCC), representing the majority of Protestant denominations, officially opposed public prayer and the use of the Bible devotionally in public schools. In *Policy, Office of Research, Evaluation and Planning* (New York: NCCC, 1951–1995), 13.5. Witness the current effort in the U.S. Congress to amend the Constitution to permit organized prayer in public schools. But here, too, the churches are sharply divided, with the majority in opposition to church-sponsored prayer.

33. So Barrett, "The New Testament Doctrine," 19.

and globally). Just as the demand for emperor worship could not be tolerated by the seer of Revelation, nor the command to keep silent by the earliest apostles (Acts 5:29), so in our contemporary setting. The twentieth century has provided us with a frightening array of contexts in which the church has been challenged to deny and resist those in authority. We need to name them in order to keep their memory alive and to observe that the church has all too often failed its God-given task to say no when necessary, regardless of the cost.

Among those crisis moments:

1. Under Hitler and the Nazis (1933–45), the church in Germany confronted a racial ideology (rooted in part in anti-Semitism) and a dictator bent on conquering Europe by technological superiority and brute force. While the church and the world outside of Germany gradually came to realize the demonic evil at work, the majority of the people and the church within Germany, both Protestant and Catholic, remained blind or indifferent or silent or subservient to those in power. Only with rare exception did Christians have the wisdom and strength and resolve to rise up against the ideology and actions of a nation co-opted by a modern tyrant and mass murderer of Holocaust proportions.[34] Here the witness of the Confessing Church and persons of courageous conviction like Dietrich Bonhoeffer represented a minority within the German nation.

2. Under Marxist-Leninist communism in its various forms, the church and the world faced both an undisguised ideological enemy (atheistic materialism) and brutal regimes that indiscriminately sacrificed human life for the perceived good of the state (Stalinism in Russia, Maoism in China, other imitators around the globe in Eastern Europe, Asia, Africa, and Latin America). With the promise of greater justice and prosperity for all, communism held deep attraction for many and a vision of equality that seemed to echo the teaching of Jesus. In many communist lands, the standard of living for the common person greatly improved, along with a more equitable distribution of wealth than under capitalist economies. Generally, however, communism failed to deliver on its utopian promise of

---

34. For a portrait of the few who did speak out and suffered the consequences, see Victoria Barnett, *For the Soul of the People: Protestant Protest against Hitler* (New York: Oxford University Press, 1992). On Dietrich Bonhoeffer, one of the leaders of the Confessing Church of evangelical Christians, martyred on April 9, 1945, see Eberhard Bethge, *Dietrich Bonhoeffer: Man of Vision, Man of Courage*, trans. Eric Mosbacher (N.Y.: Harper and Row, 1970). Bonhoeffer's writings have left an enduring legacy on the power of faithful resistance. He was one of the few who concluded that Christian resistance could even involve the taking of life (Hitler's) for a higher good. One Lutheran bishop, Hans Lilje, while imprisoned, wrote a well-known commentary on Revelation (*The Last Book of the Bible* [Philadelphia: Muhlenberg Press, 1957]), reflecting the original setting of John of Patmos.

a better life and especially failed with respect to human freedom and dignity. And, in most cases, the governments became the bitter enemy of the church and sought deliberately to destroy it. In response, the majority of church members opted out of any public Christian witness, with some notable exceptions in predominantly Catholic countries (e.g., Poland and Hungary). The church itself adopted different strategies for survival (resistance, silence, accommodation, dialogues, service). In a few former Eastern Bloc countries, the church played an active role in the collapse of the Iron Curtain (e.g., East Germany). Although the complex story remains to be written about the church under communist rule, it does not seem as though the church as a whole stood resolute and ready to resist.[35]

3. Under the apartheid regime in South Africa (1950–94), the church again encountered an ideology (white supremacy) and a government pursuing policies of discrimination against those perceived to be the inferior race (black, colored). The church in South Africa was sharply split. The white churches mainly supported the status quo of apartheid, justifying it biblically and ethically, while the black/colored churches (the majority!) obviously stood in strong opposition. There were some striking exceptions within the white churches, however, as well as among black leaders of mixed denominations who led the struggle for justice and democracy. In the end, a black Christian resistance leader, Nelson Mandela, jailed for twenty-eight years under a death sentence, was freed on February 11, 1990, and emerged to lead the nation toward a new future.[36]

During the long struggle, global churches joined the battle against apartheid. In 1982, the World Alliance of Reformed Churches declared the moment for the church in South Africa to be a *status confessionis* (confessional situation), i.e., a time when the truth of Christianity was at stake.

35. Certain communist regimes used the most thorough and systematic efforts in history to wipe out religious faith, especially Christianity. Its survival is a tribute to the church and the power of the gospel to create and preserve faith, despite my criticism of its overall failure. One compelling movie, *Question 7*, documents the struggle in East Germany for the allegiance of youth.

36. The story of this struggle is found in two books by John W. de Gruchy, *The Church Struggle in South Africa* (Grand Rapids, Mich.: Eerdmans, 1986); *Bonhoeffer and South Africa: Theology in Dialog* (Grand Rapids, Mich.: Eerdmans, 1984). Heroic figures like Bishop Desmond Tutu need to be named. On the life of Nelson Mandela, elected President of South Africa in 1994, see Fatima Meer, *Higher than Hope* (New York: Harper & Row, 1990) and Mandela's autobiography, *Long Walk toward Freedom* (Boston: Little, Brown, 1994). While apartheid became official policy in South Africa only in 1950, its roots go back much earlier, especially to Land Acts of 1913 and 1936 that created white rule in all of southern Africa (including Namibia and other territories). Like Hans Lilje under Hitler, another pastor and resistance leader in South Africa, Alan Boesak, wrote his commentary on Revelation in light of the beastly apartheid rule (*Comfort and Protest* [Philadelphia: Westminster, 1987]).

"To say Yes to Jesus Christ was to say No to apartheid."[37] Like the Confessing Church at Barmen in 1934, here apartheid was named as immoral and unchristian, a heresy that excludes one from the church. The protesting members of several denominations in South Africa also produced a powerful document of dissent in 1986, *The KAIROS Document: Challenge to the Church: A Theological Comment on the Political Crisis in South Africa.*[38] As the name *Kairos* implies, the participants understand the present moment as a time of crisis and opportunity for the church and the nation. Either apartheid is repented of or its idolatrous ideology remains.[39]

In each of these twentieth-century occasions of church-state conflict, the church was faced with governments of demonic and idolatrous proportions to whom it owed no allegiance. The church's task was to resist their inhumane policies, to speak and act in Christ's name against their tyrannical claims, and to work either for radical change or for their overthrow. That the church so consistently failed to do so begs for forgiveness and for the need to try to grasp why, beyond mere human weakness.

In the case of German Christians and the church, the reasons for failure are complex. Obviously, there was human fear in the face of pressure and threats from friends and neighbors and especially those in political authority. Perhaps Peter's denial of Jesus is of this kind (Mark 14:66-72). On another level, there is the reality of how easy it is to become caught up in the spirit and mind-set of a nation and to become captive to unchristian and inhumane ideologies and practices (e.g., "Aryan" supremacy).[40]

37. Robert McAfee Brown, ed., *Kairos: Three Prophetic Challenges to the Church* (Grand Rapids, Mich.: Eerdmans, 1990), 9. The Lutheran World Federation also declared a small German Lutheran church in South Africa in *status confessionis.*

38. See Brown, *Kairos*, rev. ed., 17–66.

39. Churches from other economically suffering parts of the world subsequently produced two more *Kairos* documents, both intended to call attention to the plight of the global poor and to plead for action by wealthier and more powerful nations and churches: *Kairos Central America: A Challenge to the Churches of the World*, 1988; *The Road to Damascus: Kairos and Conversion* (Africa, Central America, Asia), 1989 (see Brown, *Kairos*, 76–104, 113–38 for the full texts). Some U.S. Christians propose writing a *Kairos USA* response, that recognizes the urgency of a suffering world and challenges the church and nation to respond.

Robert Benne (*The Paradoxical Vision*, 175, note 54) sharply criticizes *Road to Damascus*: "This 'Christian Marxist' document, produced months before the collapse of Soviet communism, is a caricature of the danger of conflating the twofold reign of God." He is correct in noting how it falsely envisions the reign of God as a this-worldly possibility ("The Reign of God is this world completely transformed in accordance with God's plan" [p. 12]). He is wrong in failing to note the urgency of the moment and the need for Christian response and action. I also find his confidence in the justice of democratic capitalism highly questionable.

40. The research of a university colleague on the story of a police battalion under the Nazis, who were involved in the execution of Jews and others, is devastatingly insightful on how common persons could finally do such atrocious things. See Christopher Browning,

Accommodation with the spirit of the world is always the spiritual enemy of the church. Yet another reason was the constant confusion between loyalty to the nation (the Fatherland) and loyalty to God. One could be against Hitler but not see its implications for evaluating one's devotion to the nation or people.[41] A final reason, one that I find especially crucial in light of this study, may be the failure of the church to lift up the New Testament witness of the Apocalypse against the tyrannical rulers of every age. A church that knows only the ethic of subordination in Romans 13 and elsewhere has not read the whole New Testament. The book of Revelation, above all, calls the church to become a subversive community against the principalities and powers that rule the world.[42] While the imperial beast

---

Ordinary Men: Reserve Police Battalion 101 and the Final Solution in Poland (New York: HarperCollins, 1992).

41. Here the revered "throne and altar" tradition in German history led to tragic results. One signer of the Stuttgart Declaration of Guilt (1945), a Confessing Church member, Hanns Thimme, said: "All of us were compromisers, somehow, one almost has to say that, even those who were consistent opponents. . . . I was a pastor of a Confessing Church, and I never made any secret of that . . . but I always said, I am not against the state; I'm against this ideology. But basically, one couldn't separate the ideology from the state, since this ideology was the official ideology of the state. And here one made compromises . . ." (Barnett, *For the Soul*, 228). With regard to one's faith and love of the Fatherland, Barnett observes: "Historically, the German Fatherland was always more than a political slogan or even territory; it was a domain where political and religious ideals merged and in the Third Reich became demonically distorted." "But *Väterlandischeliebe* [love of Fatherland] had helped create and empower Nazism, and, after 1945, it hindered German attempts to confront the Nazi past" (ibid., 301). Martin Niemoeller, one of the most radical critics of the church said, "From the very beginning, they (German Christians) put the Fatherland above the discipleship to Christ, the national interest above their belief" (ibid., 307). After the war, "the Protestant church, which had never during the Third Reich successively confronted its own nationalism or anti-Semitism, was even less able now to do so" (ibid., 223). In the postwar Protestant church, there were two major divisions. The more radical (the Dahlemite and Darmstadt adherents) sought to end once and for all the throne and altar tradition: "A confessing church is always in the opposition, in every party, in every system, to every government" (Hans Iwand, ibid., 277). The other members sought to continue some form of alliance and to align themselves with the democratic processes and even "Christian" political parties.

On the failure to resist, Helga Weckerling, Confessing Church member, helper of Jewish Christians, said this: "But we never felt ourselves to be free of guilt, because we simply didn't go into the resistance, as Bonhoeffer did" (ibid., 230). On the failure to prevent the Holocaust, a Christian jurist wished: "In each train that drove east, where they were gassed, a Christian would have ridden along in the discipleship of Jesus Christ because it would have left him no inner peace and he'd be compelled by God to do it" (ibid., 235).

42. Similarly, Ernst Käsemann, a German theologian who lived under Nazism, made an eloquent appeal to his fellow German Christians and all Christians to resist the world powers by appeal to the Apocalypse (*Jesus Means Freedom* [Philadelphia: Fortress Press, 1972]; see chap. 6, "Those Who Hunger and Thirst for Righteousness: The Revelation of John"). He

may cause the whole earth to fall down and worship it, the saints are called to endure and keep the faith, holding up Jesus Christ alone as Lord (Rev. 13:10).

It was in this spirit that Christian leaders from the Protestant churches of Germany gathered together at Barmen, Germany, on May 24–31, 1934, to declare against the rise of Nazi ideology to all who would hear: "1. Jesus Christ, as he is attested for us in Holy Scripture, is the one Word of God which we have to hear and which we have to trust and obey in life and in death. . . . 2. We reject the false doctrine, as though there were other areas of our life in which we would not belong to Jesus Christ, but to other lords. . . ."[43] This is the witness of Revelation and the New Testament confession of Jesus Christ as Lord. There is no other.

What are the limits of Christian resistance to the state? As we have seen, the Apocalypse encourages civil disobedience, public witness and protest in defiance of the state, and acceptance of suffering and martyrdom. But it draws the line at violent resistance.[44] Despite the cries for divine vengeance on the persecuting state, these are best grasped as calls for divine justice. Moreover, it is God alone who exercises judgment on earth, not the people of God.

In the New Testament as a whole, the ethic of nonviolence and love for the enemy constitute the core ethic. Jesus rejects any armed resistance on his behalf and chooses the path of voluntary suffering. The ethic of neighbor-love permeates the other New Testament writings. But how this

---

notes that only in the Apocalypse is Christian freedom combined with "a politically revolutionary attitude" (130) that asks, "Whose is the world?" (133). So under Hitler: "Whose is the earth? . . . Did not the Nazis carry on their fight against us with the slogan: 'Heaven for sparrows and Christians, earth for us'? How many of us actually accepted it, in spite of the contemptuous method of expression! People did so because they seriously maintained that Jesus' kingdom is not of this world, or because they concluded from a questionable doctrine of the two kingdoms that, for the sake of order, even a doubtful authority had to be allowed to act on its own responsibility in political matters. The result was an attitude that resisted state interference only in church affairs and elsewhere allowed concessions and compromises up to the extreme limit, and a silence like that of whipped dogs" (134–35). Against such attitudes of acceptance of the state and idolatrous forms of nationalism, he calls German Christians to read and reread the book of Revelation (139). He concludes with its challenge to the church in all ages to defend its Lord's claim to the earth (140) and to heed its cry of hunger and thirst for God's righteousness already here on earth (143).

43. See the Barmen Declaration, text and discussion, in Arthur Cochrane, *The Church's Confession under Hitler* (Pittsburgh: Pickwick Press, 1976), appendix 7, 237–42.

44. See chap. 4. Dietrich Bonhoeffer and a few other German Christians who decided to seek the killing of Hitler did not see this as a church decision as such but as a matter of Christian conscience to which they must be obedient in exceptional moral circumstances.

ethic of love and nonviolence becomes concrete in the ongoing history of the church has remained a most difficult and debated issue. Attitudes from pacifism to just wars have been in constant dialogue with each other, with the just war tradition dominant. A Dietrich Bonhoeffer can decide that a Hitler must be assassinated, but without binding the Christian conscience of other resisters. The "liberation theologies" of the developing worlds have engaged in vigorous debate on the possibility of violent revolution against unjust governments, where no possible hope of change seems evident.[45] Whatever the actual decisions, the Christian position must always keep at its pulsing heart and center the ethic of radical neighbor-love that reaches out to embrace even the enemy. Christians pray for their persecutors, not despise them. Hostile and demonic governments who usurp their intended roles are resisted, above all, with the power of suffering love and the witness to the "word of God and testimony of Jesus Christ" (Rev. 1:9). Even Revelation, with all of its "hostility" to the beast Babylon, agrees.

To what degree does Revelation's view of the state as demonic and idolatrous reflect reality? Is this not in fact an exaggeration of the Roman government in John's time? One could argue that under the threat of persecution and the crisis of emperor worship, John understandably counters with his apocalyptic vision that depicts Rome as the satanic enemy of the church and humanity. But the reality is more ambiguous than John reveals. Despite all of its faults, Rome still preserves a reasonable measure of peace and order and justice in the world. As noted above, there were even Christian prophets in the seven churches of Asia Minor who apparently disagreed strongly with John's evaluation of Rome as the idolatrous enemy to be resisted to death (chap. 4).

The danger of Christian fanaticism always exists. John could have recognized a special danger to the church but then exaggerated its significance and demonized the enemy. This has happened before and since. But, against this possibility, I respond as follows.

1. We are never (or rarely) dealing with simple right/wrong issues in making ethical and religious judgments. A degree of ambiguity is always present. One could equally argue that the ethic of subordination to the state that fulfills its divinely intended role to uphold the good and prevent evil is an exaggeration. What government in human history has done this fully or convincingly? One could as persuasively argue to the con-

---

45. On this debate, see Jose Miguez-Bonino, *Toward a Christian Political Ethics* (Philadelphia: Fortress Press, 1983), 108–10, and his "Violence and Liberation," *Christianity and Crisis* 32/12 (July 10, 1972): 169–72.

trary. Human history, like governments, must be measured in less certain terms. Nevertheless, unless we adopt a purely cynical attitude toward life, judgments can and should be made on moral and religious questions, including governments. Relatively speaking, then, Christians can and should evaluate political institutions as good or evil, just or unjust, beneficial or demonic, open or totalitarian, friend or persecutor of the church.

2. Of all the writers in the New Testament, John sees with the greatest clarity the temptations to idolatry and tyranny and injustice that are inherent in political institutions. They possess power that can be so quickly abused. They affect the lives of people like no other human institution. They are to be held in respect as well as in fear. And their potential for mischief and evil is unlimited, unless other counterbalances to their power exist.

In Revelation, the seer rightly understands this demonic potential. He and his churches experience the "tip of the iceberg," as it were. Therefore, when the state arrogantly demands unconditional loyalty or conformity that conflicts with one's beliefs, there can be no more compromise. When the pinch of incense to "Caesar as Lord" becomes the litmus test for acceptance or survival, the word is no. To repeat, it is the Apocalypse that raises for the church in every age the question, At what point has the state become an agent of tyranny and injustice that must be opposed and changed? Without the visions of Revelation, this crucial question would not be kept alive with such forcefulness.

How can we reach consensus in the church on an ethic of resistance to an unjust or idolatrous state? Even John met with considerable disagreement in his pastoral and prophetic attempt to persuade the seven churches of the dangers. But the seers and prophets, like John, need to be heard and heeded. They see more clearly than most. They may persuade a majority or they may not, but the testimony of the few, even if on the fringe, keeps open the issue of obedience or disobedience, worship or idolatry. As I have noted, recent history has shown that the majority in the church often remain blind to the dangers and captive to the ideology of the state (German church under Nazism, white South African church under apartheid). Only later, after painful lessons of demagoguery and war and genocide, do the majority realize the truth spoken earlier by the few. Some never learn.

Finally, there is a time and place for Revelation's view of the state. The option of the ethic of resistance to the government is a Christian option. It is rooted in the New Testament, as we have taken much care to demonstrate. Some persons may not have been aware of its presence; others may wish it were not there. Still others may decide to choose one of the other options of subordination or critical distancing. But faithfulness to the New Testament requires that we hear all three, including the ethic of resistance.

All three of the New Testament attitudes toward the state need to be kept alive in the church so that it will have the means to be more faithful to its responsibility as God's servant in the world of governments and politics, both good and bad.

EPILOGUE

O UR JOURNEY THROUGH THE NEW TESTAMENT—IN SEARCH OF ITS PRI-
mary attitudes regarding the political structures and those who govern—is over. I have argued for three distinct responses in the New Testament—subordination, critical distancing, resistance—and for a serious
hearing of all three as valid options for the Christian community.

When I first began this study I thought of calling it *Uneasy* Partners:
Church and State in the New Testament. But as I looked more closely and
reflected more fully on the relationship of church and state, I became convinced *partners* goes too far in describing some kind of mutuality or inter-
dependence between church and state. History reminds us all too vividly of
the unholy alliances that have plagued these relationships or the tragic gulf
between unholy ideologies and the church, which has manifested itself so
powerfully in this past century. The New Testament, while recognizing and
upholding the state as a providential gift for the common good, finds the
state less a benevolent partner than a problematic human structure. My
revised title, therefore, is *Uneasy* Neighbors: *Church and State in the New
Testament*. This change preserves the distinctiveness of each entity while at
the same time encouraging the necessity and responsibility to live as good
neighbors. The word *uneasy* qualifies the relationship in a necessary and
significant manner.

The New Testament confession of Jesus Christ as Lord is fundamental
for the Christian community. This confession makes all other relationships
subordinate, including that of loyalty to the state. Allegiance to God and
Christ takes precedence. Christians may and do pray for good government,
wise rulers, just laws, and lasting peace, but they do so without naïveté.
They know the government is a human structure, is not perfect, and can
easily be deterred or become a force for evil. A built-in tension, moreover,
exists between the ultimate loyalty to Christ and the penultimate claims of
the state. Unconditional obedience belongs to God and God alone. Even
the practice of placing national flags in the church sanctuary alongside the

cross or other Christian symbols would seem to violate the confession of faith in only one God and Lord.

This study has illuminated the state's idolatrous potential. This has been a consistent theme, not only in the apocalyptic books, where the government is an enemy of the church and humanity, but also in the Gospels, where the story of Jesus calls into question all lesser claims relative to the kingdom. Paul would agree, despite his affirmation of the political authorities. This affirmation needs to be lifted up, since the temptation to idolatry is so powerful and subtle. The state can easily persuade its people of the rightness of its cause or the evil of its enemies. Likewise, members of nations can easily confuse love of country with love of God or one's own personal and national self-interest with the greater good. Patriotism and love of country, while in itself right and good, ought never to rival faith in God or any ultimate claims in our lives. Yet this temptation stands continually at the door.

As neighbors, church and government seek to live together and work mutually for the common good, whenever this is possible. The state has been given the unique role of ordering and promoting our life together on this globe. Here the church joins with others in assisting the government in its task. But the church always remains at arm's length from the state, lest it be co-opted by the idolatrous lure to power, control, wealth, and national self-interest. The church best performs its task by serving as a conscience for the citizens of the state and those who govern. The church should ask the deeper questions about justice and human dignity, and care for the disenfranchised and all of God's creation. The church needs to dream the dreams of a "nation under God, with liberty and justice for all." In so doing, it becomes a counter-culture community within our nations, challenging the status quo and seeking to be a voice for God's kingdom of righteousness and peace.

By and large, the church and state can live as "uneasy neighbors" under varied forms and structures of government (capitalism, socialism, etc.). We have seen, however, in this past century in particular, that governments can quickly become hazardous to the common welfare and take on demonic forms of totalitarian governments that threaten the church and humanity. These situations can occur again, unexpectedly and repeatedly. The church did not very successfully recognize or resist these dangers in the twentieth century. I hope that, in some small way, this study will enable the church to be more prepared in the future. There are times to say "yes" to good government, times to say "look out," and times to say a loud and fearless "no!" All three responses are rooted in the New Testament.

INDEX OF ANCIENT SOURCES

INDEX OF AUTHORS